Africa

Africa

A Continent Self-Destructs

Peter Schwab

palgrave

for St. Martin's Press

AFRICA: A CONTINENT SELF-DESTRUCTS
© Peter Schwab, 2001

First published 2001 by
PALGRAVE
175 Fifth Avenue, New York, N.Y.10010 and
Houndmills, Basingstoke, Hampshire RG21 6XS.
Companies and representatives throughout the world

PALGRAVE is the new global publishing imprint of St. Martin's Press LLC Scholarly and Reference Division and Palgrave Publishers Ltd (formerly Macmillan Press Ltd).

ISBN 0-312-24018-X hardback

Library of Congress Cataloging-in-Publication Data

Schwab, Peter, 1940-
    Africa, a continent self-destructs / Peter Schwab.
        p. cm.
    Includes bibliographical references and index.
    ISBN 0-312-24018-X
        1. Africa—Economic conditions—1960- 2. Africa—Social conditions—1960- 3.
    Africa—Politics and government—1960- I. Title.

HC800 .S389 2001
967.04—dc21

                                                    2001021864

A catalogue record for this book is available
from the British Library.

Design by planettheo.com

First edition: October, 2001
10 9 8 7 6 5 4 3

Printed in the United States of America.

To Albert Fried, a years-long friend who encouraged me to write this book

Contents

Through our great good fortune, in our youth our hearts were touched with fire. It was given us to learn at the outset that life is a profound and passionate thing. While we are permitted to scorn nothing but indifference, and do not pretend to undervalue the worldly rewards of ambition, we have seen with our own eyes, beyond and above the gold fields, the snowy heights of honor, and it is for us to bear the report to those who come after us. But, above all, we have learned that whether a man accepts from Fortune her spade and will look downward and dig, or from Aspiration her axe and cord and will scale the ice, the one and only success which it is his to command is to bring to his work a mighty heart.

—Justice Oliver Wendell Holmes

Acknowledgments

In the years I lived and conducted research in Africa, I came across countless individuals whose enthusiasm and/or concern about the continent and its future impressed and affected me. They are also people who provided me with insights that I might not have discovered at all or, at the least, would have taken far longer to absorb. Primarily, they gave me great pleasure and added measurably to my knowledge. Individuals who loved Africa—and the nations they lived in—have been greatly disappointed, as have I, in what the future brought.

Most important there is Amos Sawyer. A high school student of mine in Liberia, he eventually became president of the country (1990-1994) and developed into the most democratic leader Liberia has ever experienced. As a student he was highly gifted and an extraordinary conversationalist, and we spent hours together weekly, both seriously and playfully, in rapt discussion. With his infectious laugh, assiduous probing, and glorious optimism, he made my two-year-long stay in Liberia pleasurable and intellectually challenging. His impact on me was immense, and his continuing friendship is invaluable.

There was also Susan "Daisy" Broudy. A person whose optimism knows no bounds whatsoever, she taught me how to look at Liberia and in many ways how to look at life. Currently a counselor and psychotherapist in Rhode Island, she remains one of my dearest friends. Her dazzling outlook on life is irresistible.

In Ethiopia, during the several years off and on that I spent collecting data, there were many people who were extraordinarily helpful and kind to me. Among them are Abdullah Adem, Eshetu Habtegiorgis, and Norman Singer. My remembrance also to the late Gwendolen M. Carter, of Northwestern University, and L. Gray Cowan, of Columbia University, both of whom played a substantial role in launching my career in Ethiopian studies. What has transpired in Ethiopia over the past decades is tragic, but in those years we all had hope.

Finally, there are those students who attended my African Politics and Literature class at Purchase College, State University of New York, who, over time, have taught *me* a lot. I am grateful to all of them. Adamantia Pollis, of the Graduate Faculty, New School University, was my original mentor when I began my graduate studies and in that role was a wonderful guide. She and I have since worked together and over the years coauthored three books on human rights; our personal and intellectual friendship is of exceptional importance to me. James E. Churchill, Jr., executive editor at Grolier Educational Publishers, has been markedly helpful by furnishing the opportunity to sharpen my knowledge of Africa. Karen Wolny, senior editor at Palgrave, Global Publishing at St. Martin's Press, has worked side by side with me on two books. Her skill, effort, and support have been of substantial consequence to me and my work. She has my thanks and gratitude. At Palgrave too, Debra Manette provided the deftness of a talented copy editor, while the production editor, Donna Cherry, was truly adept at guiding the book through its various stages. Michael Flamini, editorial director, Ella Pearce, and Matt Ritter were also wonderful to work with.

By no means is this an exhaustive list of those I wish to thank. I have pointed out only those individuals who have meant the most to me as concerns Africa, and those who have provided me their expertise. They are the ones who have granted me their knowledge, friendship, concern, or love, and have helped to educate me about the continent.

The impact of those above not withstanding, only I am responsible for what is in this book.

Peter Schwab
New York City

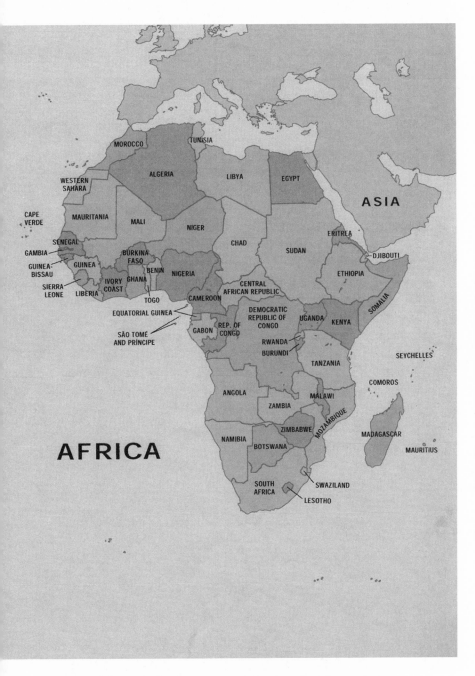

Introduction

This book has been in the making for some 40 years. I initially went to Africa in 1962 as part of the first contingent of Peace Corps Volunteers to teach in Liberia. Then in its second year of existence, the Peace Corps attracted individuals usually fresh out of college who were imbued with a hefty measure of idealism.[1] Based in the remote and isolated southeastern section of the country, in Harper City, Cape Palmas, for two years I had the opportunity to experience West Africa around the time that many African colonies achieved independence. It was an era of great expectations. It was also a time when the United States, bustling to organize its involvement in Vietnam, moved to secure many of these newly independent states into its ideological sphere of interest. Although a sleepy town, Harper, in Maryland County, offered a window to village life and to larger African currents.

In 1967 I traveled to Ghana, Senegal, Kenya, Ethiopia, and what is today Eritrea on a Fulbright-Hays award. It was the first of numerous research trips to Ethiopia, and in the following decades I published several books on Ethiopian politics and society. Already in the mid- to late 1960s the optimism of the early years of that decade had begun to fade. The hype and excitement that ensued when Ghana and Nigeria received their independence in 1957 and 1960 respectively were swiftly followed by military coups d'état that occurred in Togo in 1963, in which President Sylvanus Olympio was murdered; in Nigeria, Ghana, and the Central African Republic in 1966; in Sierra Leone in 1967; and in Mali in 1968. The continent was in a state of flux, as more and more African states moved first from multiparty to single-party rule and then to military dictatorship. Simultaneously, the Soviet Union and the United States became more heavily involved in trying to influence the ideologies and internal politics of many African states. During this time I was conducting research in parts of the Horn of Africa (comprised of Ethiopia, Eritrea, Somalia, and Djibouti) and traveling to Gambia and Senegal to study the state of relations between both countries. I also visited various nations in North, East, and West Africa, among them Morocco, Egypt, Algeria, Uganda, Nigeria, Sierra Leone, Togo, Benin (then known as Dahomey), Guinea, and the Ivory Coast.

By the late 1970s and into the 1980s and 1990s, much of the continent had devolved into chaos. Little was left of the optimism that had permeated African leaders, African specialists, and western academics who were writing about and studying the continent. Although many intellectuals including myself attempted to hold onto some enthusiasm, it really did seem apparent that Africa south of the Sahara had matriculated into a period in which pandemonium, war, predatory governments, disease, poverty, famine, and western neglect were strikingly in ascendance. As the world entered the new millennium, sub-Saharan Africa had all but collapsed into anarchy and viciousness.

On March 22, 1961, President John F. Kennedy, in a special message to Congress on foreign aid, indicated that "The economic collapse of those free but less-developed nations which now stand poised between sustained growth and economic chaos would be disastrous . . . and offensive to our conscience."[2] Some 39 years later, British Prime Minister Tony Blair, speaking at the United Nations (UN) Millennium Summit meeting held in New York City, indicated "There is a dismal record of failure in Africa on the part of the developed world that shocks and shames our civilization. Twenty-one of the 44 [sic] countries in sub-Saharan Africa are affected by conflict. . . . Nowhere are more people dying needlessly from starvation, from disease, from conflict. Deaths caused not by acts of fate but by acts of man. By bad governance, factional rivalries, state-sponsored theft and corruption."[3]

Or, as the eminent Nigerian novelist Chinua Achebe proclaimed in his novel *A Man of the People,* a rabid critique of Nigeria's corrupt political elites: ". . . I do honestly believe that in the fat-dripping, gummy, eat-and-let-eat regime just ended—a regime which inspired the common saying that a man could only be sure of what he had put away safely in his gut, or in language ever more suited to the times: 'you chop, me self I chop, palaver finish'; . . . in such a regime, I say, you died a good death if your life had inspired someone to come forward . . . without asking to be paid."[4]

The exuberance and innocence of the 1960s is gone. Violence and death have replaced the expectations of four decades ago. Internecine ethnic warfare, so well represented in the 1990s by catastrophe in Liberia, Sierra Leone, Somalia, Burundi, Angola, Sudan, the Democratic Republic of the Congo (Congo), the Congo Republic (Congo-Brazzaville), Rwanda, and the Ivory Coast, has caused states to implode, while tens of millions of people have died as a result of civil war, war, and their apprentices famine, hunger, and disease. In 2000 alone drought and famine struck 16 million people in Ethiopia, Eritrea, Somalia, Sudan, Djibouti, and Uganda.

Exceptions do exist. Democracy was finally restored in Nigeria in 1998, and in South Africa apartheid was eliminated in 1994. Political rights also flourish in Botswana, while in Ghana, Uganda, and Mozambique poverty has been somewhat reduced and some incomes are rising. But overall, sub-Saharan Africa, in the past decade, has been visited by the Four Horsemen of the Apocalypse, "the four scourges of the earth"—Conquest, War, Famine, and Death—who have begun "their mad, desolating course over the heads of humanity."[5]

Too many African countries exist in name only, and their appearance on maps is the only thing coherent about them. And while many people may claim that western news coverage regarding the implosion of Africa is biased and ethnocentric, in the case of Africa south of the Sahara that is inaccurate. The Western media has overall presented a bleak yet ordinarily accurate view of the continent in the late twentieth and early twenty-first centuries. As J. Stephen Morrison, formerly of the U.S. State Department's policy planning staff, indicated in 2000, "It is a very frightening picture that we face in Africa."[6]

The essence of Africa's plight was captured by Nigerian playwright, poet, and novelist Wole Soyinka. In 1994 he was forced to flee the country as Nigeria's brutal military dictator General Sani Abacha, who had turned prisons into torture chambers throughout the state, charged him with treason and ordered his execution. In a 1997 interview Soyinka spoke of a generic African tyrant.

> Never mind that he's just left a nation [to speak before the UN] where millions are on the edge of starvation, where medical delivery no longer exists, where the educational system has collapsed and university students have become virtually illiterate.
>
> Never mind that before or immediately after sounding off on the United Nations podium, he and his entourage detour to the most exclusive medical clinic in Wiesbaden for a routine medical checkup, then stop in London and Paris to pick up new million dollar knick-knacks. . . .
>
> Never mind that he returns home to sign a few death warrants for his alleged enemies, tried in secret with no more evidence against them than confessions wrung from "witnesses" who have been tortured so brutally that they cannot even be presented in court.
>
> [Even in the 1950s, prior to Nigeria's independence] I took one look at our first set of legislators [and] I realized that the first enemy was within.[7]

The first years of the new millennium provided a continuation of the virtual collapse of the nation-state in Africa south of the Sahara, a breakdown that can be traced to the demise of the Soviet Union and the end of the Cold War in 1991. At the time globalization and free trade were touted as the new world order, and Presidents George Bush and Bill Clinton saw both as offering vast political, social, and economic opportunity that soon would be available to the impoverished world. In large part, however, Africa has been bypassed, and a continent rich in resources, which during the Cold War was seen as vital to U.S. national security, has all but been abandoned by the sole remaining superpower. The United States chose to direct its foreign policy initiatives toward other, more vital geopolitical regions. For Africa, the new world order and globalization have proven to be merely a grotesque chimera. This is due to the continent's heritage of slavery, predominately in West Africa, and its racial aftermath, its colonial heritage, its confined geopolitical and geographical location, and its intractable social, political, and ethnic problems. *Africa: A Continent Self-Destructs* emphasizes what has occurred in Africa south of the Sahara since the end of the Cold War in 1991.

Viewed from the framework of the African slave trade, colonialism, and superpower intrusion, the book discusses how these three seminal events facilitated the elimination of opportunities that the newly independent states might have had as they approached independence in the 1960s. When freedom did arrive, it became clear almost immediately that Africa would not be left alone to sort out its own problems. Europe, the Soviet Union, the United States, and even the United Nations impinged on political and economic developments, harming Africa's ability to cope with change. As tyranny followed democracy, and as social and economic life was asphyxiated, many professionals judged individual country events as singular circumstances that could and would eventually be overcome. But they were not, and after 1991 it was evident that, in large part, Africa south of the Sahara was in the throes of a capacious and more permanent destructive cycle that was not idiosyncratic.

Within the 1990s many African states have all but ceased to exist as coherent and organized entities, with some spiraling into complete disintegration. Several were pushed into raucous tyranny, others collapsed into civil war and/or ethnic conflict, while cross-border invasions threatened international peace and security. East, West, Central, and southern Africa were convulsed by events that tore many of these societies apart. What took place in Liberia, Sierra Leone, Guinea, the Ivory Coast, Ethiopia and Eritrea, the Congo, and Zimbabwe will be analyzed from the perspective of ethnic violence, festering white/black antagonism, and internal and external wars.

Africa's most profound contemporary calamity occurred in Rwanda in 1994, when some 800,000 Tutsi and moderate Hutu were murdered in a three-month holocaust in which genocide became state policy. The issue of human rights—in this case the very right to life—

is broached by this calamitous event. The slaying, by order of the Hutu government, is assessed within the framework of human rights and the violation of these rights by western nations and a predatory indigenous government. Similar episodes in Burundi; Islamic/Christian violence in Sudan; clan antagonism in Somalia; civil war in Angola; political turbulence in Swaziland, Nigeria, and Kenya; and continuing white racism and savagery in South Africa can be observed. The issue of political rights segues into whether economic rights have any vitality in Africa south of the Sahara. The fundamental question raised, however, is whether human rights is even a consideration in Africa. The answer is exceedingly disturbing.

It is not merely political issues that have relevance. Poverty in Africa is an extraordinary problem. Indeed, Africa accounts for just 1 percent of global gross domestic product (GDP) and only 2 percent of world trade. Its per capita income is lower today than in the 1960s. Daily existence for most Africans, particularly women, is dismal—safe drinking water is atypical, two-thirds of rural Africa lacks adequate water supplies, 75 percent of its people live without appropriate sanitation, and 2 million of the continent's children die before their first birthday each year.[8] African poverty is exacerbated by the explosion of AIDS on the continent. Of those infected with the HIV virus worldwide, 70 percent, some 25.2 million people, live in sub-Saharan Africa. The continent is the epicenter of an AIDS pandemic. How AIDS and poverty impact politics and social existence is critical when studying the bleakness of Africa's prospects.

A discussion of the role of globalization and its instruments—the World Bank, the International Monetary Fund (IMF), the United States, national financial institutions, and technology companies—will highlight Africa's niche in this new ideology. Since globalization has all but ignored Africa, or often has impacted it negatively, the continent has not benefited very much from the technological integration of world markets. The key question is what bearing globalization will have on Africa's future.

Finally, how can Africa survive these multiple calamities? As all of these issues, from the repercussions of the African slave trade to the eruption of AIDS, hover, Africa's future appears particularly funereal. Certainly some African states have made real progress, and even

Equatorial Guinea may soon benefit from the vast deposits of oil recently discovered off its coastal shores. But without fundamental change—in Africa, at the United Nations, *and* in U.S. foreign policy—the previous decade will have been simply prologue to the future. In the twenty-first century many African countries exist only nominally, and unless authentic reform occurs—indigenously and exogenously—they will continue to implode. The future may well be a continuing series of political, social, and economic coups de main that will be publicized for a while and then replaced by the next and future ethnic explosion.

CHAPTER ONE

The Slave Trade, Colonialism, and the Cold War

When Aimé Césaire, Martinique's great poet, wrote in 1939 that he was a solitary black man ensnared in white who scorned the screams of a "white death,"[1] he voiced the ideology of Négritude, the concept that "represents profound reaction to the denigration of the African and his culture that marked the [slave era and the] colonial period, and which brought many of the Africans to the psychologically perilous position of questioning the basic values by which they had been taught to live. Protest was the first move to reestablish these values,"[2] so as to unearth their social, cultural, and historical heritage.

Léopold Senghor, later president of Senegal, probed a similar refrain in his poem "Paris in the Snow," as he spoke of contemptuous whites who whipped slaves, created hatred, destroyed African kingdoms, and commanded Africa.[3] The fury toward slavery and colonialism that surrounds the poetry of Négritude is again reflected in David Diop's poem "Africa." Also born in Senegal, Diop angrily wrote of African slave blood splattered over African soil by abusive whites who enslaved an entire continent.[4]

These and other black poets like them spoke of an era that constituted, in all its particulars, almost half a millennium of genocide and then an additional century of colonialism. For more than 400 years Africans were forcibly removed from their continent by Portuguese, Dutch, British, French, and other European slavers and spirited away some 3,000 miles where they had to confront entirely different cultures and populations. This appalling traffic in people would impact Africa and the Americas well into the twenty-first century. And the despoiling of Africa by whites, from the slave trade to colonialism, was accomplished only with their own pecuniary advantages in mind. The European world came to Africa and brought along a holocaust, and then occupation.

This first long-term and continual contact between the two continents—slavery—generated victims only—the moral corruption of whites, the physical degradation of Africans—but those who suffered utterly at the hands of westerners were solely African. It was a dynamic based purely and simply on barbarity and terror inflicted by Europeans and experienced by Africans, a violent phenomena situated within the collision of cultures and endless in its consequences. It was truly an association of colonizer and colonized, slaver and slave, the powerful and the powerless. The white/black, European/African connection had its origins in the awfulness of the African slave trade. Sub-Saharan Africa's slave/master association with the West would be the standard upon which all future links would be based. It was a portentous beginning.

THE AFRICAN SLAVE TRADE: THE EUROPEAN OBSCENITY

From 1441 to 1870 the Atlantic slave trade devastated Africa. Estimates vary, but somewhere between 12 million and 15 million Africans were ripped from their homes and villages and transported to the New World. Slavery turned into a torrent after the 1640s as plantation economies blossomed from the West Indies to North and South America, and labor was required to toil on the sugar, tobacco, and cotton estates. Untold millions more were taken, but they died, most during the perilous Middle Passage across the Atlantic Ocean.[5] The triangular system, or Great Circuit trade, consisted of transporting European trinkets and shabby manufactured goods to Africa, purchasing slaves from African chiefs or African traders and ensnaring others, shipping them across the Atlantic for money or agricultural and mineral resources in the Americas and the Caribbean, and finally selling these goods in Europe.

Although an extraordinarily profitable enterprise for Europe, the trade destroyed Africa and eviscerated its people. Conducted essentially in West Africa, in the region between Senegal and Angola, the slaves were savagely rounded up and captured in their villages, manacled, often taken to slave forts on the coast in places such as Goree (an island off the coast of Senegal) and the Gold Coast (Ghana), stored until the arrival of slave ships under the most gruesome and suffocating conditions, and then hounded on to the vessels.

The slaves, according to novelist Barry Unsworth, who was awarded Great Britain's Booker Prize for his narrative *Sacred Hunger,* "were forced up the ladder one by one [as] attendants . . . prodd[ed] them on with their cutlasses. The girl was very young. There were tears on her face, though she made no sound. The faces of the others were fixed and expressionless."[6]

On one boat in 1829, according to a British observer,

> The slaving ship's cargo was of five hundred and five men and women—the crew had thrown fifty-five overboard during their seventeen days at sea—and these slaves "were all enclosed under grated hatchways between decks. The space was so low that they sat between each others' legs, and stowed so close together, that there was no possibility of lying down. . . . [T]hey were all branded like sheep. . . . These were impressed under their breasts or under their arms . . . burnt with a red hot iron."[7]

Between 1500 and 1850, 4 million slaves were taken from Angola, "11,000 per year for 350 years. Politically, the slave trade created great instability." Kingdoms were "subverted or conquered in the struggle to control parts of the slave trade. New kingdoms or autarkies were formed to take advantage of the presence and greed of slave traders, but they were based on the foundations of disobedience to traditional authorities. Such fragmentation and competition for profits created political tension and military conflict." Catholic Portugal maintained that the slave trade in Angola was "spiritually positive," while the Catholic church in Cuba "had no objection to masters trading in slaves [and] remained steadfast in upholding the slavery institution."[8]

Almost as many slaves came from what is today Nigeria as from Angola. "Over the period of the whole trade more than 3.5 million slaves were shipped from Nigeria to the Americas. Most of these slaves were Igbo and Yoruba, with significant concentrations of Hausa, Ibibio, and other ethnic groups."[9] In the Gold Coast area slavery became an "accepted social institution, and the slave trade overshadowed all other commercial activities."[10]

Slaves were treated as merchandise, of which there was an endless supply. Plantations could not operate without ample field workers, but labor was used "with such wasteful folly that whole slave populations had to be replenished time after time." At the end of the eighteenth century, on the Dutch West Indian colony of Surinam, "plantation mortality was so high that 'the whole race of healthy slaves, consisting of 50,000, are totally extinct once every twenty years.'"[11] Brazil imported the largest number of slaves; between 1817 and 1843 alone more than 517,000 Africans were hauled into the country. In the same period of time Cuba took in 87,000; earlier, from 1774 to 1807, it had imported 119, 000.[12]

Perhaps no element of the trade is sadder to observe than the value placed on people in the negotiations conducted between slave traders and tribal chiefs over the purchase price per slave. Such bargaining remains a metaphor for the gruesomeness of the whole business. Basil Davidson, author of The African Slave Trade, illustrates one such event in the seventeenth century as recorded by a European participant. "A man and a fine girl" were exchanged for "One roll tobacco, one string pipe coral[,] One gun, three cutlasses, one brass blunderbuss[,] Twenty-Four linen handkerchiefs, 5 patches, 3 jugs rum[,] Twelve Brittanicas, 12 pint mugs[,] One laced hat, one linen handkerchief." In another transaction, "The factor or supercargo, having finished his sale, is to present the king again with two muskets, twenty-five lbs of powder, and the value of nine slaves in other goods."[13]

Overall the

personal suffering caused by the slave trade can never be calculated. Perhaps only 25 percent of the slaves captured in the hinterland . . . arrived at their destinations. . . . The serious wounds and violent death inflicted at the time of capture, the separation from family and friends, the hunger and thirst along bush trails, the cruel punishments by agents or guards, the diseases and injuries sustained without medical assistance, and the month-long voyage huddled in the cramped, filthy hold of a sailing vessel are aspects of the personal impact of the slave trade of which we cannot even conceive.[14]

And that does not take into account the stupefying horrors that awaited the slaves upon reaching their destination in the New World.

When evaluating the predicament of sub-Saharan Africa in the twenty-first century, one has to take into account the repercussions of slavery on the continent. Robbing Africa of its best and brightest, its farmers and workers, brought about acute economic stagnation. There "can be no doubt that on balance the economic effects of European contact worked steady and decisive damage. After about 1650, with diminishing exceptions, African production-for-export became a monoculture in human beings. It was obviously an impoverishment to send away the very men and women who would otherwise produce wealth at home."[15] Africa has had an arduous time recovering from the economic vacuum formed as its people were mercilessly removed from their communities.

The long-lasting political/psychological effects were just as marked. European whites dominated the relationship; they were in total control. They destroyed much of the traditional economic and political infrastructure and imposed their own system, a service-for-fee pattern of rudimentary capitalism. The primacy of the white "overseer" would remain the pattern of Africa's link with the West—through colonialism, the Cold War, and beyond.

African villages were thrown into turmoil "because the sellers of men infested them by night."[16] The culture, once united by its group or collective notion, had been turned on its head. Ethnic values and social structure were altered. Tribes and tribal chiefs, often along the coast, competed for the economic benefits of the slave trade, raiding interior villages of other tribes to find slaves so as to increase their power and, in many cases, to save their own villagers from being taken by the white slavers. Raids between neighboring villages often occurred when the global demand for slaves was at its height. Within this terrible aberrant institution there existed not a shred of humanity. Capitalist competition over human beings was cultivated into the system, and survival was one of its "profits." Because many Africans partnered with the slavers, societies were transformed into internally riven cultures. Traditional life was largely upended as, in Liberia, for example, there was "massive population movement and displacement with coastal peoples such as the Vai, Gola, Kru, and Bassa preying upon inland peoples such as the Kissi and Dahn."[17] "Things," in Chinua Achebe's voice, began to "Fall Apart."[18]

Slavery, however, was merely sub-Saharan Africa's first lengthy and consistent conversation with the West. Unfortunately, it was not to be the last. "The ultimate demise of slavery and the slave trade was not the end of a bad relationship, for it occurred almost simultaneously with the emergence of still another negative aspect of the Euro-African connection: the imposition of colonial rule."[19] The continent, home to the great ninth- to fifteenth-century West African centralized states of Ghana, Mali, and Songhay, in which the realm of Mali comprised "a land as large as western Europe and as civilized as most of its kind in Europe,"[20] was in the process of being turned into Europe's inextirpable servile minion.

COLONIALISM

The decline of plantation economies in the West Indies due to their ever-decreasing profitability, the rise of industrial capitalism in Europe during the nineteenth century, and the developing vitality and skill of the antislavery movement led eventually to the end of the African slave trade. In 1805 European governments began to trigger its abolition. First Denmark and eventually France, Great Britain, and the others put an end to it. Unauthorized commerce in slaves, however, continued well into the third quarter of the century.

Bridging the close of the slave trade were the developing imperial policies of European states. As the interior of Africa began to be opened up by western explorers, European monarchs and their governments organized official claims to large swaths of the continent. With Portugal, Spain, Germany, England, France, Italy, and Belgium contending for territories, the mammoth land-grab often led to conflict. Imperialism proved to be a very competitive contest, as the rival parties had enormous appetites.

So as to arrest the increasingly dangerous friction among themselves, every European power other than Switzerland, as well as the United States, met in Berlin, Germany, from November 1884 to February 1885 to establish recognized frontiers. In addition, navigation rights were discussed, including the imposition of taxes and tariffs, relating to the Congo and Niger rivers so as to abort potential problems that could arise in those venues. The conference dealt with the most trivial geographic details. Africa was minutely, almost effortlessly diced and distributed to European nations while its own concerns were given not a moment's thought. Arrangements were also made for meetings held later in 1885 and in 1886 that brought about a series of bilateral European agreements which further legitimated the carving up of the continent.

Because Europe's consideration of its own imperial interests was paramount, the conference was very specific in laying out boundaries. For example:

> France . . . was completely cut off from the mouth of the Congo. But she obtained the much coveted valley of the Niari Kwilu, which she was free to incorporate in her province of Gaboon. She also obtained the right bank of the Congo. . . . This meant that although she did not herself have free access to the sea along the Congo, she could easily utilize its upper course for the exploitation of the interior of the Gaboon. . . . Portugal retained only the Cabina enclave, which cut off as it was from the mouth of the river, was of no value in itself. Her possession of the left bank of the river [however] afforded her valuable means of access to her (now) enlarged province of Angola. Neither of these districts, however, was important to Leopold [II, King of the Belgians] for his economic and strategic security on the Congo. This was the essential to him at the conference, and this was fully and firmly assured to him at the conference, under the aegis of [Chancellor Otto von] Bismarck's diplomacy.[21]

Many of contemporary Africa's borders therefore are synthetic, almost fictional, created out of the needs of European rather than African states. Ethnic groups were often divided between territories because a river or ridge served as a demarcation point for a boundary, or because European colonists decided to divvy up tribes among two or even three spheres occupied by different nations. In many cases unrealistic borders encompassed groups with little in common culturally or sociologically. In Chad, Nigeria, Sudan, and Kenya, for example, different ethnic groups or nationalities were forced to coexist. In southwest Ivory Coast, the Cavalla River separates Kru and Grebo tribespeople from their counterparts in Liberia. And formerly British Gambia juts like a long, slim finger directly through the center of the previous French colony of Senegal. Geographical and ethnic absurdity is evident, although the imperialists appeared to have few qualms around their behavior.

Often European states selected one tribe to serve the colonial bureaucracy, creating a dependence on the colonizing nation, while other cultures were politically marginalized. As independence eventually came in the 1960s, these preferred ethnic groups commonly, although not always, gained control over the new state. Resentment by other groups or nationalities intensified. "Divide the land, divide the people" became the all-but-stated imperial policies of the European colonizers.

The interaction of colonizer to colonized was constructed on a base of racism traced directly to the era of the slave trade. According to Albert Memmi, the Tunisian-born author who wrote the classic study *The Colonizer and the Colonized*, "although the economic aspect of colonialism is fundamental . . . racism sums up and symbolizes the . . . relation which unites colonialist and colonized." It was a "consubstantial part of colonialism."[22]

The fascism of the colonial experience entailed removing the colonized from history by denying that they were subjects of history; usurping any role the colonized may have wished to play; negating their objective political and personal importance by destroying their humanity; socializing the colonized to internalize their inferiority; and manipulating the occupied peoples to accept the fact that they were "out of the game."[23] As Cameroonian novelist Ferdinand Oyono so sensitively expressed it in *Boy!* through his protagonist, Toundi Ondoua, who is tortured to death by his French oppressors, "Brother, what are we? What are we blackmen who are called French?"[24]

Nuruddin Farah, the magnificent Somali novelist, bitterly reviews the experience from the perspective of the colonized.

> Africa, for nearly a century, was governed with the iron hand of European colonial economic interests; these ran Africa as though it were a torture-chamber. Africa has known the iron rod, the whiplash, thumbscrewing and removing of testicles: Africa has been humiliated one way or another. I am not saying anything new if I add that whether British, French, Belgian, Spanish, Portuguese or Italian, the colonial mafiadoms which, on behalf of the civilized world, administered the colonies barbarously, savagely, never considered it expedient to allow their sub-human species under their administration the same democratic rights as they themselves had. . . . For the colonies, they created a small elite that, in a world of make-believe, behaved as though they were on a par with their European classmates.[25]

Frantz Fanon, the Martinique-born psychiatrist whose radical books on colonialism in Algeria summed up what oppression meant for all the wretched of the earth, stated that "The colonial world is a world cut in two. The dividing line, the frontiers are shown by barracks and police stations. In the colonies it is the policemen and the soldier who are the official, instituted go-betweens, the spokesmen of the settler and his rule of oppression. . . . But it so happens that when the native hears a speech about Western culture he pulls out his knife—or at least he makes sure it is within reach."[26]

The British and French, who colonized a great deal of sub-Saharan Africa, applied different imperial philosophies in governing their territories. For Great Britain, the application of indirect rule essentially entailed using traditional chiefs to administer its colonies under instruction from European overseers. According to its architect, Frederick Lugard, Britain's high commissioner to northern Nigeria from 1900 to 1914 and to a united Nigeria from 1914 to 1918, "By allowing local rulers to exercise direct administrative control over their people, opposition to European rule from the local population would be minimized. The plan . . . had the further advantage of civilizing the natives because it exposed traditional rulers to the benefits of European political organization and values. This 'civilizing' process notwithstanding, indirect rule had the ultimate advantage of guaranteeing the maintenance of law and order."[27]

Lugard had served in colonial offices in India, Egypt, and East Africa and played the formative role in installing the British in Uganda. To ensure that indirect rule would work in Nigeria, he "systematically subdued local resistence, using armed force when diplomatic measures failed. From Lugard's point of view, clear-cut military victories were necessary because their surrenders weakened resistence [to British domination] elsewhere."[28] Control, rather than "civilizing" the population, was, of course, the primary objective.

In Chinua Achebe's *Arrow of God,* a superb novel considering the issue of indirect governance, in part as a mechanism of divide and rule, the author speaks directly to what really amounts to a pestiferous issue. Through the district officer, Captain T. K. Winterbottom, who is stationed in Okperi, in eastern Nigeria, indirect rule is spoken of a bit differently from the high-minded sounding policy of cultivating and educating the colonized Africans. "What do we British do? We flounder from one expedient to its opposite. We do not only promise to secure old savage tyrants on their thrones—or more likely filthy animal skins—we not only do that, but we now go out of our way to invent chiefs where there were none before. They make me sick." Concurrently, his assistant reads from a book on British policy: "But . . . for those who can deal with men as others deal with material [we can] lead the backward races into line."[29] For Achebe, racism is a key component of the British attitude.

France considered its colonies from a different perspective. Direct rule, the theoretical cultural assimilation of Africans—making Africans into Frenchmen—and association—confirming the dominant position of France and creating a separate system of laws for French citizens in the colonies and for those who were its subjects—were the overall administrative goals. Organized and run out of Dakar, Senegal, a center of French rule for all of West Africa, in the Ivory Coast, for example:

governors appointed in Paris administered the colony . . . using a system of direct, centralizing administration that left little room for Ivoirian participation in policy-making. The French colonial administration also adopted divide-and-rule policies, applying ideas of assimilation only to the educated elite. Africans . . . were allowed to preserve their own customs [only] insofar as they were compatible with French interests. Except in remote rural areas, the colonial government gradually destroyed the traditional elite by reducing the local rulers to junior civil servants and by indiscriminately appointing as rulers people with no legitimate claims to such titles.[30]

Everywhere in West Africa the colonized "were subjects of France and had no political rights." Indeed, in the Central African Republic "forced labor, pillage, atrocities, and wanton killings left the countryside totally alienated, distrustful of all policies . . . and simmering with bitter hatred of Europeans. Moreover, the authority and status of the chiefs were greatly tarnished [as France] pulverized traditional values, proletarianized large masses of people, and caused population dislocations, all of which further detraditionalized society, and weakened the hold of chiefs over their kinsmen."[31]

The newly empowered urban African elites were largely used as intermediaries to keep the traditionals, urban civil servants, and proletariat in line so as to disallow any active response to colonial rule. In Senegal, as expressed in Sembène Ousmane's glittering novel of an African-led railroad strike, *God's Bits of Wood,* the African gentry are sharply criticized for representing the values of whites as opposed to Africans: "A campaign to demoralize and undermine the unity of the strikers . . . had been undertaken by the men who were their 'spiritual guides.'" One African, a deputy in the French parliament, castigates his fellow Africans: "you will accomplish nothing by defying [the whites]."[32]

But as Memmi indicates, no matter the philosophy, whether direct rule or indirect rule, be it French or British control, the entire system was fundamentally "colonial racism . . . built from three major ideological components: one, the gulf between the culture of the colonialist and the colonized; two, the exploitation of these differences for the benefit of the colonialist; three, the use of these supposed differences as standards of absolute fact." Assimilation was nonsense, a fanciful mirage used to dupe Africans since "the colonialist could not favor an undertaking which would have contributed to the disappearance of colonial relationships."[33]

The colonial policy of Belgium in the Congo, Rwanda, and Burundi was openly based on racism. It was also deadly, as in the Congo millions died under genocidal schemes. Paternalism, the concept that Africans were unprepared for "civilized" life and had to be readied for it over a never-ending period of time, allowed Belgium to treat its colonized as little more than toddlers. Education was, for example, largely ignored. When Rwanda won its independence, it had one African high school graduate while the Congo had merely five college graduates. The trauma evident in all three nations after independence speaks to the criminal activities of Belgium in the territories it once dominated.[34]

Overall, then, colonialism was a terribly destructive force. It vanquished societies and individuals. It created African elites, functionally removing them from traditional society, but refusing to permit them to truly assimilate; the result was a new culture of Africans who fit comfortably in neither one community nor the other. Zimbabwean author Tsitsi Dangarembga sizes up the widespread impact of the horror of colonial governance and the newly contrived noncentered heritage in her somewhat terrifying novel, *Nervous Conditions*. Nyasha, a young African woman of Zimbabwe's elite and the book's ill-fated heroine, has a nervous breakdown as a result of the stress placed upon her by colonialism. During one of her seizures she proclaims in all her anger and fury, "do you see what they've done? They've taken us away. Lucia. Takesure. All of us. They've deprived you of you, him of him, ourselves of each other. We're groveling. Lucia for a job, Jeremiah for money. Daddy grovels to them. We grovel to him. I won't grovel. Oh no, I won't. . . . They've trapped us. They've trapped us. . . . I'm not one of them but I'm not one of you."[35]

The colonial experience is emblematic of man's inhumanity to man and woman. According to one observer in Dangarembga's novel, "it'll kill them all if they aren't careful."[36] Often spoken of by Europeans of the time as an ennobling experience for Africans, in much the same way Israelis, more recently, absurdly considered the occupation of the West Bank as enriching for Palestinians, colonialism was neither. It was an encounter that brought about "the mental sedimentation and . . . the emotional and intellectual handicaps which resulted from" more than 100 years of political, social, and economic oppression in Africa.[37] It was parasitic fare that like a tapeworm sucked the life from the body politic.

THE COLD WAR

Just as the African slave trade proceeded seamlessly to colonial rule, so colonialism segued into the doctrinaire conduct of the Cold War. When, in the 1960s, most African states attained independence, the United States and the Soviet Union (and often European states) moved into the vacuum created by the departure of the imperialists and extended the ethnic and tribal divisions so that their own interests could be served. Colonization was replaced by a form of Cold War neocolonialism—control of the new nations (or the old ones, for that matter) of Africa via their economies and through the national elites who had been cultivated by the Europeans. One superpower would buttress the elites empowered by the colonial authorities, while the other often backed the opposition, as each supported a different client and a different agenda. If elites could not be controlled they were often dismissed or eliminated, replaced by others more patronizing to the superpowers. In Somalia and Ethiopia (a nation never traditionally colonized), for example, different politicians were served by one or the other of the major powers. By continuing the colonial intrusions, while pouring billions of dollars worth of weaponry into client states, superpowers trained political elites to use the arms to support the vital interests of the respective superpower and to resist competing indigenous forces.

The United States, as the only western superpower, moved to supplant the now-marginalized countries, such as France and Great Britain, as their colonies were freed. It filled the vacuum left by the departure of the colonizers so as to prevent the spread of communism and radical nationalism, which would threaten American interests. The Soviet Union represented just such a menacing and alien communist ideology. The Cold War credo, expressed in the Truman Doctrine of 1947, provided the framework of containment within which the United States resolved to pursue a policy of intervention in Africa.[38] For the Soviet Union, these newly independent states offered opportunities to expand its sphere of interest. From the 1960s to 1991, the year the Soviet Union collapsed, the respective interests of the U.S. and the USSR often clashed in Africa. Each side "undertook for what it honestly saw as defensive reasons actions that the other honestly saw as unacceptably threatening and requiring countermeasures. Each succumbed to the propensity to perceive local conflicts in global terms, political conflicts in moral terms and relative differences in absolute terms."[39]

The United States and the Soviet Union frequently fanned the fires of ethnic diversity, since their support of one group or one leader primarily meant that tribes and nationalities not represented by the American-financed or Soviet-supported leadership were left out in the political cold. Frustration and alienation with the ruling classes easily germinated since the same policy of divide and conquer had been the colonial fare. Little had changed. But now, with independence, and with military arms pouring into the region, the ruling nobility was not in Paris or London but in Accra, Lagos, Kinshasa, or Bangui, and African army commanders and the ranks of the enlisted had weapons or access to them. The political upper class was no longer unreachable and untouchable.

Clans, ethnic groups, and nationalities in a given state frequently did not consider other cultures part of their tribal nation, or were socialized by the colonizers to see dissimilar ethnic societies as alien. Once the constraints limiting political behavior had dissolved with the departure of the European overlords, the violence that often accompanied the ensuing struggles for indigenous control or superpower hegemony was awesome and destructive. In Africa, those not seen as part of the national sphere were frequently viewed outside the boundaries of normal political discourse and were deemed to be ominously threatening.

Both the Soviet Union and the United States, however, pursued their own interests irrespective of the internal political dynamics of African states. As long as their concerns converged with those of the respective ruling elites, domestic politics interested them not at all.

Concurrently, the elites utilized the apprehension of the superpowers to buttress their own power vis-à-vis disgruntled domestic forces. Internal political friction was thus exacerbated and inflamed by the two world powers.

Ethiopia, Somalia, and the Superpowers: Neighborly Truculence

Ethiopia received enormous U.S. military assistance beginning as early as 1953. Located on the southern littoral of the Red Sea, which flows into the Suez Canal in the north and the Gulf of Aden in the south, the country was seen by President Dwight D. Eisenhower as vital to America's geopolitical interests. Preventing the Soviets from blockading western oil lanes was an indispensable element to the economic security of the West, while keeping the Red Sea and Indian Ocean open for Israeli and Israeli-bound shipping also ministered to U.S. interests.

The strategic geographic location of Ethiopia served it well in that Emperor Haile Selassie I was able to obtain funds and military supplies from the United States; in return, the United States obtained base rights, which allowed it to keep tabs on the Red Sea/Indian Ocean area. A mutual-defense treaty was signed between the two nations in 1953 that laid the basis for the modernization of Ethiopia's military and was to be used to maintain the country's internal security, its self-defense, and to permit the United States to participate in the defense of the area.

Between 1953 and 1974 the United States supplied Ethiopia with over $200 million in military assistance. Until 1970 this represented nearly half the total U.S. military support to all African states. In 1953 Kagnew, an American military base near Asmara, in Eritrea, which was then part of Ethiopia, was set up for tracking space satellites, relaying military communications, and monitoring radio broadcasts from Eastern Europe and the Middle East. Thirty-two hundred U.S. military personnel were quartered there.[40] By 1960 Eisenhower had secretly committed to oppose "any activities threatening the territorial integrity of Ethiopia." In 1970 the U.S. Senate Foreign Relations Committee, then chaired by Senator William Fulbright, uncovered data indicating that, in 1964, President Lyndon B. Johnson moved three separate counterinsurgency teams to Ethiopia, which were instrumental in facilitating that nation's efforts to oppose the secessionist Eritrean Liberation Movement (ELF). David Newsom, President Richard Nixon's assistant secretary of state for African affairs, indicated in testimony given at the hearings that Ethiopia "is an area in which we have very substantial interests."[41]

To be sure, most of the military equipment received by Ethiopia was used to combat internal opponents—most particularly the Eritrean liberation fighters who, after 1962, were engaged in a titanic, and eventually successful, 31-year struggle to secede from Ethiopia. Since the military was indispensable to Haile Selassie's power, the U.S. munitions also had the effect of reinforcing the soldiers' support. Indigenous political forces, markedly alienated by the totalitarian and feudal policies of Haile Selassie so richly endowed by the United States, were eventually unleashed in a deadly and ultra-violent political explosion in 1974 that was amazing in its Marxist fervor and anti-American sentiment. United States nourishment of the emperor was significantly responsible for the vehemence of the advocates of the 1974 revolution.

Initial military assistance agreements between the civilian government of Somalia and the Soviet Union, calling for $35 million in grants and credits, were signed in 1963. After 1969, when the civilian government was overthrown by the armed forces, the Soviets approved an additional $50 million in grants. Furthermore, Moscow assisted Somalia in constructing port facilities at Berbera, overlooking the Red Sea. Naval support networks, including two Soviet communications facilities, were opened there in 1972, and a Soviet air base was unveiled at Harghessa the same year. By October 1977 the Soviet Union had granted more than $250 million in military aid to Somalia, while 2,300 Soviet personnel and military advisors were stationed in the country.[42]

The United States and the Soviet Union were locked into a Cold War conflict on the Horn of Africa. Contending information installations, competing naval forces, air force overflights, land-based military counselors, insurgency activity, counterinsurgency efforts, harsh martial rhetoric, and hundreds of millions of dollars in armaments were centered in the region. Superpower rivalry within the African Horn was intense and somewhat threatening to regional stability.

The absurdity of the Soviet/U.S. dynamic was played out for all the world to see in 1977. By then Ethiopia was under Marxist rule, and

Somalia, trying to take advantage of the revolutionary turmoil playing itself out, invaded Ethiopia's Ogaden region in a foolhardy attempt to annex it. The Soviets, enamored of the Ethiopian revolution, airlifted 1,500 military advisors and $875 million in arms to Ethiopia, and persuaded Cuba to send 16,000 military troops to sustain Ethiopia's defense. President Jimmy Carter, although unsympathetic to Somalia's invasion, moved eventually to send economic aid to the Somalis as U.S. diplomatic personnel were expelled from Ethiopia and given four days to leave the country. At the time it was suggested (only partly in jest) that the planes of the Soviet Union and the United States passed each other in the skies over Ethiopia and Somalia as they each shifted allegiance and relocated military personnel to the nation each had originally viewed as the opponent's client.

By 1984 the Soviets had supplied Ethiopia with an additional $3 billion in military aid and had developed an anchorage in the Dahlak islands off Ethiopia on the Red Sea. Through 1981 the United States had delivered $40 million in "defensive" military aid to Somalia; the American State Department, then peopled by President Ronald Reagan's administrators, announced the aid was "part of a strategic framework in response to the Soviet threat in the region."[43]

Years later all this military hardware would be used against domestic opponents as Somalia entered a period of ferocious civil strife in 1991 that continues today, while from 1998 to 2000 Ethiopia and Eritrea engaged in one of Africa's bloodiest wars.[44] Russia, one of the successor states to the now-defunct Soviet Union, and the United States have only their Cold War military policies to blame for the anarchy that presently passes for government rule in Somalia and the blistery destructive war that convulsed Ethiopia and Eritrea. Many other African states, as the evidence will demonstrate, have been left reeling by the hangover generated by Cold War policies. It is a repugnant heritage.

A CRIPPLING TRILOGY

The slave trade, colonialism, and the Cold War left Africa with a ruinous heritage that has been exceedingly difficult to subdue. For more than five centuries, first Europe, then the United States and the Soviet Union have done what they could to eviscerate Africa and its people. According to Fanon, who spoke merely of the industrialist states, "For centuries the capitalists have behaved in the underdeveloped world like nothing more than war criminals. Deportations, massacres, forced labor, and slavery have been the main methods used by capitalism to increase its wealth, its gold or diamond reserves, and to establish its power."[45] Fanon went on to maintain that it is "a just reparation which will be paid to us. This help should be the ratification of a double realization: the realization by the colonized peoples that *it is their due,* and the realization by the capitalist powers that in fact *they must pay.*"[46]

Whether reparations ever take place or not, they will hardly compensate for the paralysis imposed history has caused in Africa. Historiography offers compelling evidence that the predicate of independent Africa gave it little opportunity to begin the era of freedom with much of a chance for political or economic success. Economies were destroyed, resources were all but stolen and removed to the western metropolises, people were enslaved, ethnic harmony was sundered and often replaced by fratricide, elite/traditional dichotomies were provoked as normative and customary authorities were made impotent, politics was treated dismissively, while obsequious politicians were infantilized.

Indeed, the wide-ranging force of nationalism, which was often explosive in other sectors of the globe, appeared in Africa only intermittently. Upon independence or shortly thereafter, most new presidents and prime ministers were content to indicate, as did Gabon's first president, Léon M'ba, that nationalism had little appeal to the new elites: "Gabon is independent, but between Gabon and France nothing has changed; everything goes on as before."[47]

Quite a few African nationalists who did appear on the scene, such as Ghana's first prime minister and president, Kwame Nkrumah, who was a fervent leftist, found themselves fairly rapidly out of power or, in the case of Guinea's president Sékou Touré, isolated.[48] Some of course did flourish and had impressive careers; Kenya's Jomo Kenyatta and Julius K. Nyerere of Tanzania are two imposing examples, as is South Africa's Nelson Mandela, who underwent his own personal and political ordeal while spending almost three decades in prison. But, overall, "embryonic nationalisms which had already begun to develop [in 1939] among certain African peoples are nowhere discussed,"[49] because in most cases they were stillborn.

In the bitter harvest of slavery, colonial rule, and Cold War politics, nationalism in sub-Saharan Africa was replaced by greed and the struggle for power. As Achebe, in his literary assault on the new age, raged, "to occupy a 'European post' was second only to being a European. It raised a man from the masses to the élite whose small talk at cocktail parties was: 'How's the car behaving?'"[50]

All in all, prior to 1991 independence had never really arrived. Until the removal of the Soviet Union to the dustbin of history Africa was still slave to foreign demands. Even after that portentous year Africa south of the Sahara remained unable to thrust itself onto a level international playing field. With the end of the Cold War and the elimination of U.S. national security interests, the continent was all but abandoned by the United States. Post-1991 independence entailed virtual isolation and compelled negation as the West absolved itself of any responsibility for its past dealings with the continent. The playing field was essentially bequeathed to the African seekers of power whose ethical and humane political antennae were nonexistent. The killers and marauders were pretty much left alone to do as they liked. As the slave era evolved into the colonial period, and as colonialism shifted to the Cold War, so too the non-Soviet era, which sallied forth from the Cold War, would offer sub-Saharan Africa another mortifying period from which it would be hard-pressed to recover. There would be No Sweetness Here.[51]

CHAPTER TWO

Civil Wars, Wars, and Political Collapse

Since the end of the Cold War in 1991, a host of African states have all but ceased to exist as functioning entities. Many have disintegrated entirely. The only circumstance that defines them is an orderly set of connected lines drawn on a map that distinguish them from their neighbors and in the middle of which the name of a country is designated. These so-called nations are currently demarcated solely by civil wars, ethnic conflict, tumultuous tyrannies, cross-border invasions that threaten international peace and security, countless refugees, long-harbored racial animosity, and brutalities that are often of an unspeakable nature.

They are frequently agriculture-based entities with one-crop and sometimes no-crop economies, or mineral-rich with the resources commonly used to fund civil strife; many find themselves characterized by the United Nations as among the least developed countries in the world, and just as often as amid the most corrupt. "It is noteworthy that in the 1999 Transparency International Corruption Perceptions Index, five of the ten worst offenders were in Africa."[1]

check out indicators

Corruption

The corruption begins at the top of the political order and sinks to the bottom, seeping into everyday existence. Nigeria and the Congo are notorious in that regard. In both, virtually everything, including getting in and out of the airport and even retrieving one's luggage, has its price, or "dash" as it is called in much of Africa. "So it went [at Congo-Kinshasa's Ndjili Airport]; with a few banknotes shed every twenty feet, no more than five dollars in all, he spirited me through passport control, check-in, and customs in fifteen minutes flat, while around me I watched sweating men and women endure hour-long shakedowns as their passports disappeared for 'closer inspection' or their luggage was rifled through sock by sock."[2] Leaving Guinea's airport in the capital, Conakry, I was once forced to spend four hours in a taxi, with my luggage locked in the trunk, because I refused to pay an exorbitant bribe to redeem my bags, while the local police, who took an interminable time to arrive, shrugged their shoulders, smiled, and championed the driver.

Nigeria's Chinua Achebe wrote a splendid novel savagely attacking the wholesale state of corruption in his nation. In *No Longer at Ease,* in which very few characters remain untainted by the affliction, Achebe, through Obi Okonkwo, the book's primary protagonist who eventually succumbs to the disease of bribery, reflects on the subject. "'What an Augean stable!' he muttered to himself. 'Where does one begin? With the masses? Educate the masses?' He shook his head. 'Not a chance there. It would take centuries. A handful of men at the top. Or even one man with vision—an enlightened dictator. People are scared of the word nowadays. But what kind of a democracy can exist side by side with so much corruption? . . . Perhaps a half-way house— a sort of compromise.'"[3]

In much of Africa, because of the ethnic factiousness that is a remnant of the colonial era and the uncommon poverty that strangles the continent, the struggle for power is seen as a contest for survival. In a region in which a middle-class bourgeoisie hardly exists, and where few countervailing institutional structures endure to provide wealth and opportunity on a scale provided by government or the military, securing and holding on to the sole venues of power engenders what I would term the "cling abstraction." Particular individuals attain control any way they can and mercilessly cleave to it.

Achebe makes the same point but, naturally, in a literary setting. In his novel *A Man of the People,* he proclaims:

> A man who has just come in from the rain and dried his body and put on dry clothes is more reluctant to go out again than another who has been indoors all the time. The trouble with our new nation . . . was that none of us had been indoors long enough to be able to say "To hell with it." We had all been in the rain together until yesterday. Then a handful of us—the smart and the lucky and hardly ever the best—had scrambled for the one shelter our former rulers left, and had taken it over and barricaded themselves in.[4]

From the 1990s to the present, East, West, Central, and southern Africa were overwhelmed by ordeals that tore many societies asunder. Beset by bedlam initiated, harnessed, or aggravated by despotic leaders, civilians found themselves battered by events and engulfed by confusion. Drought, famine, and starvation were additional plagues that tore through populations as they fled advancing armies or rebels. In the process millions perished, perhaps hundreds of thousands were murdered, while other millions were driven out of their homesteads and converted into refugees.

Buchi Emecheta, in her novel of the 1967 Nigerian civil war and the secession of the eastern region, which survived for three years as the state of Biafra, speaks of the timeless turmoil of refugees everywhere in Africa. The plight of African outcasts in any decade, whether by the handful or in the scores of thousands, speaks to dread and apprehension: "When it was completely dark . . . the four women backed the babies and led the older children into the bush, but not before the widow had fed them hot yam porridge, spiced with pepper and laced with chunks of bush meat. That, at least, would last them through the night. . . . They hugged her and left in single file, refugees of the darkening night setting out on their long journey through the thick . . . bush."[5]

Certainly, not all countries underwent such thoroughgoing hardship. But enough did that by 2001 calamity just about became the norm by which much of the continent was appraised. The states considered next are prototypes of what Africa has experienced within the past few years when abomination rampaged through the continent.

WEST AFRICA: THE IVORY COAST, SIERRA LEONE, AND LIBERIA

The Ivory Coast

The latest, but perhaps most telling, implosion occurred in the Ivory Coast in the final months of 2000. Once known as a country of wealth and stability, the nation metamorphosed into an ethnically perilous space. Although certainly by far not the most explosive country in West Africa, the events, as they unfolded, certify that what appear to be the most stable of nations, are in actuality on the edge of an abyss. Thus, I begin with the latest blowup.

One of the world's major producers and exporters of cocoa, the country had been dominated for decades by President Félix Houphouët-Boigny. Intent on "creating a climate of confidence and stability favorable to foreign interests," he developed a program of economic liberalism and economic planning that led to the creation of "the infrastructure and guarantees necessary to growth—roads, ports, buildings, telecommunications, etc."[6] Until the 1980s economic growth rates averaged an astounding 8 to 10 percent annually, while ethnic differences "proved to be of minor significance." In 1985 the gross domestic product growth rate remained a powerful 4.9 percent.[7] Holding to a conservative political philosophy, Houphouët-Boigny cooperated closely with France from the time of independence in 1960 until his death in December 1993, and, in turn, the Ivory Coast's economic miracle served as a poster boy for French economic policy in West Africa.

But his passing changed everything. One month later Henri Konan Bédié was elected president of the ruling party and took over control of the country. In 1995 multiparty elections were held. Although Bédié won the presidency, it was the result of the promulgation of an election code that barred northern Muslim Ivoirians from seeking the office. A number of parties boycotted the vote, and the stage was set for the development of ethnic/religious conflict.

The country was also thrown into a furor when, in 1996, it got caught up in Liberia's civil war as more than 350,000 refugees fleeing the conflict poured into the Ivory Coast. Despite international appeals, thousands more were turned back as they attempted to enter the Southwest by boating across the Cavalla River, which demarcates the border between the two nations.

By late 1999 troops overthrew the unpopular president due to what they claimed were unpaid wages, widespread corruption, unemployment, and government-supported ethnocentrism aimed at separating Christian southern Ivoirians from northern Muslim "outsiders." General Robert Gueï took power as head of a military junta promising speedy elections and a return to democracy and civilian rule. Within months, however, despite international opprobrium, he inflamed the antinorthern atmosphere and resolved to run for the presidency in 2000. The military coup d'état, along with ethnic and religious discordance, had arrived in the Ivory Coast. A new and more threatening politics was now in the offing as the country began its course along a thoroughfare of misery.

As a result of the Arab inrush across the Sahara centuries ago, Islam dominates Ivoirian culture in the North, while Christianity, brought to Africa by Europeans involved in the slave trade and seeking riches, is ascendent in the South. Until 1993 few religious problems existed. Bédié, however, created the concept of "Ivoirité,"or Ivoirianness. It was, in effect, a concocted distinction between "pure" Ivoirians from the South and Muslim "immigrants" in the North. In addition, people with merely one native parent (presumably the other progenitor would have emigrated from the bordering state of Burkina Faso, Mali, Guinea, or Ghana) were defined as outside the rubric of Ivoirité. Muslim immigrants from Mali and Burkina Faso, who were primarily employed as fishermen, were brusquely expelled from the Ivory Coast, while a Christian xenophobic campaign against Muslim northerners was launched. Discrimination became officially sanctioned. With 40 percent of Ivoirians being Muslim, 30 percent Christian, and the balance largely animist, the country's integrative history was in the process of being torn asunder.

In September 2000 General Gueï, who had inflamed the antinorthern atmosphere by attacking believers in democracy as xenophilous, escaped an assassination attempt. His political opponents claimed the endeavor was bogus, that it was merely a theatrical stunt devised to shore up citizen support for Gueï and his policies. Nonetheless, scores of Muslim military personnel were arrested. The second and third in command of Gueï's military junta, who were supporters of Alassane Ouattara, the head of the opposition party Rally of the Republicans and a northern Muslim candidate for the presidency, were ousted from their positions.

To exclude the popular Ouattara from the ballot—he was an economist with the International Monetary Fund (IMF) and held the post of prime minister from 1990 to 1993—so as to ensure his own election, Gueï had the constitution amended to require presidential candidates to be born of Ivoirian parents. Gueï accused Ouattara, his foremost opponent and in a free election a possible victor, of being the son of persons who were from Burkina Faso. Ouattara, who was born in the northern city of Kong, angrily rejected the charge.

In a country whose politics have been dominated by Christian ethnic groups, Ouattara's popularity and his northern/Muslim heritage were seen as threatening to supporters of Gueï. By October the Supreme Court, intimidated by the general, ruled that Ouattara and eight other Muslim candidates were ineligible to run for the presidency. Five Christian nominees, including Laurent Gbagbo, leader of the third largest party, the Ivoirian Popular Front, were allowed on the ballot. Gbagbo, a so-called socialist, had also organized his campaign around Christian ascendancy and his representation of ethnically pure Ivoirians. His political platform was based chiefly on xenophobia against northerners. The Rally of the Republicans, along with the late Houphouët-Boigny's seasoned Democratic Party, beseeched their supporters to boycott the election.

Halfhearted attempts by the Organization of African Unity (OAU) and ten African heads of state, in meetings held in Togo and the Ivory Coast, to pressure Gueï to accede to democratic electoral processes failed. The OAU, the European Union, and the United States then canceled plans to send observers to oversee what they termed an "undemocratic election," while international foreign donors withdrew promised financing to pay for the election's cost.

The balloting took place on October 22, 2000. Despite Gueï's political machinations, it became clear within two days that Gbagbo was far ahead in the vote count, although turnout was exceptionally low. Gueï dissolved the electoral commission posthaste and declared himself the winner. Gbagbo responded by calling upon his supporters to "stand up against the imposter," while France, the former colonial authority and still a commanding presence in the country—20,000 of its citizens work there and the place is home to a garrison of French troops—demanded "the military junta respect the will of the people."[8]

For a moment something new to Africa transpired as tens of thousands of unarmed citizens spontaneously took to the streets of the commercial capital, Abidjan, to condemn the electoral putsch and were joined by elements of the armed forces, police, and security services. Democracy, as represented by the broad-based popular movement, appeared to have taken hold as on October 25 Gueï, stunned by the demonstrations, vacated his position and relinquished power. Gbagbo then declared himself president and was swiftly inaugurated.

But democracy was short-lived. Ouattara rejected Gbagbo's political legitimacy and authority to govern and called for new and fair elections that would also encompass the northern/Muslim-based political parties. Supported by the military and the French government, Gbagbo defied Ouattara's demand, promptly setting off vicious street battles between Muslim supporters of Ouattara and Christian devotees of Gbagbo.

Parts of Abidjan, a lovely, modern, and architecturally exquisite city consisting of neighborhoods largely divided along the black/white divide, were torched. A number of the city's mosques were burned and trashed. Almost 200 people were killed, many executed by the security forces and dumped into a garbage dump. The bitter ethnic/religious divisions brought into play by Bédié, Gueï, and Gbagbo, in their effort to hold on to or achieve power, rapidly ended any hopes for a democratic, economically viable Ivory Coast. By 1998 the average annual GDP percentage growth rate over an eight-year span had slipped to 2.9 percent.[9]

The extremely dangerous tribal divisions that were the emblems of many of its African neighbors had oozed into the Ivory Coast. These divisions were punctuated after the protests by the Supreme Court's refusal, once again on ethnic grounds and issues of nationality, to permit Ouattara to seek parliamentary office in 2000. Gbagbo supported the decision and gave an incendiary speech all but declaring war against northerners. More riots and deaths followed, while Ivoirians gave more credence to talk of civil war and secession by the North. The country would not be the same again.

Sierra Leone

In 2000 the *New York Review of Books* referred to Sierra Leone as "the worst place on earth."[10] An agriculture-based country, its rural population and city traders rely largely on the export of cocoa, coffee, and palm oil and on the production of rice and cassava, while the urban elite has benefited from the corrupt diversion of public funds into its hands and the consignment of diamond mining to foreign firms.[11] This netherworld has been convulsed by civil war since 1991. Indeed, Sierra Leone qualifies as a state whose military personnel have spent the better part of their efforts tormenting and persecuting their people. For the past ten years the country has turned upon itself in a manner that most of humanity would find incomprehensible.

In 1991 a group of Sierra Leonean rebels invaded the country from northwest Liberia and moved into the diamond-rich region of Kailahun. Within a year the president, Joseph Momoh, was ousted in a military coup, but fighting between government forces and the rebel Revolutionary United Front (RUF), led by Foday Sankoh, continued. Although Sierra Leone has been beset by numerous coups d'état since it received its independence from Great Britain in 1961 and Sir Milton Margai became prime minister, the events that began in 1991 were the most profound and painful the country had ever confronted.

By 1994 most foreigners had been evacuated, while tens of thousands of Sierra Leonean civilians fled into Guinea. That same year Sankoh took control of the country's diamond, bauxite, and titanium mines, enabling him to acquire the funds to dramatically expand his campaign, while his terroristic maneuvers, which consisted of burning villages, murdering civilians, and kidnapping tribal chiefs, were expanded within the southern and eastern regions of the country. Nine hundred thousand people (out of a population of 4.8 million) had, at that point, been turned into refugees.

One year later Sankoh's forces were poised to capture the capital, Freetown, when another military coup occurred. The new military junta, however, pledged to hold free elections, and in early 1996 Ahmad Tejan Kabbah, of the Sierra Leone People's Party, was elected president. Kabbah, in an attempt to settle the ongoing civil war, reached an accord with Sankoh, which was brokered by the Ivory Coast, that permitted him to participate in the affairs of state. Within months, however, Major Johnny Paul Koromah overthrew the government, Kabbah fled to Guinea, and in 1997 the country once again collapsed into civil war. Nigerian troops, which had originally been dispatched to Freetown to prop up Kabbah, organized the military opposition to Koromah. Within two years, more than 1,000 of their soldiers were killed. By 1998 the Economic Community of West African States Monitoring Group (ECOMOG) sent in thousands of Nigerian, Ghanaian, and other West African military forces under its command to oust Koromah and try to stabilize the country. The endeavor was also supported by fighters from a London-based private mercenary organization. Koromah was neutralized, Kabbah was reinstalled, but the country and the economy were in shambles. Yet, amazingly enough, this was just the beginning. The politics of mutilation was only now getting under way.

Soldiers of the RUF, whom U.S. Ambassador to the United Nations Richard C. Holbrooke labeled "a bunch of ragtag, machete-wielding murderers,"[12] swarmed into Freetown in 1999 randomly murdering babies, women, and the elderly. Scores of thousands of civilians, including children, in the capital and elsewhere had their hands or arms, legs, and lips cut off, while huge swaths of the city were put to the torch. Towns and villages throughout the country were razed, tens of thousands killed, and 25 percent of the population driven from their homes. Women were kidnaped and turned into sex slaves, villagers were prevented from farming, while famine spread. For Sankoh, unadulterated terror was plainly an avenue to power, since it was predicated on pressuring the population and government to accept his authority knowing that only then would the horrors finally cease. Some 600,000 people were now piled into refugee camps in Guinea, while in Freetown alone more than 200,000 were displaced and 5,000 killed as fighting raged between the troops of ECOMOG and the rebels.

Finally, in mid-1999 a peace agreement was signed in Lomé, Togo, in which all parties agreed to a permanent end to hostilities. Sankoh was given the government portfolio that placed him in charge of the diamond mines, he and his rebel fighters were to be given a full amnesty for crimes committed during the civil war, and the RUF was to be transformed into a political party. Later that year the UN Security Council dispatched 6,000 peacekeepers, subsequently expanded to 13,000, including troops from India, Jordan, Kenya, Ghana, and Nigeria, in an effort to ensure order.

In May 2000, after a politically stormy ten-month lull in internecine fighting, Sankoh resurrected his war against the government and people, hoping finally to attain the absolute power he had been seeking since 1991. The killings and mutilations began anew. Simultaneously 500 UN peacekeepers were taken hostage by the RUF. Over the next two months their release was negotiated or they were plucked from captivity. Because of the continuing impotence of ECOMOG and the UN peacekeepers, Sankoh was once again on the verge of capturing Freetown. Great Britain then sent 1,000 crack troops to secure the capital, while an additional 500 British sailors and marines were stationed offshore. Although Sankoh was finally captured and arrested by combatants supporting President Kabbah, the RUF maintained its horrific warfare throughout the state well into 2001 as two-thirds of the country remained under its control. The battle for Sierra Leone appears unending despite a defunct cease-fire agreed to in Nigeria at the end of 2000.[13]

Besides the human toll, the decade-long crisis has been an economic and social calamity. Sierra Leone ranks 174—last—on the Human Development Report index. Life expectancy is 37 years, while the infant mortality rate is 169 per 1,000 live births. In 1997 GDP annual growth was -20.2 percent. The country is ranked 47 out of 48 sub-Saharan African states in gross national product (GNP) per capita; Somalia is last. After 1990 annual palm oil export growth plummeted to an average -21.7 percent, cocoa exports declined from 13,000 metric tons in 1991 to 3,000 in 1997, while the average annual growth rate of coffee exports averaged -7.6 percent in the 1990s. Sixty-seven percent of the population is illiterate.[14] More than 25 percent of the citizenry have been transformed into refugees. Hunger and starvation are mounting problems.

The enduring anarchy also impacted exogenous military and political authorities. As conflicts arose among the various peacekeeping forces because of their frustration at not being able to bring the fighting to a halt, India withdrew its contingent of 3,059 soldiers under UN command at the end of 2000. Soon thereafter Jordan's 1,800 soldiers exited the country.

The United States, unwilling to enter the fray, but fearful that it would be accused of sitting by while another African soldiery was slaughtering its people, dispatched hundreds of servicemen to Nigeria to train an additional 7,500 Nigerian and Ghanaian troops to eventually bolster the UN contingent to 20,500. Concurrently, the UN Security Council voted to increase their number and security functions and to establish a war crimes tribunal to try Sierra Leonean "crimes against humanity." It also, *finally*, imposed a global ban on diamond exports from Sierra Leone for a three month period and, as the gems have largely fueled the civil strife, declared that diamonds can only be purchased from licensed Sierra Leonean dealers—a restriction which is utterly unenforceable.

Liberia's president, Charles Taylor, supported Sankoh. It was Taylor who advised him to use barbarity in support of politics, and, according to the UN Security Council, Taylor and President Blaise Compaore of Burkina Faso serve as conduits for selling Sierra Leonean diamonds abroad to subsidize the revolt and enrich all three men who are reported to have taken a large cut of the profits. Many of the gems are said to pass through Gambia. In 1999 alone Liberia exported $300 million worth of smuggled Sierra Leonean stones. By 2001 the UN moved to bar all diamond exports from Liberia unless its support for the RUF is terminated. Taylor and Compaore remain serious benefactors of the Sierra Leonean rebels.

Liberia has also sent its armed forces on intermittent forays into Guinea, which had given sanctuary to 675,000 Sierra Leonean and Liberian refugees. More than 300 civilians were killed in crossfire between Guinean and Liberian troops through early 2001, while hundreds of others were massacred by Liberia's military. Relief agencies were forced to flee the area. Representatives of the United Nations High Commissioner for Refugees (UNHCR) have been killed and abducted. Guinea responded by sending its army into northern Sierra Leone in periodic raids against opposing forces. Guineans are presently caught up in battles among Liberian, Sierra Leonean, and Guinean armies, and the contending rebel forces of each country; Guinea's political leaders are unable to control the maelstrom.

The role of the United States and the United Nations has been abysmal. The United States has been unwilling to get involved in any meaningful way. Intimidated by its failure to resolve the chaos in Somalia, where 22,000 troops had been dispatched from 1992 to 1993 and then abruptly withdrawn in 1994 when 18 U.S. soldiers were killed, Washington had no appetite for further involvement in the internecine warfare spreading throughout Africa. More important, with the collapse of the Soviet Union in 1991, the United States found that it no longer had any national interests to speak of in Africa. "With the end of the Cold War, the U.S. strategic interest in Africa is minimal. Africa is simply not commanding the kind of attention in the new world order to keep it from dissolving into new world disorder. 'GLOBAL ECONOMY' is the foreign policy king, and there has been no economic rationale for dealing with sub-Saharan Africa, especially since the continent began its freefall in the 1980s."[15]

Not wishing to be dragged into a quagmire by the United Nations, the United States used its extraordinary influence in the Security Council to ensure that any military commitment of UN forces to Sierra Leone would be minimal. Indeed, until the 500 peacekeepers were taken captive, the relatively tiny contingent of UN troops were permitted to carry only light firearms. Even when the United States finally moved in Sierra Leone, it acted merely to train African troops in Nigeria. Other armies, under UN command or African stewardship, would have to take responsibility.

The overall position taken by the United States and the other permanent members of the Security Council—France, the United Kingdom, China, and Russia—concerning peacekeeping and peacemaking in Africa so angered UN Secretary-General Boutros Boutros-Ghali that, as early as 1992, his first year in office, he began to complain publicly of their neglect of the continent. His comments, reiterated often, dramatized President Bush's and later President Clinton's isolationist African policy, and eventually his leverage in Washington was severely eroded.

But Boutros-Ghali was correct. United Nations requirements that a cease-fire be in place before peacekeepers can be introduced inhibits problem-solving in Africa. Additionally, it "is obvious that without securing adequate resources the United Nations can be expected to do little. Long neglect by the United States and other powers has taken a heavy toll. . . ."[16]

The end of the Cold War worked to the disadvantage of Sierra Leone. As the United States saw it, national security interests lay elsewhere in the world; Africa was now virtually off the radar screen. Most of its countries no longer mattered to America's vital concerns, and what went on in the continent could be safely ignored.

Liberia

Although Liberia's disabling civil wars began in December 1989, its antecedents lay in the events of 1980, when the country's house of cards came crashing down. Indeed, an argument can be made that Liberia's contemporary grief had its origins in the nineteenth century.

With assistance provided by the U.S. government and private colonization societies, in 1822 freed American slaves and Africans rescued from slaving ships were transported to what is today Liberia. Since that time and until 1980 the land had been ruled by a so-called Americo-Liberian elite who traced their heritage to that original class of repatriates. By 1847 the first sovereign black republic in Africa had been declared and 17 distinct cultures lived astride one another—16 tribal groups and the dominating Americo-Liberians. In essence, from that time forward the indigenous tribal population lived under the yoke of a paternalistic ruling class. According to scholar Christopher Clapham, "As a settler regime . . . it was less inhibited than the colonial governments in restraining, as repressively as the occasion required, any systematic politicization of anti-government sentiments."[17] It was an uneasy alliance. Ironically, a form of compulsory labor was imposed on indigenous inhabitants, who were forced to work as field hands—

such servitude, which was analogous to slavery, was ended only in 1930—while many tribes were compelled to submit to new trading patterns determined by this unique ruling class. A dubious association it certainly was, but it lasted for 133 years.

The long period of Americo-Liberian control crumpled in 1980, and it did so with a bang. In April of that year 17 soldiers, led by 28-year-old Master Sergeant Samuel K. Doe, a Liberian of Krahn ethnicity, assassinated President William R. Tolbert and seized power. A military junta was constituted under the rubric of the People's Redemption Council, and Doe became the first person of indigenous origin to head the Liberian political order. Initially met with rejoicing, the junta revealed what uncontrolled military rule signified. Within 10 days 13 high-ranking Americo-Liberian officials of the Tolbert government were taken to the beach in the capital, Monrovia, tied to trees, and executed by firing squad. It was a gruesome scene to behold, yet the event was televised and reporters were invited to cover the story. In a sense, the executions opened a political Pandora's box and foretold what was to come.

By 1984 "the sense of mission and optimism had all but evaporated. Almost no one had anything good to say about Doe. . . . There was an outpouring of animosity toward the military and toward Doe in particular."[18] During his remaining years in office Doe moved to crush democracy and constitutional government.

Amos Sawyer, the pro-democracy constitutionalist who advanced the concept of civilian ascendancy over the military and who had chaired a constitutional commission, was arrested and falsely charged with treason by Doe. With his staunch republican credentials intact, and as a dean at the University of Liberia who had verbally stood up to the excesses of the Tolbert and Doe regimes, Sawyer attracted huge student and public support. Doe sent his troops onto the campus to arrest and beat Sawyer's many university devotees. Although Sawyer was released after ten harrowing months, Doe's position was weakened as his tactics were made clear for all to see.

In 1986 Doe, who had doctored election results, manipulated himself into the presidential office in a Second Republic. Over the next years opponents were arrested, beaten, and tortured; journalists were imprisoned; and the constitution, which was largely Sawyer's handiwork, and which Doe had initially supported, was steadily under-mined. It was clear that the Second Republic was merely civilian cover for a military autocracy.[19] Sawyer concisely sums up this era:

> No sector of Liberian society escaped military repression. Upon seizing power, the military banned all political activities, decreed strikes to be illegal, banned student campus political organizations, closed newspapers, imprisoned editors, and looted business houses. People of the interior did not escape military terror. . . . The only consistency about military rule in Liberia was the repression rained upon the people and the looting of the society.[20]

For the United States, during these last years of the Cold War, Doe was a tolerable leader. The sanctity of the sizable holdings of the Firestone Rubber Corporation, which initially had set up plantations in 1926, was guaranteed, anticommunism was upheld, attacks on Soviet policy were fashioned, diplomatic relations with Israel were reestablished, and the historically strong connection with the United States was reiterated. United States Ambassador Edward Perkins, who was appointed by President Ronald Reagan, had no "hangups about democracy for Liberia. What mattered was that Washington had a close 'friend' in Monrovia. The politics of the Cold War had eclipsed the chances for building democracy in Liberia."[21] The democratic values so revered and upheld by Sawyer were swept under the carpet by the Reagan administration, which was intent on securing Liberia's support in the Cold War.

As the Soviet Union's empire was rapidly disintegrating in 1989, a rebel force, led by Charles Taylor, invaded Liberia from neighboring Guinea. Taylor, whose lineage is traced to the America-Liberian culture, organized his force around very young, liquor- and drug-addled adolescents. As they made their way deep into the countryside, these undisciplined warriors, whose number quickly rose to 10,000, and many of whom were merely children, slaughtered, raped, and executed civilians, particularly Mandingo and Krahn tribespeople, who were seen as supporters of Doe. Government troops responded in kind by attacking, and often murdering, Mano and Gio ethnics, who were perceived as pro-rebel. Tribal antagonisms were brutally unleashed as both sides used terror—the wholesale rape of women, the killing of children, roadblocks where citizens were haphazardly stopped and massacred, the burning of villages—as an instrument of power politics.[22]

Dissident factions arose from among Taylor's forces as the rebels approached Monrovia. One such group was led by Prince Johnson, who in 1990 kidnaped President Doe as he left the Executive Mansion. In a scene out of hell, which represented everything Liberia had evolved into, Doe was tied up and then brutally tortured as his ears were cut off and his body eviscerated. Covered with blood and begging for his life, while his tormentors, drunk and laughing, taped the event, eventually he was slain. The ignominy of Doe's political life and of the manner of his death are truly metaphors for what has happened to much of Africa.

In never-ending ferocious battles, Monrovia was eventually laid to waste as the armies of Doe, Taylor, and Johnson used artillery to blast away at each other within the confines of the city. Refugees, who had inundated the town, were caught in the triple crossfire, and scampered to find refuge in the blown-out husks of former high-rise buildings and homes. Currently scavengers prowl the city's garbage dumps for food, just trying to keep alive. There is no electricity, no running water—where they exist, wells are used, where not, holes are dug—no functioning sewer network, hotels and hospitals have been gutted, and the school system has shut down. The capital, which was once a vital bustling town of Liberian and Lebanese shopkeepers and traders, has been transformed into a netherworld where every standard public service has all but been destroyed, employment opportunities have evaporated, and even grocery stores hardly exist. Monrovia is a dying hell hole.

As Taylor controlled the hinterland and most of its resources, the capture of Monrovia would have completed his takeover of the country. By late 1990 the Economic Commission of West African States (ECOWAS), composed of Gambia, Ghana, Mali, Nigeria, Senegal, Burkina Faso, Guinea, Sierra Leone, and Liberia, organized a peacekeeping force of 9,000 troops, later expanded to 18,000 (from the first five ECOWAS members listed), to secure Monrovia, separate the three opposing forces, and prevent Taylor from taking power. It also appointed Amos Sawyer as interim president. Taylor ignored the appointment of Sawyer, while his rebel force challenged the peace-keepers. There were now four contending armies in Monrovia, while much of the rest of the country was securely dominated by Taylor.

Sawyer, who was never able to neutralize Taylor diplomatically, spent much of his time outside Liberia. His government controlled only a few neighborhoods in Monrovia while Taylor tightened his grip on the country. With proceeds from the sale of diamonds smuggled from Sierra Leone and the export of Liberian diamonds, lumber, and iron ore, Taylor developed a financial war chest, with help from Libya, which allowed him to conduct his war with fiscal impunity.[23]

By 1994 Sawyer, who despite his democratic credentials received no support from the United States, was forced to relinquish the presidency. Taylor moved to the brink of political authority under the rubric of a transitional government and one year later of an interim Council of State. For two more years fighting continued to rage the length and breadth of the land. Finally, in 1997, the wars seemed to come to an end as Taylor was "freely" elected president by a population certain that if he did not win the havoc would continue.[24] Within a year, however, other factions arose challenging Taylor's rule, and intermittent civil war lingered.

The personal, social, and economic damage inflicted on society was harrowing. More than 6 percent of Liberia's population of 2.6 million were killed, countless numbers of whom were first mutilated and tortured. Almost 1 million people were transmuted into refugees, with many fleeing to Guinea, Sierra Leone, and the Ivory Coast—countries that were undergoing their own political traumas. Monrovia was destroyed. The World Bank and the United Nations reveal few economic indicators for Liberia for the period of the war years, as the economy, quite simply, stopped functioning. What economy existed had been taken over by Taylor for his own personal or political benefit. For all practical purposes, as a state, Liberia no longer exists.

The war did serve to highlight once again the changing role of Africa's relationship with the West. The United States, despite its long-standing association with Liberia, took no action in trying to resolve the drama, other than to help finance the ECOWAS military coalition and deny U.S. visas to Liberian officials. Africa, post–Soviet Union, was seen to be of no vital interest to the United States, so neither Presidents Bush nor Clinton saw fit to do anything else but—to put it bluntly—send their sympathies to Liberia. Western nations looked on in stupefaction but did nothing. The United Nations, despite imposing an arms embargo, stood by as the carnage went on year after year.

But events in both Liberia and Sierra Leone did underscore Nigeria's formative new role in Africa. As *the* regional power in West Africa, Nigeria began to flex its muscle. In trying to bring about some stability in both nations, Nigeria indicated that it would do whatever it could, particularly in military terms, to disallow a spillover effect in West Africa. As the hegemon of the region, and with some 121 million people, "Nigeria is Africa's equivalent to Brazil, India, or Indonesia. It is the pivot point on which the continent turns."[25]

It is more than likely, particularly since democracy is once again ascendent in Nigeria, that bilaterally, multilaterally, or under the auspices of regional or international organizations Nigeria will enhance its hegemonic posture to secure its own vital interests in West Africa. The United States would be more than willing to help fund such peacekeeping operations. That would permit the United States to remain out of the multiple African quagmires that it truly does not understand, while at the same time giving it some voice in influencing events in the direction of its own national interests, at least where they exist. The needs of Nigeria and the United States, where they do intersect, can stimulate a coordinated approach that might serve to complement their respective foreign policy concerns in Africa, whether they be limited, in the case of the United States, or expansive, in Nigeria's circumstance. In that sense the United States does have a real interest in supporting Nigeria in its efforts to strengthen democratic values within its own country.

EAST AFRICA:
ETHIOPIA AND ERITREA—AFRICA'S DEADLIEST WAR

Africa's bloodiest traditional war was fought over a barren and inconsequential 160-square-mile patch of wasteland—the Yiagra Triangle—separating the 600-mile never-formalized border between

Ethiopia and Eritrea. In a titanic struggle, by means of trench warfare, air bombardment, and tank combat that lasted from 1998 to 2000, 85,000 soldiers were killed, 500,000 Eritrean civilians were turned into refugees (out of a population of 3.8 million), and the economies of both countries fell into disrepair. Even without the carnage of war both are labeled by the United Nations as among the 10 least developed nations in human terms, while World Bank estimates establish that life expectancy at birth is 43 for Ethiopia and 51 for Eritrea.[26]

Eritrea, which was colonized by Italy in 1890, became part of Italian East Africa in 1936. Occupied by Great Britain in 1941, in 1950 the United Nations resolved that Eritrea be federated with Ethiopia; the association was sealed in 1952. By 1962 Eritrea was formally incorporated into Ethiopia and became one of its 14 regions. From that year until 1991 it was engaged in a fierce, and ultimately successful, liberation war against Ethiopia. In 1993 it became an independent state.[27]

Ethiopia was the only quarter of Africa, other than Liberia, that was never colonized by Europeans. Although it battled Italy in the nineteenth century and was occupied by it from 1936 to 1941, it has been an independent entity for centuries. Once known as Abyssinia, it was alluded to by both Homer and Herodotus, and is referred to in the Old Testament. Ruled by kings and emperors who imposed a harsh feudal system—Emperor Haile Selassie I was the last of its monarchs—in 1974 a military junta took power, promoted a Marxist/Leninist ideology, and proceeded to impose a stern—nonideological—tyranny upon the population. President Mengistu Haile-Mariam led a Leninist regime that, until it was toppled in 1991, was viewed as the most revolutionary in Africa. It also evolved into one of Africa's cruelest.[28] It was while Mengistu was in power that Ethiopia confronted the harshest famine it has ever known. More than 1 million Ethiopians died between 1983 and 1986.[29]

Ethiopia and Eritrea had been relatively close allies since 1993 as the present rulers of the two countries had struggled together against Mengistu's government since its inception. But that changed in 1997 when economic tensions arose between the two states. By mid-year 1998 Eritrea sent its military forces into the Yiagra Triangle to expel

Ethiopian troops and administrators, asserting that Italian colonial boundaries had placed the region within its jurisdiction. The border dispute was not new—the countries had been discussing the issue peacefully since 1993—but military confrontation emerged as an instrument to be utilized by Eritrea because of unresolved trade and currency disputes. For two years the conflict constituted the largest war on the planet.

Ethiopia mounted a significant counterattack one month later. Its warplanes bombed Eritrea's capital, Asmara, and battles broke out near Assab, an Eritrean port on the Red Sea. Since then the port has been closed. For its part, Eritrea attacked Mekele, the capital of Ethiopia's Tigre region. By 1999 ferocious battles within the triangle had been under way for the better part of a year when Eritrea's major port, Massawa, was assaulted by Ethiopian fighter bombers. Extensive damage was caused to port facilities and oil depots. Furious battles along the Mereb River, east of the Badme region of the triangle, erupted and thousands of lives were lost. Fighting continued unabated with troops of both sides occupying various sections of the triangle while attempting to dislodge opposing forces.

The combat was developing in the midst of an extraordinary famine that affected 8 million Ethiopians and 800,000 Eritreans. The devastating famine was caused by a three-year drought exacerbated by the war. Neither country, however, was prepared to withdraw as issues of sovereignty clearly took precedence over their starving populations. As Ethiopian prime minister Meles Zenawi indicated, "you do not wait until you have a full tummy to protect your sovereignty."[30]

Under increasing pressure stemming from the United Nations to terminate the war peacefully, in 2000 Ethiopia launched a massive blitzkrieg against Eritrean troops in the triangle. Storming the region along three fronts, 350,000 troops supported by tanks and artillery moved with lightning speed from west to east capturing towns and villages while flushing out Eritrea's 300,000 soldiers. The Ethiopian air force engaged in comprehensive bombing of Eritrea, while its ground troops penetrated 65 miles deep into the country, ensnaring scores of hamlets in the south. Tens of thousands of Eritrean soldiers were captured, and thousands killed. Eritrean refugees poured out of the southern regions and fled north. A monumental refugee crisis was in the offing. Beset by misery, economic collapse (exports fell by 80 percent), military defeat, and humiliation, Eritrea indicated it was prepared to accept a cease-fire under terms dictated by Ethiopia. On June 18, 2000, a cease-fire agreement was reached and Africa's most destructive war finally came to an end.

The international community had made several unsuccessful attempts to settle the dispute. Rwanda and the United States had suggested a demilitarization of the border area with the simultaneous initiation of negotiations, even as the OAU and the UN failed in their efforts to promote peace. Either one side or the other frustrated the armistice bids. At the same time war profiteers came calling as Bulgaria and Russia sold arms to Ethiopia, while Ukraine sent heavy weaponry to Eritrea. Romania, China, and North Korea also poured munitions into the region. Djibouti's port on the Gulf of Aden was used as a gathering point for the transfer of armaments to both states. And although the World Bank and the IMF curtailed some funding, and the West suspended most aid programs, Ethiopia and Eritrea remained unmoved. In fact, Ethiopia spent $480 million on military equipment in 1999 and $1 million per day in 2000 despite the cutoff in funds.

The additional threat to withhold international food relief to Ethiopia for its starving millions so as to pressure it to negotiate with Eritrea also failed. As Ethiopian foreign minister Seyoum Mesfin proclaimed, "This is Africa and the situation in Africa always gets a response from Europe or the international community when people start to see skeletons on screens."[31] He was correct. Shortly before the war ended the European Union pledged 430,000 tons of food aid, while the United States agreed to contribute an additional 432,000 tons. Thereafter, the World Bank and the IMF pledged debt relief of $1.3 billion to Ethiopia, amounting to 23 percent of its outstanding foreign debt.[32]

The document officially halting the war was brokered by the OAU, the UN, the United States, and Algeria. But the reality is that the war was brought to an end only by Ethiopia's military success on the battlefield. The cease-fire accord also called for a 15.5-mile buffer zone along the border within Eritrea, in effect acknowledging Ethiopia's military success and Eritrea's responsibility for the war due to its initial aggression; a 4,200-strong UN peacekeeping force, known as the United Nations Peacekeeping Mission in Ethiopia and Eritrea

(UNMEE), to patrol the main areas of the Yiagra Triangle, consisting of troops from Algeria, Jordan, Zambia, Tanzania, Kenya, Ghana, Canada, China, India, Bangladesh, Peru, Uruguay, Ukraine, Sweden, Poland, Romania, Spain, Finland, Italy, Holland, and Norway and led by Dutch Major General Patrick Cammaert; the demarcation of the border between the two nations, which will be decided by UN cartographers using colonial treaties of 1900, 1902, and 1908 recorded by Ethiopia and Italy. A few days after the signing Ethiopia agreed to withdraw its troops from captured Eritrean territory, and by December 12, 2000, a formal peace treaty was concluded and endorsed.

The United Nations, pressured by the United States and the major European powers, was unable to use its clout to intercede effectively. The industrial nations were focused on other areas of the globe, no national security interests were at stake, and the turmoil spreading throughout Africa was seen as political and military quicksand. Ironically, during the years of the Cold War, the United States viewed the Horn of Africa as vital to its national security due to its strategic location on the Gulf of Aden, the Red Sea, and the Indian Ocean.[33] By the 1990s, however, Africa had lost its appeal to the West and particularly to the United States; without the Soviet Union, the Horn of Africa signified just another area of the continent that had succumbed to adversity.

The war between Ethiopia and Eritrea was simply a footnote to the more prominent foreign policy interests of the West, notwithstanding drought, famine, a horrific refugee crisis affecting hundreds of thousands of people, and the deaths of 85,000 combatants. United States rhetoric regarding the importance of a peaceful settlement to the dispute was in overdrive. Performance, however, was limited to supporting the creation of UNMEE but otherwise constraining the UN Security Council from acting more constructively. European nations generally mirrored U.S. views, and their only substantial involvement came *after* a cease-fire had been agreed to.

SOUTHERN AFRICA: CHAOS IN ZIMBABWE

Two decades ago, in 1980, Zimbabwe gained its independence as its former appellation, the white-controlled Rhodesia, passed into history.

Robert Mugabe, one of Rhodesia's prominent black African freedom fighters, was elected prime minister, as his political party won an absolute majority in the new parliament. The evening of his election Mugabe addressed the nation; "he spoke of turning swords into plowshares to rebuild the war-torn nation, of the need for reconciliation and not recrimination, and he assured the whites that they had a place in the country—as Zimbabweans." "Let us deepen our sense of belonging," he said, "and engender a common interest that knows no race, color or creed. Let us truly become Zimbabweans with a single loyalty. Long live our freedom!"[34]

A Marxist, and head of a dynamic guerrilla organization in the brutal struggle against racist white rule, the protracted phase of which began in 1972, Mugabe's radical stand against white and black opponents during the war years earned him an international reputation as a hard-liner. His nationalist forces were the mailed fist of the freedom fighters and bore the burden of much of the struggle, during which 20,000 people were killed, even as from 1964 to 1974 he was held in detention by Ian Smith's white government. The United States, on the eve of Ronald Reagan's election victory, would view him with great mistrust, while Mengistu in Ethiopia and Cuba's Fidel Castro saw in him a fellow Marxist revolutionary.

Perceptions aside, Mugabe initially proceeded to reach out to rivals, such as his former ally Joshua Nkomo, even while white emigration to South Africa, Australia, New Zealand, and Great Britain swelled. Whites, who owned the best land, most of the tobacco farms and controlled the financial institutions, thus dominating the economy, maintained title to their property, but many were fearful of the future and fled.

Within a short time a more imperious Mugabe began to show his hand. The basic parliamentary system was superseded by a presidential structure in 1987 so that Mugabe would not be dependent on parliament for election to office, one-party rule was installed, and Mugabe, as president, became far more intolerant of domestic criticism. One of the great revolutionary nationalists of the 1970s, Mugabe, now 77 years old, has evolved, after more than two decades in power, into a "kleptocratic" ruler "hard to control and harder to oust."[35]

By 2000 he had brought his country to the brink of economic ruin, initiated a rampage against Zimbabwe's remaining white population, and fought a desperate battle to politically emasculate his domestic political opposition—all with the sole purpose of retaining authority. The youthful revolutionary had become an aging despot, intent on doing whatever it required to sustain his absolute power, even at the expense of country and fellow citizens. He is currently the unequivocal archetype of Achebe's allegorical sovereign "who has come in from the rain" and is "reluctant to go out again."

In his effort to secure eroding black support in the June 2000 parliamentary elections, Mugabe encouraged thousands of his supporters, some veterans of Zimbabwe's independence struggle, others unemployed rowdies paid for their nefarious activities, to storm and either seize or destroy the farms of white Zimbabweans. By midyear squatters had forcefully occupied more than 1,000 farms, many of them having been burned to the ground, numerous white farmers and scores of their African employees were murdered, while thousands of black agricultural workers lost their jobs and close to 400,000 others had their employment jeopardized. Of 4,500 white settlements, the government listed 3,270 for confiscation and redistribution under its black resettlement program.

Feverishly intent on holding on to power after two decades of authoritarian rule, Mugabe proclaimed he would neither brook domestic opposition nor accept any foreign criticism of the policy despite the raging chaos. And while whites had purloined the land in the heyday of colonialism during the nineteenth century, whatever government purchases of white-owned property occurred after independence were largely transferred to Mugabe's cronies. The insignificant acreage poorer Zimbabweans received was of pathetic quality. The confiscation policy of 2000 was meant to steal the land back without offering any compensation whatsoever. According to Mugabe, if Great Britain, the original colonizer, wished to offer compensation, fine, but Zimbabwe would not accept responsibility.

The concept of due process was deemed irrelevant, particularly in light of Zimbabwean court orders, including a determination by the Supreme Court declaring the occupations illegal and the fact that some months earlier Zimbabweans had voted down a referendum to give Mugabe the legal right to appropriate the farms without compensation. "The courts can do whatever they want," Mugabe railed, "but no judicial decision will stand in our way."[36] Indeed, in 2001 the chief justice, Anthony Gubbay, resigned after the government refused to guarantee his safety.

Even criticism from South Africa's president, Thabo Mbeki, who fears a spillover of refugees and violence into his own country, failed to persuade Mugabe. "These things are wrong," Mbeki proclaimed. "These things must stop. They must be addressed. And we'll continue to say those things."[37] As Anthony Caldwell, chairman of the business development committee of the United States-South Africa Business Council, put it: U.S. investors "hear Mugabe is taking over land and they wonder if it's going to trickle down to South Africa." In Botswana too "the crisis in Zimbabwe has had a negative impact on both the tourism industry and the flow of foreign investors' funds into [the] stock exchange."[38]

With unemployment above 50 percent, inflation close to 100 percent, an estimated 70 percent of the population living below the poverty line, the GDP growth rate having plummeted from 7 percent in 1990 to -1 percent in 1999, trade growth less GDP growth at -2.5 percent, and corruption rampant "the people of Zimbabwe are one-third poorer than they were at independence."[39] They also live shorter lives; from 1990 to 1998 life expectancy in Zimbabwe declined from 56 years to 51.[40]

The occupation of tobacco farms—tobacco being Zimbabwe's largest currency earner since it makes up half the country's exports—only added to the economic misery. Many white farmers fled the country. Most others were forced to halt planting or harvesting altogether, while processing ground to a halt and countless numbers spent most of their time appealing to the courts and the government or defending their lives. There are merely 70,000 whites—less than 1 percent—out of a total population of some 12 million, and the attack on these core producers clearly had a profound impact on the overall economic and social health of society. Zimbabwe does not have the entrepreneurial skilled labor to successfully run the complex tobacco agro-industry developed by the white farming elite.

Although Mugabe's Zimbabwe African National Union–Patriotic Front (ZANU-PF) held on to power in the elections through dubious means, Morgan Tsvangirai's opposition group, Movement for Democratic Change (MDC), increased its representation dramatically by securing 57 of the 120 contested parliamentary seats. Opposing the land resettlement program and the use of 11,000 troops—one-third of the army—in the Congo's civil war in an implausible effort to increase Mugabe's influence in Central and southern Africa, and railing against the economic dislocation and corruption, all of which were bleeding the once-wealthy country of its capital, Tsvangirai rallied a surprisingly large portion of the population to stand up to Mugabe.

But, at least in the short run, to little avail. The MDC remains in the minority even as Tsvangirai has come under political attack by the government. Mugabe is still chief executive and will be until the 2002 presidential elections. He continues to encourage violence and lawlessness in his occupation scheme: "Our party must continue to strike fear in the heart of the white man, our real enemy." The country is in an economic imbroglio and riddled by strikes, work stoppages, government violence directed at the media, and an increasing number of political murders. Black professionals are fleeing the country while foreign investment tumbled by 89 percent between 1999 and 2000. HIV/AIDS is of epidemic proportions. Yet Mugabe proclaims proudly that his domestic policies are finally ridding the nation of its colonial heritage. As he said in the waning days of 2000, before a delirious crowd in the capital, Harare, "they think because they are white, they have a divine right to our resources. Not here! Never again!"[41]

Ama Ata Aidoo, the gifted Ghanaian short story writer, sensitively and tenderly describes through her fiction the plight of women in the world of Africa's "big men." But her sketches are wondrous parables of what it is like for men and women alike who live under the sway of the gun in Africa. And although she speaks of Ghana, her words have resonance in Zimbabwe: ". . . but the big man . . . he can ruin them if they do not give him what he wants. 'O Allah, what times we live in. What rulers we have. How can men behave in this way who are our lords?' All women are slaves of our lords. 'But . . . the masters of the land are always bad, or they have been bad for a long, long time. . . .'"[42]

CENTRAL AFRICA: CONGO—AFRICA'S FIRST WORLD WAR

Congo, once also known as Zaire, is the second largest African state. With endless mineral and energy resources, it previously furnished "two-thirds of the free world supply of cobalt . . . half its industrial diamonds, approximately a third of tantalum and germanium, and slightly under 10 per cent of its copper. The [Congo] River could also conceivably light up all central Africa."[43]

Twenty-two years later "basic infrastructure is in total decay. Major sections of trunk 'A' roads are not usable. Smallpox, diarrhea, sleeping sickness, among others have come back into force, while AIDS, malaria and poliomyelitis continue to devastate a population already weakened by undernourishment. . . . More than 60 percent of the country's working population is not at work."[44]

With a 300 percent inflation rate, a defunct economy, overdue debts to the IMF and World Bank totaling $798 million, a nonexistent infrastructure, per capita income at $866—and falling—among the lowest in Africa, life expectancy of 51 years, 45 percent of its children suffering from malnutrition, safe drinking water virtually unheard of, and net foreign direct investment tumbling 100 percent within the past 15 years, the Democratic Republic of the Congo can surely be considered the ultimate basket case of Africa.[45] Indeed, for more than 20 years it has experienced an average annual *decline* in its GDP growth rate of between 6.6 percent and 1.5 percent.[46]

What happened to the potential of this behemoth of a country surrounded by nine African states? Unquestionably, the corruption and malevolence of its leadership over the past 40 years have, quite simply, driven this nation—or what's left of it—into the proverbial ground.

In 1960 Congo received its independence from Belgium. A country that was formerly viewed as largely the personal property of Belgium collapsed five days later as the army mutinied, Katanga province seceded, and Prime Minister Patrice Lumumba, a leftist and radical nationalist, was deposed by the head of the army, Joseph Mobutu. Lumumba was arrested shortly thereafter and murdered by 1961. The polity split asunder as various leaders established their own duchies. A UN peacekeeping force entered the fray, while the United States and the Soviet Union competed for influence among different factions as the country was seen as a valuable domino in the Cold War.

By 1962 Katanga was returned to central government control, and representative government was restored. But the following year political turmoil erupted anew as multiple political actors vied for control of the state. Parliament was shut down by President Joseph Kasavubu, repression increased, and the economy fell into disrepair. By 1964 "Insurrection engulfed the Congo" once again as the "tides of rebellion swept away central authority in five provinces out of twenty-one, and in portions of eight more. At high-water mark in August 1964, the complete collapse of the . . . regime appeared a real possibility."[47] From 1964 to 1967 the Congo underwent another destructive cycle as rebellion once more overwhelmed the nation. The UN quit the country in despair. The OAU tried its hand at peacemaking as Belgian paratroopers and European mercenaries traversed the state. Over time the rebellion self-destructed.[48] By 1965 General Joseph Mobutu had overthrown the government and taken control. Under the nom de guerre Mobutu Sese Seko, he held virtually absolute power until 1997.

Philip Gourevitch accurately assesses Mobutu's impact upon the Congo. A man who owned spectacular and luxurious homes in France, in Switzerland, and in numerous Congolese provinces, who traveled the world with an entourage of hundreds of sycophants each time spending hundreds of thousands of dollars on hotel rooms, jewelry, and other trinkets, as Mobutu socked away multiple billions of dollars in U.S. aid in Swiss banks, while in the last year of his rule the country's external debt was $14 billion:

> President Mobutu Sese Seko . . . had named the country Zaire and robbed it to ruin for thirty-two years. . . . Even now, Mobutu remains fixed in the international imagination as the grotesque apogee of the postcolonial African bullyboy. Spectacularly corrupt, insatiably predatory . . . he kept himself swaddled in luxury, and buttressed by doting Cold War patrons in Washington, Brussels, and Paris, as he sponsored cross-border insurgencies against neighboring countries and crushed or bought off all domestic opposition. He liked to call himself Papa, the nation's "founder" and "guide," but he treated its children with rank disdain, systematically reducing their lot—body and soul—to a condition of want and disarray akin to that of orphanhood.[49]

For 30 years Laurent Kabila led an obscure guerrilla movement that was quartered in the Southeast. And for 30 years it was nothing more than a pin prick for Mobutu. But, in late 1996, with massive support from Rwanda and more limited assistance from Uganda, Kabila's army attacked Congolese forces in the Northeast—directly across the Rwandan border. Although initially a localized rebellion, as Congolese troops went into a full retreat Kabila moved to overthrow the Mobutu government. The rebels, who were primarily ethnic Tutsi, were then reinforced by even more Rwandan troops, who essentially took over direction of the war effort. For Rwanda the war had two purposes: to eliminate the Rwandan Hutu warriors who had fled into the Congo in 1994 after massacring more than 800,000 Tutsi and who continued to cause havoc within Rwanda via cross-border military excursions[50]; and to see to it that Mobutu, who harbored the criminals, was deposed.

As Rwanda clandestinely poured troops into the battle, the Rwanda/ Kabila combatants rapidly moved east toward Kinshasa, slaughtering tens of thousands of exile Rwandan Hutu as they scrambled to flee on foot the entire width of the country. As cities, towns, and villages fell to the advancing forces, the battle became a rout. The army of Mobutu decomposed, took out its fury on local villages, which were razed and stripped, and fled. In May 1997, seven months after the war began, Mobutu bolted the country and escaped to Morocco.

Not long after Kabila declared himself president, he came under increasing pressure from his own people. Accused of being a stooge of Rwanda, he eventually dismissed Tutsi commanders from the army command, allied himself with the now Congo-based genocide leaders of the Hutu exile community, and ordered all Rwandan troops out of the country. Incensed by Kabila's actions, the Rwandan government withdrew its military, but within one month it was back in force as Rwanda invaded the country again in August 1998 and this time organized a rebellion against Kabila, aimed at his elimination. Rwanda was intent on placing the Congo within its sphere of influence. The country was to be overseen by Rwanda and its roughly 25,000 troops.

To stave off Rwanda's increasing political and military clout—it had the best-organized and most efficient army in the region—Angola and Zimbabwe entered the war to support Kabila. Uganda then sent in additional battalions in support of Rwanda, bringing the total number of its soldiers to 10,000, while Burundi's army, under Tutsi control and sympathetic to Rwanda, came into the fray. Chad and Namibia sent their armed forces to support Kabila. For more than three years "seven African nations and more than a dozen guerrilla and rebel forces have been fighting . . . in a conflict so messy, so broad, and so resistant to any comprehensive resolution that it is sometimes spoken of as Africa's First World War."[51]

The motives for the multiple involvement were a struggle for power by indigenous groups; as in Sierra Leone, the grabbing of diamonds for personal and political benefit; hubris and dubious glory for Zimbabwe's President Mugabe; Angola's aspiration to secure its border from rebel National Union for Total Independence of Angola (UNITA) forces led by Jonas Savimbi; and Rwanda's desire to eliminate its Hutu assassins. Other nations, such as the Central African Republic and Zambia, have gotten caught up in a massive refugee crisis. In fact, the Congo is also home to scores of thousands of Angolans who have fled to escape the never-ending battles between UNITA forces and government troops.

By 2000 at least two Congos existed. Rwanda, Uganda, and its rebel allies controlled the eastern part of the country, while Kabila and his supporters managed the western part. Fighting continued, however, in both sectors. Villagers throughout the war-torn nation have been caught in the constancy of crossfire, and the International Rescue Committee estimated that between 1998 and 2001 alone more than 3 million people have died in the multiple and complex Congolese civil wars, while another 3 million have been displaced. The imbroglio's intricacy is indicated by the fact that intermittently raging battles have occurred between erstwhile allies—for example, Uganda and Rwanda—and their respective rebel clients.

As for the role of the United Nations in the Congo, there is little positive to be said. In 2000 the Security Council agreed to send in 5,537 "observers" to "verify" that the multiple countries and rebel groups pull back and eventually withdraw their forces and to monitor a nine-mile buffer zone separating the combatants. By 2001 the number was reduced to 3,000 as the warring parties agreed to a phased withdrawal of their troops. The observers entered the country to prop up the miniscule UN force of 600 after the respective brigades vacated to agreed upon staging areas, something they finally achieved, but had heretofore hesitated to do even in the face of a cease-fire signed in 1999 in Lusaka, Zambia—an accord that Kabila all but declared invalid. In other words, in a country the size of Western Europe, the UN teams have small numbers, few teeth, and little enforcement power. And while the UN imposed a global ban on diamond exports from Angola in 1998 and did the same in 2000 to Sierra Leone, no sanctions have been imposed on gems from the Congo. Ban enforcement on diamonds from nations ravaged by civil strife has been left to private marketing groups, largely based in Antwerp, Belgium, whose extremely lax controls have made all such embargoes ineffective. For all practical purposes, the UN is at the mercy of the many foreign powers in the Congo, a place that Richard C. Holbrooke called "daunting."[52]

The Congo remains a god-awful mess. Kabila was murdered by a bodyguard in January 2001, and immediately replaced by his 29-year-old son Joseph Kabila, a man raised and educated in Tanzania and with no political experience whatsoever. Propped up by Angolan and Zimbabwean troops, he has attempted to placate his opponents. And although the invading armies once again agreed to withdraw from the Congo and even removed some of their troops, as Joseph Kabila appeared to be willing to negotiate, rebel forces and foreign troops continue to thwart UN peace efforts. It remains highly doubtful that the country can crawl out of its chaotic condition.

The Congo has been in a state of acute crisis for almost the entire period of its existence as an independent state. In more than 40 years of war, civil war, and rebellion, refugees have become life's norm, as death, murder, disease, hunger, and famine prowl the countryside. With the confluence of multifarious African states into the never-ending conflict, indigenous rebellion has been transformed into an African world war.

Truly, the Four Horsemen of the Apocalypse arrived in the Congo some time ago and settled in for a long stay. The object—a more accurate appellation than nation, state, or country—remains the center of a maelstrom that refuses to subside. For all practical purposes, this is a place that has hardly known a day of normal existence; and normality does not appear to be in the offing. As the political scientist M. Crawford Young indicated as early as 1970, "only the most consummate leadership can forestall yet another rendezvous with rebellion."[53] And that dominion is still nowhere to be seen.

CONCLUSION

According to the political scientist Inis L. Claude Jr., an expert on international organizations, "the necessary assumption of collective security is simply that wars are likely to occur and that they ought to be prevented. Collective security . . . is intended only to forestall the arbitrary and aggressive use of force."[54] But collective security as it relates to Africa south of the Sahara is negated by an absence of western, even nonwestern, national interests, as evidenced by the performance of the major powers that sit as permanent members of the United Nations Security Council. Thus, as J. L. Brierly, the noted internationalist and scholar of the law of nations, stated some years back, the real issue is not collective security but "the tolerance which the system has hitherto perforce extended to the persistence of war."[55]

The United Nations does not function in a vacuum. It is often consigned to take its direction from policies established by the superpowers, particularly those western states that have a history in Africa and currently view it as outside the realm of large-scale intervention. There is a threshold of obligation set by the large powers that they will not go beyond, and it would be absurd to expect that the UN can accomplish what they disallow it from performing.

At the same time it should be obvious that despite the absence of vital interests, western nations, and in particular the United States, would be foolhardy to jump into the bog that is currently Africa. Unless and until indigenous leadership arises that is intent and willing to put its nation's interests above personal aggrandizement, there is little that can be done to resolve the complex and bloody civil strife operative in so many African states. Western populations would not support intervention or peacekeeping/peacemaking endeavors—other than perhaps the short-term feeding of hungry people, or a quick strike to arrest genocide—and such efforts would not be sanctioned by their leaders. Indeed, it seems obvious that elected western officials have little comprehension of the internal dynamics of most African cultures, and because their countries have few remaining national interests, they have no need to engage in on-the-spot learning.

In the final analysis, it is up to Africa and Africans to finally take the initiative to fix what is broken and to address the problems confronting their respective states. These are clearly not nations where there is public loyalty to established politically legitimate institutions. Even in Zambia, in 2001, mayhem sallied forth as President Frederick Chiluba ordered a crackdown on political opponents and public meetings after he unsuccessfully sought to revise the constitution so that he could seek a third term. In the Central African Republic rebels continue to push for the removal of the government. There are many cultures, many loyalties, and few national structures that are not riddled with graft and at the mercy of wanton leaders. No conspicuous anchor is available to tie the ship of state to while exploring solutions. Until more pilots are unearthed who resemble South Africa's Nelson Mandela or Liberia's Amos Sawyer—and when they arise they should be given foreign support—the future of African states will remain bleak. Neither the United States nor the United Nations can accomplish very much. At this point in its history, Africa holds the future in its own hands. What it does with it remains to be seen.

CHAPTER THREE

Whither Human Rights?

In 1986 the Commission on Human Rights, under the jurisdiction of the United Nations Economic and Social Council, initiated a procedure by which it would select "basic reference works on human rights for use by United Nations information centers."[1] Among the initial three books chosen was *Human Rights: Cultural and Ideological Perspectives,* which was authored and edited by Professor Adamantia Pollis and me.[2] It was one of the earliest books on the subject that differentiated among political rights and economic and social rights, and explored "the extent to which the [political] doctrines of human rights as embodied in the Universal Declaration of Human Rights may not be relevant to societies with a non-Western cultural tradition or a socialist ideology."[3]

The Universal Declaration of Human Rights was passed by the General Assembly of the United Nations on December 10, 1948. It is *the* consecrating document on human rights, and it was a recommendation to all nations that they adhere to what the UN then categorized as universal provisions. An analysis of the declaration indicates clearly that the underlying philosophy was the Western concept of political liberty and democracy. The rights and freedoms enumerated in its articles are, among others, life, liberty, the illegality of torture, equality before the law, prohibition against arbitrary arrest, fair trial by impartial tribunal, the right to be presumed innocent until proven guilty, freedom of travel, the right to marry freely, the right of individuals to own property, and freedom of assembly. The primacy of political rights in the declaration is certain: Of the 30 articles, only three, one of them dealing with property rights, can be considered as enunciating economic rights.[4]

The United Nations International Covenant on Economic, Social and Cultural Rights entered into force in 1976. And although it promoted the right to employment, education, and the warrant of everyone to an adequate standard of living including food, clothing, and housing, the document remains a de facto subaltern to the Universal Declaration.

It seemed apparent that the Commission on Human Rights praised our book because the volume gave equal importance to the Third World interpretation of human rights, which accentuates economic prerogatives, and viewed the Western perception of rights—based on the notion of atomized individuals possessed of certain inalienable rights in nature—as marginal to Third World nations. We maintained that the basic unit of traditional society—the kinship system, the clan, the tribe, the local community—with its emphasis on the group rather than the individual had as much validity as western-based individualism.[5] In other words, polygyny can be as measured a custom as is monogamy; collective or kinship ownership of property—where land is thought of as belonging to ancestors and is held in trust for them—is as acceptable as the concept of private ownership of estate; and the traditional role of a paramount chief, who embodies traditional authority and makes decisions in coordination with a council of chiefs, and where the populace plays little, if any, role in the potentate's selection, may have as much sophistication and can encompass as much democracy as that of a president or prime minister in a western parliamentary political structure.

To that end we argued that western notions of political rights—speech, elections, association, private ownership of property, and the like—were a conception of popular sovereignty and individual rights that had as their basis the writings of western political philosophers—among them Hugo Grotius, John Locke, Baron de Montesquieu, Jean-Jacques Rousseau, and Thomas Jefferson. Overall, Third World states did not have a cultural heritage of individualism, the doctrines of inalienable human rights were neither disseminated nor assimilated, and the emphasis was not on Jeffersonian principles of political rights based on natural law (the law of God) but on the collective, or the community, which ensured, through the sovereign or the state, economic, social, and cultural rights—food, clothing, shelter, ethnic values, and the like. Political rights were peripheral. As Vietnam's foreign minister, Phan Van Khai, indicated in November 2000, in language that explicitly clarifies the dichotomy between the two value systems, "we . . . have different definitions of human rights. [We have] to worry about the rights of Vietnamese to eat and get an education."[6]

Pollis and I essentially confirmed that the state, as observed in and by the Third World, is "a substitute for the traditional communal group [and] has become the embodiment of the people. [The] individual has no rights or freedoms that are natural or outside the purview of the state."[7] *But,* as we illustrated, the social contract between people and state did insinuate that economic and social rights would be confirmed to the population who in return would accede to the rule of the sovereign. The social contract in the nonwestern world was, therefore, utterly in contradistinction to the officiating order upon which western society is based. It was a marked and notable distinction that was recognized by the United Nations Economic and Social Council when it highlighted our book and its thesis.

Of course we acknowledged that a

certain minimum of values indispensable to a dignified human existence must be described as immune from all claims of derogation at all times. Notably among these are the right to life, freedom from torture and inhuman treatment, freedom from involuntary human experimentation, freedom from slavery, the slave trade and servitude, . . . the right to recognition as a human being, and freedom of thought, conscience and religion. These rights and freedoms are indispensable to a dignified human existence and remain wholly intact from derogation upon grounds of crisis. . . . It can never be necessary to encroach upon these rights and freedoms.[8]

Twenty-one years and two human rights books later we modified our thesis somewhat in that we became "aware that the dichotomy between universalism and cultural relativism has been overdrawn. Initially, the argument for cultural relativism was an essential corrective to the Western natural law-based philosophical universalism of civil and political rights."[9] We now recognize that both paradigms have a fluidity that encompasses elements of the other, and while they also have a fixity that rejects the basis of the other, it has become apparent that the two theoretical concepts can approach each other in cross-cultural dialogue. What earlier appeared as an impasse or as a dichotomization could be refashioned so that a merger or synthesis might be reconstructed into a new form of universalism not monopolized by a western design.

In terms of contemporary Africa, however, a number of unconventional, salient, and in many ways appalling issues pertaining to human rights must now be raised. First of all, whether from the perspective of political rights or of economic and social rights, do any human rights endure? That is, putting aside the issue of whether different theoretical perspectives sometimes violate their own human rights social contract, do African states as a group (recognizing there are always exceptions) consistently, and as a matter of course, violate the human rights of their people to such a degree that for all practical purposes human rights do not exist?

Just as germane an inquiry is: When there is no state, where there are few or no public authorities who care about their people, are there human rights? Obviously, in many "African countries . . . state institutions have been eroded and there is no [effective] government to impose order, administer [real] justice, or guarantee . . . human rights. These social units cannot be analyzed within any of the existing mainstream human rights categories—civil/political versus economic/social rights, or universalism versus cultural relativism."[10]

As an adjunct to this point of view, how are African states and leaders to be categorized when the violation of the human rights of their subjects is, for all practical purposes, a matter of public policy, or a strategy invoked when rebel commanders and their bands attempt to grab power? In other words, when the violation of human rights becomes the norm, and adherence to them either nonexistent or exceptional, how can human rights even be part of the prevailing political or social conversation?

In 1968 Tanzania's president and national icon, Julius K. Nyererę, insisted that there

> is a continuing need for an extension of human rights throughout the world; that surely is incontrovertible. We cannot rest where we are because some of us are comfortable or content. Those of us who are free to develop ourselves and our nation have no right to demand that the oppressed, the victims of discrimination, the starving, and the persecuted, should acquiesce in their present condition. If we do make such a demand we are ourselves becoming their persecutors and their oppressors. . . . We have no right to be patient with the wrongs suffered by others.[11]

Nyerere's plea has essentially gone unheeded in sub-Saharan Africa. Privation, corruption, the neglect of AIDS, ethnic horrors, civil turbulence, murder, oppression of dissidents, a refugee emergency, hunger, famine, and genocide are the social norms that reverberate within the geography of Africa south. The concept of human rights appears to have little resonance in a society that is a crumbling mess. From what should be relatively minor issues of political discourse to genocide itself, too many African leaders have all but abandoned any consideration of the human rights of their people. And even in states where democracy is more or less raised to a higher level, violations of human rights are not taken very seriously. Sub-Saharan Africa appears to be living out a time where chaos is king and human rights go begging. The people seem to be considered no more than fleas—when they get in the way of rebels and autocrats they are swatted and squished.

PERSECUTORS AND OPPRESSORS

In 1966 Colonel Jean-Bedel Bokassa overthrew his cousin, President David Dacko, and took power in the Central African Republic. Referring to himself as emperor, "Bokassa's every fancy and idiosyncrasy—however irrational or infeasible—became state policy. His power was absolute. . . ." He "governed the Central African Republic as if it were his personal fiefdom for thirteen years."[12] A country of 80 different ethnic groups, previously ravaged by Arab slave raids and brutally exploitative French colonial rule, was now in the hands of a megalomanic who had no compunction about ordering arbitrary executions and plundering the state for personal excess.

Five years later, in 1971, Idi Amin, the commander of the army, took out Uganda's president, Milton Obote, in a coup d'état and for eight years led a lunatic and horror-filled reign of terror. Elimination squads were developed, which were little else but organized assassination teams. The viciously mislabeled Public Safety units purged ethnic groups of political opponents while tracking down and murdering key military officers. "The disaffection of a single officer, the discovery of a plot, an assassination attempt, or the voicing of the slightest criticism (even the rumor of any occurrence) was more than sufficient grounds for a wave of indiscriminate killings of entire groups of people. Amin's colossal brutalities in office defy cataloging. . . . As crimes against humanity they rival those of Nazi Germany."[13] In 1972 the entire 70,000-strong Asian community, made up largely of Indian and Pakistani merchants, was expelled from the country and given three months to leave. Since they controlled much of Uganda's trade, the economy collapsed. Amin's regime was based on whimsical terror; no one was safe and citizen insecurity translated into regime assurance, at least for eight years.

Bokassa and Amin were forerunners of those pitiless leaders who would rise to power by the barrel of the gun. Both often personally tortured their victims, and both were accused of ritual cannibalism. But their rule, merciless as it was, remained idiosyncratic and personal. It was far less organized and coherent than would be that of their political disciples. From the 1970s to the new millennium semifascistic leaders would rise to power, inflicting organized terror upon their people. The era of tyranny and dictatorship was under way.

In the following vignettes some of Africa's other contemporary persecutors and oppressors—individuals and ethnic groups—are sculpted so as to provide another face to the pulverization of African society within the context of human rights.

Swaziland

In lilliputian Swaziland, at the end of 2000, the government of King Mswati III resurrected what is known as the Makhundu Order—an emergency preventive detention regulation that gives police the power to deal with political and labor unrest by arresting opponents, strikers, or journalists for up to 60 days without trial. The order can then be extended for another two months. In a country of less than 1 million people, which is bordered by South Africa on three sides, the "only absolute monarchy in sub-Saharan Africa" (although Lesotho is ruled by King Letsie III) was intent on seeing to it that "all demonstrations have been crushed [and] threaten[ed] treason charges against public servants who attended . . . pro-democracy meetings. Human rights activists say this is probably the first step toward banning the union movement [since] the government banned all political meetings."[14] Opposition political parties were prohibited in 1999.

The immediate cause of the unrest that incited the population on to the streets and provoked the government was the king's dethroning of two traditional chieftaincies in favor of his older brother, Prince Maguga, who wished to appoint his own political cronies to the posts. As a result of this uncharacteristic, untraditional, and threatening style of patronage, one of the deposed chiefs fled for his life to South Africa; the second went into hiding. The concrete reason for the government's use of repression, however, was the bold civic activism of advocates for a multiparty democracy in this politically sterile and undemocratic country. Since 1996 Swaziland has been affected off and on by protests and strikes demanding an expansion of democracy and an end to the king's absolutism. Union leaders and demonstrators have been detained intermittently since then. Normal political discourse and dissent are treated as akin to treason, while marches and remonstrations are viewed as sedition. So is the way of human rights in Swaziland.

Kenya

Another style of absolute monarchy, under the guise of a presidency, is alive and flourishing in Kenya. Daniel arap Moi has been president since 1978. Moi is only Kenya's second chief executive; he was vice president and became head of state after the death of the father of Kenya's independence movement, Jomo Kenyatta, who wrenched his country away from British colonial rule in 1963.

Single-party rule, election rigging, deep-seated corruption, the arrest of journalists, political violence, and economic misrule are inherent features of Kenya's "democracy" under Moi. As early as 1982 Moi instituted a one-party system, while in 1989 he empowered the police "to monitor public places, such as bars, hotels, and restaurants, to identify those who opposed the Office of the President."[15] Another highlight of Kenya's politics is the intense dislike many ethnic Kikuyu and Luo politicians have for Moi, a member of the Kalenjin tribal minority. Indeed, as occurs every so often, ethnic and political dissidents are whipped by soldiers, police, or internal security officers in the streets of Nairobi, the capital city, when they violate Kenya's security laws and dare to publicly protest the policies and practices of the president who has enjoyed absolute power for 23 years.

In 1997 opposition demonstrators caused the central quarters of Nairobi and Mombasa, a major urban and commercial center on the Indian Ocean, to be shut down. Moi sent in the police who used ax handles and tear gas against worshipers praying for free speech and democracy. Police were also accused of torturing and murdering student demonstrators at the University of Nairobi. That same year Kenya's High Court dismissed charges against representatives of Kenya's ruling party, the Kenya African National Union, who were accused of having illegally smuggled abroad $430 million, an amount that was equal to 10 percent of the country's GNP. Nicholas Biwott, a former energy minister, was reappointed to the president's cabinet in 1997 despite being arrested in 1991 as a suspect in the 1990 murder of Foreign Minister Robert Ouko, a Luo ethnic politician. At the time Ouko was engaged in an investigation of corruption deep within the president's circle, and had also run afoul of Moi over foreign policy issues. It was rumored—although no proof has ever been unearthed—that Moi had ordered Ouko's assassination.

A country noted for its animal reserves, Kenya is a magnet for foreign tourists who arrive to go on safari. But travelers, obviously taken by the modernity of Nairobi, its available tourist amenities in places such as the New Stanley Hotel, their wanderings through the Highlands Region, seeing the Rift Valley as well as the thrill of experiencing wild animals, are largely indifferent to or unaware of the domestic political violence that swirls throughout Kenya. Indeed, they might be oblivious to it; on the other hand, since they are there to enjoy themselves, if they are informed of it, they may not really care.

Sudan

The Sudan has been in a state of civil war for almost 20 years, just somewhat less than half the period of its existence as an independent state. During that timespan well over 2 million people have been killed. Divided between an Muslim/Arab North and a Christian/black South, southerners have viewed the central government in Khartoum as racist and discriminatory, particularly after the Islamic *shariah* penal code was introduced state-wide in 1983; its attempted implementation in the South was viewed as particularly oppressive, smacking as it did of a colonizing country imposing its alien values on a colonized territory. Concurrently the South has viewed relations between the "imperial state and the society it governed [as exacerbating] communal feelings. Yet, that contrast not only of identity but of political incorporation between the leading sects on one hand, and the distant southern communities on the other, was only one manifestation of the contrast between the central and peripheral areas of the Sudanese state."[16]

The southern secessionist forces are led by Colonel John Garang, who directs the Sudan People's Liberation Army (SPLA). Militarily supported off and on since 1983 by Ethiopia, which has accused Sudan of fueling secessionist fervor in its country and fears Muslim encroachment, Garang has often found sanctuary for his troops in southwest Ethiopia. The northern forces are now led by the Sudanese president, Omar Hassan Ahmed al-Bashir, who is also head of the government-controlled political party, the National Islamic Front (NIF). In 1989 al-Bashir took power in a military coup.

Over two decades numerous international organizations and various African and European states have tried their hands at mediating the conflict, but to no avail. The civil war in its ethnic, religious, and imperial/colonial context appears to leave little room for compromise and negotiation. It is a zero-sum game in which secession will not be compromised by southern forces, nor will national unity be risked by the North. Each component views military victory as the only game in town. Within the civil war too there is intense, and often violent, internecine struggle inside both groups, which plays a substantial role in each side's refusal to reconcile. Such struggles are recurrently politically vicious, and sometimes deadly.

The endless and bloody war has seen violations of human rights by both sides. In 1994 the United Nations issued a report that accused Sudan of inherently violating the human rights of southerners through the implementation of Islamic law. Massacres of civilians are a regular component of the battles; in 1987, for example, over 1,000 civilian Dinka—the largest tribe in the South—were slaughtered by Arab warriors in a single occurrence.

Slavery too is a common feature of the ongoing struggle. Southern forces regularly seize tribal civilians, coercing them into servitude so as to prop up drudge support for southern soldiers. Christian Solidarity International, a Swiss organization, periodically buys the freedom of these slaves at $33 per head, although the UN and most human rights nongovernmental organizations (NGOs) condemn the buyout procedure because they believe it adds an incentive to the practice, notwithstanding the fact that it saves lives. In late 2000, 4,400 slaves were purchased in southern Sudan, bringing the total number freed to 38,000. The SPLA socked away more than $1.2 million in gross profits. Slave selling has become a lucrative business for the southern rebels. Obviously, they do not care about the prohibition against slavery in Article 4 of the Universal Declaration of Human Rights. Neither do northern forces, who have also apprehended thousands of southerners for use as slaves in the North.

Eighteen years of civil war have generated a conspicuously large number of refugees. Well over 250,000 remain in exile in Ethiopia, while 2 to 3 million others endure refugee status inside the Sudan. In the South "from a population of around 5 million, perhaps half had been forced to seek refuge, often in terrible circumstances, and the very few reporters able to get into the south confirmed the impression of massive displacement, with villages lying empty and sometimes destroyed, with untended crops around them. Relief agencies suggested that up to 2 million, mostly southerners, were in destitution, many verging on starvation. The overall picture of the South was clearly one of widespread devastation."[17]

Southern civilians have unquestionably been caught within the vise of two armies confronting one another. It remains indisputable that neither side is at all concerned with the emaciation, lives, or human rights of those unfortunates encased within the virulence of a secessionist struggle that is one of Africa's wars without end. Making matters even worse was a lethal drought which struck the Sudan and many of its neighbors in 2000. Indeed, in 2001 the United Nations reported that 3.2 million people, largely southerners, were confronting food and water shortages, while 1.7 million were being fed by the World Food Program. While the country lies in tatters its people must endure the forces of nature, the ruins of war, and the cruelty of their so-called leaders—and they must do so pretty much on their own.

Somalia

Violence also continues to engulf Somalia, which has been in a total state of anarchy since 1991. An entity—it is neither a state nor a nation and it hardly qualifies as a country—that has been without a government for ten years, it is ruled by clan warlords who have divvied it up into separate dominions. Even Mogadishu, the capital, is partitioned between the forces of two warlords à la an invisible Berlin Wall.

From 1992 to 1993 the United Nations and the United States tried their hands at peacemaking. A combined international force under UN auspices, which comprised 31,000 peacemakers, 70 percent of whom were Americans, was sent in and by 1994 hurriedly withdrawn. General Mohammed Farah Aidid, a prominent Somali warlord, had defeated the UN troops by organizing an effective military strategy, which led to the deaths of 24 Pakistani and 18 American soldiers in daring attacks in 1993. Television images of Somalis dragging dead U.S. soldiers through the streets of Mogadishu soured the U.S. public on the enterprise. Convinced that the United Nations and the United States were attempting to recolonize Somalia—is it possible that any nation would want the responsibility?—Aidid struggled effectively to achieve the removal of western forces. Even African states were frustrated; the OAU "proved largely irrelevant as Somalia's tragedy unfolded. . . . "[18]

By 1993, when the civil war was just two years old, 1 million Somalis, out of a population of some 7 million, fled to refugee camps in Ethiopia, Djibouti, Kenya, Yemen, and Saudi Arabia, while malnutrition and starvation impacted a further 1.5 million. At the time the "consequences of Somalia's mayhem were described . . . as 'the greatest humanitarian emergency in the world.'"[19] And although the immediate threat of famine was dealt with by tons of food relief shipped in by western nations, in 2000, 750,000 Somalis, afraid to return home, remain outside the country. Presently, in addition to being split up among different clans, the Somali entity has three separate autonomous regions that relate to each other as three distinct and separate countries—Somalia, Somaliland, and Puntland.

During the latter part of 2000 representatives of Somalia's multiple clans convened for five months in Arta, Djibouti, in a problematic effort to form a central government. Although bearing no electoral legitimacy whatsoever, the group appointed 245 of its members to a Transitional National Assembly that in August selected Abdikassim Salad Hassan as president. The president and assembly leaders maintain, somewhat illusorily, that they serve as a transitional government. The conference had been organized by Djibouti's president, Ismail Omar Guelleh, who had been anxious to bring peace and stability to the Horn of Africa. With Ethiopia and Eritrea at loggerheads and Somalia deep in the throes of anarchy, Guelleh was fearful that his tiny country would be engulfed by the ongoing upheaval.

Hassan's selection as president was rejected by the heads of four major Somali clans, the most important of whom is Hussein Muhammad Aidid, the son of General Mohammed Farah Aidid (who was killed in 1996 during a street battle with a rival clan). The four indicated that the Arta peace conference included officials of the country's former dictator, Muhammad Siad Barre, who fell from power in 1991, and they demanded that other nations disavow the outcome.

The new "president"—who was deputy prime minister under Siad Barre—heads a state whose capital is without water, electricity, police, or schools, even as the country itself remains fragmented. When most of the representatives of the new assembly returned to Mogadishu, they were shot at and attacked; Hassan's arrival was more peaceful. Whatever the basis of his legitimacy, it is clear that the new leader—if he ever really achieves that status—has a formidable job in administering a divided state convulsed by bedlam.

Somalia is another example of how sub-Saharan Africa has been transformed. Mayhem, starvation, millions of desperate refugees, clan friction, and civil war are the appropriate new labels that define contemporary Africa. Human rights mean nothing. People mean nothing. Life itself is meaningless to Somalia's warlords. A country that was harshly and dictatorially ruled for 22 years by Siad Barre, and that invaded Ethiopia in 1977 in an abortive attempt to annex part of its territory, exploded into a frenzy during the last days of his governance; the ferocious battle for Mogadishu in 1991 led to 4,000 civilian deaths and the destruction of the city. The country and its people have never recovered.

The United States and the United Nations Security Council, stung by the attack of the UN secretary-general, Boutros Boutros-Ghali, on them for neglecting Africa, did take a stand, but then withdrew as things turned sour swiftly. Africa once again proved so inconsequential to western national interests that even unmitigated pandemonium affecting millions of Somalis could neither keep nor focus their attention.

Africa is on its own; Somalia is on its own. Unfortunately, the people of Somalia do not have effective rule, good government, or decent leadership; there is no political entity that can address their grievances. There is no one to petition. Somalia is a striking example of how African governments are at war with their own people.[20] The people of Somalia also are on their own.

Congo-Brazzaville

Congo-Brazzaville has been thrashed by civil war since 1997. Fighting erupted as soldiers loyal to President Pascal Lissouba and rebels supporting former military dictator General Denis Sassou-Nguesso, who had been president from 1979 to 1992 and had brought the country close to bankruptcy, battled it out. From June to October fighting convulsed the capital city, Brazzaville, and the port town of Point-Noire. Both municipalities were leveled as the cities' populations sought refuge from the firestorms. Lissouba fled to Burkina Faso, and Sassou-Nguesso once again took control of the country. Neither side seemed the least concerned that the Congolese people—who had watched as their neighbor across the Congo River, Congo-Kinshasa, had disintegrated—were now living through their own drama. A nation of some 2.5 million people was tossed into bedlam as splits within the rebel movement pushed the civil war into 2001 even as a questionable peace accord was signed.

The struggle for power took place in a state whose major sources of foreign exchange are petroleum, timber products, sugar, and the reexport of diamonds smuggled in from Congo-Kinshasa. Part of the problem was that Angola supported the rebel forces because Lissouba was seen as a supporter of Angolan rebels seeking to displace their government, while France, the original European colonizer, saw its oil magnates also sustain the rebellion out of fear that their profitable investments would be impaired. Because of France's strong presence in the country, the rebellion could not have succeeded without its support. Foreign interests played a major role in sustaining the rebellion and seeing that it was successful.

United Nations Secretary-General Kofi Annan recommended to the United Nations Security Council that peacekeepers be sent in to stabilize the country. But the permanent members of the Security Council, with their attention directed elsewhere, pretty much decided that if any international actor was to become involved it should be France, which, in fact, did have vital interests at stake.

According to Samuel Decalo, a noted specialist on the rule of the military in Africa, "authoritarian rule has become ingrained as the norm in much of the [African] continent."[21] Congo-Brazzaville is simply just one more illustration of that truism. The coup occurred because an African potentate wanted once more to "come out of the rain." There was no other reason to destroy cities, disrupt the lives of a citizenry, or bring about bedlam. It was simply power for power's sake.

Burundi

In 1966 the political scientist René Lemarchand wrote that Burundi is too "often dismissed as a feudal backwater in a seething continent [and] has hardly received the attention it deserves. . . . This neglect is unfortunate on several counts, not the least being the sense of dismay of certain Burundi elites upon discovering that so few westerners are even aware of the existence of Burundi on the map of Africa."[22] Grievously for Burundi, that is no longer the case.

Ethnic violence between Hutu and Tutsi ethnic groups is today's trademark of Burundi politics, where, since 1993, well over 200,000 people have been killed, 500,000 remain in displacement camps, while hundreds of thousands of others are either internal or external refugees. With a population of merely 5.7 million people, this is a calamity of the first order.

Melchior Ndadaye, the first Hutu leader to be freely elected president since the country received its independence from Belgium in 1962, and several cabinet officials were killed in a Tutsi-led coup d'état in 1993, only four months after assuming power. Although the president had been freely elected to his post, the army, the economy, and most government positions were dominated by Tutsi. Ethnic fighting then flared between Hutu and Tutsi, which led immediately to the deaths of 100,000 people and forced hundreds of thousands of refugees to flee to Rwanda, the Congo, and Tanzania.

The Tutsi, who constitute 15 percent of Burundi's population, and the Hutu, who represent 80 percent (the Twa encompass the other 5 percent) had been at each other's necks even before then. In 1972, 250,000 mostly Hutu were slaughtered in another major outbreak of ethnic violence. Until independence "cyclical competition . . . tended to mitigate ethnic tensions,"[23] despite Belgium's policy of creating divisions between the two groups, but since then, in a continuing struggle for cultural power, ethnic violence has been explosive.

By 1995, with the presidency again in the hands of a Hutu and the army controlled by the Tutsi, the tension between the two groups continued to escalate. It was also chaotically worsened as 500,000 Rwandan Tutsi had earlier bolted in a frenzy to Burundi due to the genocidal policies of Rwanda's Hutu-led government in 1994. Tanzania closed its border to Rwandan and Burundi refugees. Then, in 1996, Burundi's army seized control of the government and named Pierre Buyoya, a moderate Tutsi, president. Despite economic sanctions imposed by Tanzania, Kenya, Uganda, Rwanda, and the Congo, civilian rule was not restored and Buyoya's military government easily survived the pressure placed upon it.

Despite intensive efforts by the former South African president Nelson Mandela, and a brief trip to Tanzania by President Bill Clinton in 2000, no progress has been made in resolving Burundi's ongoing cataclysm. Mandela, who had taken on the task of mediating the conflict in 1999, convened a conference in Arusha, Tanzania, in the summer of 2000 in which 19 separate Burundi groups were to sign a peace accord. On the eve of the conference Hutu rebels and Tutsi hardliners launched attacks on Burundi's capital city, Bujumbura, while President Buyoya warned Tutsi militants who opposed the conference not to stage a coup.

The peace treaty called for the eventual return to power of the Hutu majority, but with rights and protection for the Tutsi. A three-year transitional government would be established before any new elections were to be held. A unique legislative body to be evenly split by ethnicity, and brandishing broad veto powers, would be created, while the army would also be divided equally for ten years. A genocide tribunal and a peace and reconciliation commission would be composed to consider the torture and murder of some 200,000 people since 1993.

Clinton's one-day visit was meant to pressure the warring factions to sign the covenant, but it failed. Two of the main Hutu groups refused to attend, some parties declined to sign the pact, and Mandela concluded the meeting by scolding the conferees on their shameful failure. A follow-up summit meeting held in Nairobi to try to seal the Arusha compact also ended in failure as the parties refused to agree to a cease-fire. The presence of Mandela, along with the leaders of Tanzania, Kenya, Uganda, and Rwanda, had no beneficial impact on the contentious representatives, although Burundi authorities did agree to release 350,000 of the 850,000 civilians in displacement camps. By 2001 intense fighting again erupted in Bujumbura and its suburbs, while attempts to overthrow the government persisted.

What is there to say? If one does a little arithmetic and totals the numbers, they are heartbreaking. Since 1972 some half a million people have been killed, many of them civilians; perhaps 1 million others have been forced to flee their homes. Torture, malnutrition, some starvation have become everyday phenomena since at least 1993, while the entire society has been everted.

Human rights? No one seems to have any rights in Burundi—neither political rights nor economic claims. The ethnic struggle for power obstructs all assertions to civilized behavior. Outside forces can do little when political elites refuse to do *anything* that would bring this bloodshed to a halt. Burundi is another entity on the planet that cannot be defined as a state, nation, or country. Perhaps the best definition of what Burundi is would be a nightmare without end. The state has ceased to exist.

Rwanda

Hutu/Tutsi savagery is also a hallmark of Rwandan politics. In 1994, in an orgiastic firestorm, some 800,000 Tutsi and moderate Hutu were slain when the *interahamwe*, the strike force of the Hutu government, went on a three-month rampage. In what can be compared to the genocide executed by the Nazis in Europe during the 1930s and 1940s, in which some 6 million European Jews were slaughtered, or to the murder of 2 million Cambodians by the Khmer Rouge from 1975 to early 1979,[24] the Hutu policy of eliminating all Tutsi was one of the last century's crimes against humanity.

Like the Congo and Burundi, Rwanda's disintegration is in large part due to the colonial policies invoked by Belgium in its Central/East African empire. "Whatever Hutu and Tutsi identity may have stood for in the precolonial state no longer mattered; the Belgians had made 'ethnicity' the defining feature of Rwandan existence. [Belgium perfected] the administration of an apartheid system rooted in the myth of Tutsi superiority." Accordingly, the Belgian policy of divide and rule was essentially conjured up as "you [the Tutsi] whip the Hutu or we will whip you."[25] To observe what has befallen the Congo, Burundi, and Rwanda since each achieved independence is to illuminate the fiasco that was known as Belgian East Africa.

The Tutsi make up 14 percent of Rwanda's population of 8.2 million people; the Hutu, 85 percent; and the Twa, 1 percent. Following independence in 1962, with the policies of Belgium as the operative framework, the murder of Tutsi by the new Hutu government became unofficial policy. To escape the oppression some 500,000 Tutsi fled to Uganda. (Many had already exited in 1959 when an earlier anti-Tutsi rampage had been initiated.) By the 1970s France had replaced Belgium as the prime European actor in the country and established a strong patron/client relationship with the Hutu leadership. Arms, which were used against the Tutsi minority, poured into the country. When a small Tutsi-led rebel force, the Rwandese Patriotic Front (RPF), invaded Rwanda from neighboring Uganda in 1990, the anti-Tutsi sentiment became even more ingrained within the Hutu Power leadership.

On April 6, 1994 the Hutu president Javénal Habyarimana was killed when the plane he was in crashed. (Burundi's president, who was aboard, was also killed.) Habyarimana, a relative—very relative—moderate, had signed a peace agreement with the RPF in 1993 so as to reach accommodation with the Tutsi, thereby fully alienating the radical Hutu. Although no evidence was ever unearthed, it is more than probable, although clearly merely a hypothesis, that the Hutu Power elite had arranged for the plane to be shot down. Nonetheless, organized rumors that the airplane had been shelled by the RPF were spread over Hutu-controlled radio stations. The Hutu population was instantaneously assembled to employ a "final solution" to the Tutsi problem. The Hutu saw the Tutsi as "the other," as aliens in a Hutu land, resulting in a perspective that whatever happened to them was of small consequence to the "pure" inhabitants of Rwanda. Worked into a frenzy by the Hutu Power radicals, a mad, berserk, and very well organized tide of slaughter swept the nation.

Within 100 days hundreds of thousands of Hutu people massacred almost 1 million Tutsi. Led by the *interahamwe*, the Tutsi, including women and children, were bludgeoned to death; killed by machete, screwdrivers, or knives; machine gunned in their homes; or lured into churches by Hutu priests and nuns and burned as the churches were set afire. Orphans, priests, lawyers, teachers, hospital patients, doctors, intellectuals, politicians, laborers, everyone that mobs could get their hands on was brutally slain. "During the genocide, the work of the killers was not regarded as a crime in Rwanda; it was effectively the law of the land, and every citizen was responsible for its administration."[26]

Meanwhile the RPF, under the command of the Tutsi General Paul Kagame, which now had 20,000 fighters under its control, moved rapidly to evict the Hutu government and overthrow the *génocidaires*. In early July it seized the capital, Kigali, and took over administration of the state. As the RPF forces closed in on the metropolis, the Hutu elite and their followers took flight. More than 1 million frightened Hutu, along with most of their genocidal leadership, scrambled into the Congo, where they were given protection by President Mobutu and fed by international aid agencies. The Hutu chiefs organized the Congolese refugee camps as their personal fiefdom. All relief supplies had to go through them; much of it was then sold to the bedraggled masses, and arms were purchased to organize military forays inside Rwanda. Another 600,000 refugees fled to Tanzania. Kagame assumed power in Rwanda.

During the Rwandan holocaust the United States, and in particular President Clinton and Madeleine Albright, then U.S. representative to the United Nations, did everything conceivable to keep the UN from taking any action, including denying the ongoing annihilation. In fact, while the killing was under way, the UN slashed its United Nations Mission to Rwanda observer force by 90 percent, leaving only 270 troops to do virtually nothing but watch. With the Somalia fiasco still fresh in America's consciousness, Clinton refused to sanction any forceful UN Security Council endeavor. "The desertion of Rwanda by the UN . . . can be credited almost single-handedly to the United States. . . . Rwanda had a genocide; the world's powers left Rwanda to it."[27]

Rwanda, however, was not merely left to stew in its own homicide. France continued to airlift weapons to the Hutu government, while its president, François Mitterand, maintained that "genocide" in countries such as Rwanda "is not too important."[28] Racism has rarely been so eloquently expressed; the bigoted implication evident in his statement requires no further elucidation.

In 1998 President Clinton briefly visited Rwanda to apologize for U.S. behavior and vowed the country would no longer remain aloof.

But Hutu attacks on Tutsi from inside the country and from across the border in the Congo continue intermittently; more than 7,000 mostly Tutsi Rwandans have been murdered since the 1994 butchery. As Auschwitz and Adolf Hitler's other concentration camps became public knowledge, the allies of World War II ascribed to themselves the maxim "never again." Still, as western abandonment of Rwanda during its time of trial demonstrated, words are cheap.

Kagame tried to calm the population and restore equilibrium in Hutu/Tutsi relations; but his shattered domain had more than half of its remaining 7 million people displaced. A government was established that included Hutu moderates, and appeals were made to noncriminal Hutu exiles in the Congo to return without fear of retribution. Most were prohibited from coming back by the Hutu who controlled the refugee camps. Tanzania forced Hutu refugees to return to Rwanda; they were permitted to peaceably merge back into Rwandan society.

Meanwhile, some 125,000 Rwandan Hutu were charged in domestic courts with genocide and arrested pending trial; by 2001 more than 120 of 4,500 individuals tried were found guilty and sentenced to death, while others were given life sentences. An International Criminal Tribunal for Rwanda was established by the United Nations. The trials, dealing with genocide, conspiring to commit genocide, crimes against humanity, encouraging mass rape campaigns, and outrages upon personal dignity are held in Arusha, Tanzania. But by 2001 fewer than 50 individuals had been indicted, among them the former Hutu prime minister (who pled guilty to genocide and crimes against humanity), foreign minister, and ministers of commerce and health. Merely eight people have been convicted. Most of the prominent suspects remained in the Congo, while others fled to Europe, the United States, or other countries in Africa where some were arrested and handed over to the International Tribunal. Others are being tried in Belgian courts. General Kagame, president and the bona fide authority in Rwanda, fretted about the sluggish pace of the international judicial process and mused that the West continued to underplay the importance of what had transpired in Rwanda. Within the country, so many legal officials had been slaughtered that there were few judicial personnel left to officiate. Clearly, the juristic procedures are agonizingly slow.

Paul Kagame is a decent leader who has tried to bring about reconciliation. That definitely sets him apart from the numerous tyrants who populate sub-Saharan Africa. But the odds against his success are striking. With the problems in his nation more or less still ignored by the international community, and the country forced to go to war with the Congo to preserve the sanctity of western Rwanda and to eliminate the exiled Rwandan killers still in attack mode, Kagame will need all his intellectual and military resources to succeed in the long term. He will get little help from the United States.

In the matter of Rwanda the role of the United States was the nadir of an African policy based on negation. Certainly no vital U.S. interests were in jeopardy. But as the moral leader of the Western world and as the only remaining superpower, it was clearly incumbent upon the United States to intercede. It has been estimated that 5,000 armed U.S. or UN forces could have prevented the bloodbath. The United States might have easily provided a peacemaking strike force. It would not have required a change in its African policy—a policy based on the reality that without national interests at stake there are no compelling reasons for engagement. Such a move could have been a short-term commitment. That the United States not only refused to intercede but developed the proposition that a holocaust was not under way, although it knew better, was an infamous declaration that, in all but the very rhetoric used, remains an affirmation of Mitterand's racist dictum that genocide in Africa is inconsequential.

In 1951 the United Nations Convention on the Prevention and Punishment of the Crime of Genocide came into force. It defined genocide as a crime under international law and obligated the attestant states to condemn, thwart, and punish acts that are intended to annihilate ethnic, national, racial, or religious groups.[29] The United States is a signatory to the convention. Why didn't the United States and the United Nations, in all of their moral rectitude, demand that the convention be adhered to in Rwanda? The answers have already been explicitly recounted. Essentially, the United States didn't really care about what was transpiring in a country far away and having no vital interests to be troubled about. And, as such, the United Nations could not be permitted to drag the Western world into the quicksand.

That, of course, does not exonerate the Hutu Power killers. They are fully responsible for the havoc wreaked upon Rwandan Tutsi. It is incumbent on the signatory states to the Genocide Convention to see to it that the responsible parties are brought before the International Criminal Tribunal for Rwanda, and in a timely fashion. Without such litigation human rights, insofar as Rwanda is concerned, will remain in the shadows of history.

Angola

Civil war consumed Angola even 10 years before it received independence from Portugal in 1975. But from the moment freedom came the three African nationalist entities, broadly representing different ethnic/ cultural groups—the Bakongo, Mbundu, and Ovimbundu—that had been battling Portuguese colonialism and each other turned inward with a vengeance. Initially part of a transitional, if fractured, government, violence was promptly unleashed, massacres took place, and a struggle ensued for control of the state. Additionally, as a country occupying a strategic geopolitical position, rich in mineral resources, and with one of the factions, the Popular Movement for the Liberation of Angola (MPLA), having a Marxist bent, the country was ripe for Cold War intervention.

The Soviet Union supplied military equipment to the MPLA, while Fidel Castro's Cuba supported it with 20,000 troops. The United States and the Congo (Zaire) threw their firearms and military muscle behind the National Front for the Liberation of Angola (FNLA). The third element, the National Union for Total Independence of Angola (UNITA), led then, as now, by Jonas Savimbi, was supported by troops from apartheid South Africa. Within a year the MPLA gained control of the capital, Luanda, and seized absolute power, the FNLA had been routed, and Savimbi's UNITA melded into the interior, gaining control of much territory there. The United States then shifted its support to UNITA. The battle between the MPLA and UNITA for mastery of the nation would continue for another quarter of a century and beyond, much of the time being prodded along by the United States and fended off by Cuba and the Soviet Union. It is another of sub-Saharan Africa's endless wars.[30]

The place is resource-rich. Diamonds, oil, iron, gold, uranium, manganese, and copper are richly deposited while fruits, coffee, tobacco, and sugarcane once were plentiful. But the resources have gone to support the almost four-decades-long war. Savimbi's force of 30,000 troops survive on diamonds smuggled out of the country and sold abroad despite a 1998 UN-imposed embargo that prohibits their purchase, while the Angolan government has used its vast deposits of oil in the northwest province of Cabinda to subsidize its part of the struggle. In 1998 the United States indicated that half of a $900 million windfall in oil earnings was spent on weapons, while the rest was stolen by Angola's leaders. The $900 million went unrecorded in the nation's budget. Some 7 percent of imported U.S. oil comes from Angola, making it America's eighth largest petroleum supplier. Despite its wealth

> today Angola has virtually no productive industries (except for artificial limb factories). Nearly everything that is consumed is imported, even drinking water. Eighty-two percent of the country's twelve million people live in poverty, and a similar number are unemployed; three out of ten children die before the age of five; only forty percent ever go to school. The average life expectancy is forty-two. More than two million people are internal refugees and more than a hundred thousand are amputees; victims of the countless numbers of land mines strewn across the country.[31]

Some 2 million people have already died in this interminable war. Widespread starvation is ever-present despite the fact that more than 1 million people are fed by international aid agencies. Fifty-three percent of children under five suffer from severe malnutrition; each day some 500 die from undernourishment, exploding land mines, and disease. Maternal mortality of 1,500 per 100,000 live births is among the highest in sub-Saharan Africa, while 2.1 percent of the population has AIDS or the HIV virus. Leprosy too runs rampant.[32]

Much of the countryside has been destroyed, and cities lay in ruins. A land, once a Cold War centerpiece for the United States, which abetted Savimbi to the tune of hundreds of millions of dollars, has now been all but abandoned, except for foreign oil interests. Even the United Nations Observer Mission, which has 1,000 peacekeepers on the ground (their number is slowly being reduced) is impotent. Indeed, in 1998 the UN special representative to Angola, who was trying to arrange an accommodation between Savimbi and President José Eduardo dos Santos, who has been in power for 21 years, died in a plane crash under very suspicious circumstances. According to the United Nations Security Council, UNITA is the primary cause of the crisis in Angola. Peace intermittently intrudes but then is swept away by recurring warfare.

As if all this were not enough, Angola has sent military troops into the Congo to fight alongside the forces of President Laurent Kabila, and after his assassination, those of Joseph Kabila. The incentives are to prevent Savimbi's battalions from being supplied through the Congo and to isolate UNITA so as to preclude the Congo from becoming a safe harbor for its soldiers. Angola is currently helping to prop up the Joseph Kabila regime. In return it expects the Congo's support in facilitating the closing of the border to UNITA. Given Joseph Kabila's fragile political and military position, it appears to be a fool's dream.

In 2000 civilians organized protests in Luanda against corruption and oil revenues lavished on the military—more than 6,000 people marched through the streets demanding peace. The president responded by proposing legislation in which journalists writing articles that questioned or criticized the government would be jailed from two to eight years.

The civil war continues to boil. Some 50,000 Angolans fled into the Congo toward the end of 2000 as the war escalated once again between UNITA and government forces. The United Nations ferried food supplies into southwestern Congo to feed the terrified civilian refugees. In 2001 the IMF demanded and received authorization from Angola to have its auditors analyze government figures on oil revenues, which make up 90 percent of export income, so as to try to constrain the use of such receipts for the war effort. Future IMF loans were conditioned on receiving approval. Great Britain accused Savimbi of breaking the UN embargo on the traffic of diamonds by conducting sales through Gabon.

It remains doubtful, however, given Angola's history of internecine strife, that the IMF, Great Britain, the UN, or Angola's population can bring about a halt to the fighting. The suffering will continue; the violation of Angolans' political, economic, and social human rights will endure. Peace does not appear to be in the offing. The fruitless struggle for power continues. Jonas Savimbi would rather see his country—or what's left of it—hurled further into the depths of social and economic depravity than give up his vain search for ultimate political puissance. Angola remains an African human rights calamity.

Nigeria

Nigeria has been ruled by military dictators for most of its independent existence. Upon attaining freedom from Great Britain in 1960, it had six tumultuous years of civilian rule. From that point forward, with few exceptions, army control was standard. Nigeria also passed through a bruising civil war from 1967 to 1970 as the eastern region seceded and declared itself the Republic of Biafra. Some 2 million Nigerians, mostly easterners, died of the effects of war and starvation. The most populous country in Africa, with 121 million people—20 percent of the population of all of sub-Saharan Africa—Nigeria is the colossus of West African states despite its tempestuous history.

With some 250 different tribes, Nigeria is a potpourri of subcultures and languages. But four ethnic groups stand out—the Hausa and Fulani in the North, the Yoruba in the Southwest, and the Igbo in the Southeast. Most of the military heads of state have come from the Islamic North, while the government has also been controlled by northerners, who make up the majority of the population. Deep resentment among the mostly Christian ethnic groups in the South has been a by-product of Muslim dominance. Indeed, the secession of Biafra was largely caused by the tyranny inflicted upon southern traders in the North and the sense of oppression and inequality southeasterners felt within Nigeria as a whole. As Biafra's leader, Lieutenant Colonel Chukuemeka Odumegwu Ojukwu, said at the time, "you cannot get African unity by just submerging your identity."[33]

But in 1993 Nigerians, with all the autocrats and trauma they have lived through, were brought up short by the rule of arguably the most vicious despot they have ever encountered. Toward the end of that year

General Sani Abacha ousted an interim civilian government and proceeded to virtually destroy the country along with its oil-rich economy. A throwback to the personal tyrannies of Uganda's Idi Amin and Jean-Bedel Bokassa of the Central African Republic, Abacha was

> perched imperiously on the throne of power, running Nigeria not so much as a country, but as his personal fiefdom. Billions of dollars [in oil revenues] were siphoned off into overseas bank accounts controlled by Abacha, his family, or his cronies, while the masses simmered in anger at their deepening poverty. Literally millions of Nigerians had fled into economic and political exile. Newspapers were shut down, and trade unions were banned, while human rights activists, journalists, intellectuals, and opponents imaginary and real were jailed, or, in a few cases, eliminated by state-sponsored death squads.[34]

Moshood Abiola, a Yoruba media magnate who had apparently won the presidency in elections held earlier in the year but could not claim the office because the military refused to release the results, was arrested in 1994 by Abacha and died of a heart attack in prison. His treatment during his incarceration was appalling; he was kept in virtual isolation, poorly fed and in ill health, until his death in 1998. Ken Saro-Wiwa, a courageous political activist, playwright, short story writer, novelist, and television personality who championed the rights of the Ogoni people, was hanged in 1995. His only "crime" was that he stood up for the Ogoni tribespeople by demanding financial compensation for the poverty and environmental devastation inflicted upon them by the foreign oil companies—Shell, Agip, Elf—and Nigeria's petroleum corporation, which pumped billions of dollars worth of oil from their land in southeastern Nigeria.[35]

At the time of Saro-Wiwa's arrest, "troops entered towns and villages [in Ogoniland] shooting at random, as villagers fled to the surrounding bush. Soldiers and mobile police stormed houses. . . . Villagers who crossed their paths, including children and the elderly, were severely beaten . . . and sometimes shot. Many women were raped."[36]

Former head of state Lieutenant General Olusegun Obasanjo, a Yoruba Christian and hero of the civil war, who led Nigeria from 1976 to 1979 and then returned the country to civilian rule, where it remained briefly, was arrested in 1995. The following year Kudirat Abiola, wife of the imprisoned president, was murdered, presumably on orders from Abacha.

Meanwhile, with all the disorder, the value of Nigeria's currency plummeted, the banking system collapsed, inflation soared to above 53 percent, and Nigeria's external debt rose to $30 billion. As Nigeria defaulted on its outstanding debt, the United States and European countries cut off their aid programs. Nigeria was in complete disarray.

In what has been termed "a coup from heaven," Abacha died of a heart attack in 1998 while cavorting with a pair of prostitutes. Soon afterwards the political landscape was fundamentally altered. Obasanjo was released from prison and, after a seven-month period of constitutional reform, was elected president in free and democratic elections held in 1999.

Despite intense, but intermittent, eruptions of ethnic and political violence in Lagos, the commercial capital, in Ogoniland, and in the northern city of Kaduna, where thousands have been killed in street battles between Muslims and Christians largely over the imposition of *shariah* law in 11 of Nigeria's 36 states, President Obasanjo appears at least to be moving Nigeria into a new era where problems are faced rather than fueled. He seems determined to satisfy Nigeria's economic and political interests.

To sanctify Nigeria's return to republican values and to help legitimize the democratic resurrection after 16 consecutive years of military autocracy, President Clinton paid a four-day state visit in August 2000. "The world," he said, "needs Nigeria to succeed."[37] To that end the United States beseeched European states, which have provided most of Nigeria's loans, to reschedule repayments and appealed to them to consider debt relief if Nigeria remains on the path of reform. The United States also developed an aid package of $128 million, $20 million of which is to be used for primary education and disease prevention.

Success will be difficult. Ethnic and religious problems remain explosive, while social cohesion is nonexistent. Nigeria's infant mortality rate is 77 per 1,000 live births, while 4.1 percent of its adults, perhaps some 4 million people, have HIV/AIDS.[38] The average pupil/teacher ratio in primary schools is 37 to 1, secondary school-age children are grossly underenrolled in educational institutions, and 25 percent of children under 14 are fully active in the labor force. Nigeria's illiteracy rate is 40 percent. Forty-four percent of Nigerians live below the poverty line. GDP growth is merely 1.8 percent while the country's foreign debt is approaching $33 billion. Merely to service the debt costs $1.3 billion annually.[39] Historically, its human rights record has been abysmal. A germane question is: How patient will the population be? They have had to survive decades of military governance. Their entire national patrimony has been squandered, while they have sunk ever deeper into deplorable poverty. It's hard to be optimistic.

Still democracy has, at least for the moment, been restored. Obasango offers Nigeria the best leadership it has had in a very long time. The nation now has an advocate who can move to restore human rights values—both political and economic—which have been sorely lacking. The establishment in 1999 of a truth commission—the Human Rights Violation's Investigation Commission—was an attempt by President Obasango to cleanse Nigeria by ferreting out past human rights abuses. Although the commission has no subpoena power, and can offer no amnesty, there is at least a framework by which past human rights violations can be investigated. The president's success in this and other venues will in large part determine the future of human rights in Nigeria. Indeed, his impact, whether he succeeds or fails, will be felt throughout Africa.

South Africa

Although all apartheid legislation had been repealed in 1993, the election of Nelson Mandela to the presidency one year later brought about its de jure termination in South Africa. The event was of profound importance to Africa in the arena of human rights. Recognizing the vitality of apartheid's peaceful abolition, the Nobel Prize Committee awarded its 1993 peace prize to Mandela and his negotiating partner, President F. W. de Klerk, South Africa's last white leader. As Mandela indicated the year he received the prize, "we are convinced that a genuinely democratic South Africa will be [a] reliable partner as the international community continue to grapple with such critical matters as a democratic world order [and] human rights. . . ."[40]

The creation of a Truth and Reconciliation Commission (TRC) in 1995 to document the human rights abuses inflicted by the apartheid regimes and to exchange freedom for truth for those whites willing to testify regarding their own excesses were immense steps toward reconciliation. Although the "exchange value for truth" has been questioned,[41] there is little doubt that a fully integrated peaceful South Africa, through an attempt to rouse the population to honor the significance of human rights, was a principal consideration. Just one year later the adoption of a constitution ennobling human rights consecrated those freedoms.

Although Mandela and his successor, President Thabo Mbeki, have emphasized the importance of the expansion of human rights for all South Africans, it is clear that for many whites, the discarding of apartheid meant little. In late 2000 six white policemen unleashed attack dogs on three black immigrants. As the whites laughed and cavorted, "for about an hour [the blacks] were repeatedly savaged by four dogs while they screamed and begged for mercy. The policemen . . . beat the victims when they tried to fend off the dogs."[42] The event was videotaped.

Because the racist episode was a metaphor for the extensive lingering of apartheid comportment, it raised the ire of the press and the people. According to South Africa's *Mail & Guardian,* "in the first six months of 1998 [there were] 607 reports of deaths [of black citizens] at the hands of the police. The statistics reflect little change since before 1994. Amnesty International expressed concern that the legacy of police complicity in acts of brutality and human-rights violations 'does not appear to want to go away.'" As the newspaper indicated, old habits die hard.[43]

Other conventions die just as hard. Some conservative white local councils have tried to establish their own private companies to take over municipal services prior to the councils' imminent electoral transfer to black hands. Thus, the maintenance of roads, garbage removal, park and recreation control, school construction, the development of library facilities, bus transportation routes, and so on would remain in the hands of whites. The result, of course, is that black councils would hold little power in those communities, few social services would be provided to the black townships, and white residential areas would receive the most social, cultural, and environmental attention. Tourist facilities, such as hotels, can then legally remain off-limits to blacks, while South African blacks may also constitutionally be evicted from their homes. In such fashion white councils can hijack black towns.[44]

Although there is absolutely no doubt that democracy and human rights are now at the forefront of the South African political order, there is also no disputing the fact that acts which represent apartheid values remain deeply ingrained within white South African society. Certainly no reasonable person should have expected that 46 years of racist politics would disappear overnight. Yet it is certain that the South African Human Rights Commission (SAHRC), with its responsibility to develop a culture of human rights, must act more forcefully to help purge the country "of racist images and assumptions."[45] Its role and obligation, as laid out in chapter 9 of the constitution, to "promote the protection, development and attainment of human rights; and monitor and assess the observance of human rights in the Republic . . . so as to promote respect for human rights and a culture of human rights," needs to be more rigorously pursued. What also requires attention is the explosive crime rate that is the bête noire of urban centers in particular. Living within high-security walled compounds has become a necessity for the middle and upper classes.

South Africa, along with Nigeria, offers Africa an alternate model of rule and some hope for the future of the continent. The development of democracy by sub-Saharan Africa's two regional giants and South Africa's accentuation of human rights are vital components of a return to overall political sanity vis-à-vis Africa and its leadership. These efforts must be supported by the international community. The prompt U.S. allocation of some $50 million in development aid to South Africa after the fall of apartheid and further help since then were important indicators of encouragement.[46] Far more must be done. Increased aid, debt relief, tariff reduction, or even a trade pact similar to the North American Free Trade Agreement (NAFTA) should be considered for both nations. Democratic leaders must be supported if the happy occasion of restored democratic rule is to spread to the decomposing nations of Africa.

THE GLOBALIZATION OF HUMAN RIGHTS

In 1999 a military coup overthrew the government of Guinea-Bissau. Civilian government was restored in early 2000 and then made temporarily impotent when, late the same year, the junta generals indicated they would not take orders from the elected president. The generals were then shot dead. A second coup sans a military coup d'état, followed by outright murder. In 1999 also the president of Niger was assassinated. In Mozambique, where democracy has made inroads following a vicious 17-year civil war that was brought to a close in 1992, reporters critical of the government are sometimes slain, while prison overcrowding amid suffocating conditions led to the deaths of almost 100 prisoners in November 2000. Transparency International, founded by former World Bank officials in 1995 to expose corruption among officials worldwide, placed Nigeria, Angola, Chad, and the Cameroons as among the world's worst offenders during 2000. Children from Togo, Benin, and Mali, sold into slavery in the Ivory Coast and Gabon by impoverished families, continued to be used in the harvesting of cocoa and coffee. Child slavery, organized by African "businessmen," also persists in other parts of West and Central Africa, and effects some 200,000 children. Clearly, disorder and the violation of human rights in Africa continue unabated. The long, uncheckered history of extraordinary human rights abuse in Africa south of the Sahara must, finally and decisively, be confronted.

Bemoaning the widespread absence of political and economic liberties does little good in bringing a solution to bear on ever-increasing rights violations. Information is important but action is necessary. Bilateral, although perfunctory, strategies have proven to be relatively fruitless, whereas South Africa's noble and courageous efforts to induce equality in its society are laudatory. United Nations peacekeeping ventures have hardly been successful. A global, more universal approach to the problems as they exist in Africa might be broached. Worldwide economic sanctions imposed on apartheid South Africa were quite effective and validated an international approach to domestic human rights violations. The formation of international tribunals in Tanzania to try individuals for the Rwandan genocide and in the Netherlands to bring to trial Bosnian war criminals are also components of an effective transcontinental tactic.

When former Chilean dictator General Augusto Pinochet was seized and arrested in London in 1998, in an attempt to bring charges of genocide and crimes against humanity against him, another measure was established for responding to crimes committed by African leaders against their people. Despite the fact that for medical reasons Pinochet was eventually released and sent home to Chile, the action "set a precedent whereby state sovereignty will no longer be a safeguard for individuals accused of gross violations of the right to life."[47] "Furthermore, the indictment of former Yugoslav president Slobodan Milosevic by The Hague Tribunal in May 1999 for crimes against humanity in Kosovo, his arrest in Yugoslavia, and removal to The Hague for trial in June 2001 signals a further uncertainty for sitting governing elites if they engage in crimes against humanity."[48]

These startling and precedent-setting acts should be reviewed to determine when they can be appropriately imposed on African heads of state who have violated the UN's Convention on Genocide, its Universal Declaration of Human Rights, and its International Covenant on Economic, Social and Cultural Rights (which the United States has refused to sign). The initial step taken to convene a war crimes tribunal in Sierra Leone is a positive beginning. So is the continuing attempt to arrest the former ruler of Chad, Hissène Habré, for the alleged execution of 40,000 people. The war crime trials of Rwandan citizens in domestic courts in Belgium gives further impetus to international accountability. They should be expanded continent-wide. Charles Taylor, Foday Sankoh, Jonas Savimbi, Denis Sassou-Nguesso, Robert Mugabe, Idi Amin (who currently resides in and is protected by Saudi Arabia), and their ilk should not be permitted to freely put their populations through hell. War crimes trials and the arrest of leaders should be seriously considered by the international community. The precedent is now available and should be used. Indeed, when the 1998 Rome Treaty on the International Criminal Court comes into force—which the United States signed on December 31, 2000, but which must be ratified by 60 countries—another instrument, a permanent world court, will be available to bring to justice perpetrators of genocide, war crimes, and crimes against humanity.

State sovereignty is no longer an issue. It cannot be manipulated as a convenient shield to hide behind. International criminal charges should be brought against African (and other) leaders and rebels who have unambiguously violated the human rights of their people in the most egregious fashion. Of course there will be an outcry. Some authorities will proclaim that such actions violate Article 2, paragraph 7, of the UN Charter, which states, in part, that "Nothing contained in the present Charter shall authorize the United Nations to intervene in matters which are essentially within the domestic jurisdiction of any state."[49] But Pinochet tried to use that argument and he failed.

As early as 1964 Leland M. Goodrich, then Columbia University's distinguished scholar of the United Nations, maintained that, in practice, the domestic jurisdiction clause "has not had the restrictive effect which was feared. . . . It would be difficult to establish that in any instance the domestic jurisdiction principle has been the decisive factor in causing an organ of the United Nations to refuse to take action."[50] Currently, hiding behind domestic borders is internationally untenable, and domestic jurisdiction is less relevant than it once was.

It is time that the world community via the United Nations or, eventually, the International Criminal Court goes after these killers. If slaughter, torture, slavery, rape, ethnocide, genocide, and crimes against humanity in Africa are to stop, the perpetrators must be blocked. And the way to do that, so as to truly enshrine human rights—political, economic, and social—as a cluster of fundamental freedoms is to indict, apprehend, arrest, try, and if found guilty, punish them. Such a course, should it ever be adopted, could very well serve as a deterrent in that future leaders might think twice about the consequences before imposing their viperous policies upon their peoples.

CHAPTER FOUR

African Poverty and the AIDS Crisis

SCARCITY AND MISERY

In West Africa, climate, which is often extreme, afflicts Africa's people in myriad, and recurrently detrimental ways. Average yearly rainfall can exceed 156 inches but in exceptional years may climb to over 400 inches. Although annual totals generally hover around 60 inches per year, in the rainy tropical region higher quantities are not unusual. Cameroon, for example, has been hit with 158 inches of precipitation; Sierra Leone, by 137 inches; and the Congo, in Central Africa, gets 40 to 80 inches with 150 inches not uncommon.[1] States along the Guinea Coast—Gabon, Liberia, Ghana, the Ivory Coast, Benin, and the central and southern parts of Nigeria—suffer through inordinate drenchings—between 80 and 200 inches per year—while humidity and temperature usually linger near 90. As a result, a luxuriant vegetation has grown that makes "penetration of the African rain forest difficult. Here also insects, pests, intestinal parasites are constant plagues. Malarial mangrove swamps flourish along many of the rainy tropical and wet-and-dry savanna coasts."[2] On the other hand, dry grassland

and desert regions, such as Somalia, with 17 inches per year, and Niger have precious little precipitation. Still, much of Africa south of the Sahara is impacted by a hot, rainy, and humid climate that takes its toll on the health of the population.

In Uganda, for example, malaria is the most serious health problem by far, accounting for 20 percent of all hospital admissions. While it "has been hit hard by the AIDS epidemic, malaria and diarrheal diseases . . . still cause more deaths annually."[3] "Ghana has the full range of diseases endemic to a sub-Saharan country. Malaria and measles [are] the leading causes of premature death. Among children under five years of age, 70 percent of deaths are caused by infections compounded by malnutrition. Guinea worm reached epidemic proportions . . . in 1988-89."[4] Common diseases in Ghana, and elsewhere in Africa, also include cholera, typhoid, pulmonary tuberculosis, tetanus, yellow fever, hepatitis, trachoma, schistosomiasis, dysentery, river blindness, and poliomyelitis—afflictions that have been all but eradicated or constrained in much of the rest of the world. In 2001 a cholera outbreak struck South Africa—earlier it had impacted Zambia—while in late 2000 various villages in Uganda succumbed to the Ebola virus—one of the most gruesome, lethal, and contagious viruses known—killing hundreds of people. Elephantiasis, a disease usually marked by the excessive enlargement of the legs or scrotum, caused by a roundworm carried by mosquitos and parasitic when in the blood, is a common sight in the interior of Liberia. Often the scrotum is so overenlarged that it has to be lifted on to a makeshift wagon so that the affected man can move around the village.

Overall, "health in Africa is . . . wretched in comparison with that in Western countries and also worse on average than in most countries in other parts of the world."[5] According to the United Nations, Africa's malaria infection rate has soared by 60 percent over the past 30 years, while 2 million of Africa's children die before reaching their first year of life. In Niger 41 percent of children under five suffer from moderate to severe stunting due to malnutrition; in Madagascar the figure is 48 percent. In Mauritius and Botswana, where the economy is on the upswing, the figures are 10 percent and 29 percent respectively. Two hundred fifty million Africans live on less than one dollar a day; in Guinea-Bissau it is 88 percent of the population.[6]

In sub-Saharan Africa, 70 percent of Africans have no access to clean drinking water. In Madagascar, clean water is unavailable to 96 percent of its rural population; in Equatorial Guinea, the figure is 69 percent; in Chad 83 percent; and in South Africa, 67 percent. In Botswana, on the other hand, 77 percent of rural people have access to safe water.[7]

The overall physician-per-population ratio in Africa south of the Sahara is 1 for each 25,000 people. In Rwanda, it is 1 per 31,000; in Swaziland, 1 per 9,277; in the Central African Republic, 1 per 27,000; and in Ethiopia, 1 per 35,000. In Botswana, the number is 1 per 4,000.[8] But even these horrifying figures are quite deceiving since more than 80 percent of all medical personnel reside and practice in urban areas, notably in the capital city. Those who have escaped village life have no interest in returning, while doctors brought up in cities wish to remain there. Indeed, 20,000 professionals emigrate from Africa each year, many of whom are medical workers. Thus, most people who live in the villages of the interior have extremely limited access to any medical assistance—if they have entrée at all. As a result, most go to country doctors or faith healers for treatment, a tribal class whose resources are, quite simply, limited to the use of medicinal leaves, herbs, roots, prayer, and witchcraft.

For example, in the case of pregnant women in traditional Nigerian Igbo society, prenatal care does *not* often include stressing "the importance of diet, including adequate intake of folic acid and calcium . . . as well as the importance of avoiding alcohol and other personally toxic exposures."[9] It does sometimes encompass a ritual that in some parts of the culture has "survived unchanged" to aid in "warding off evil spirits. On the day of this ritual, a *dibia* [a practitioner of traditional medicine] would take the girl before the first cock crow, and take her to the evil forest. There, he would prepare a concoction which [she] would throw into the evil forest, and then walk to her husband's home without looking back."[10] In my own experience in West Africa, I often came across individuals in the interior who chose to seek the counsel of a traditional country doctor; of course, "African medicine" would be prescribed. Cultural values remain strongly ascendant in village life and bear a commanding influence over the lives of individuals.

In some areas of Africa other transforming problems loom. In parts of East and southern Africa, and in the Sahel—that group of countries stretching from Senegal to Chad on the southern flank of the Sahara—there is often very little or no rain. Over the past three decades these regions of Africa have been rocked by drought and famine as rainfall declined to the lowest tabulated level in 100 years and as the Sahara inched its way south. For 20 years, beginning in the late 1960s, the Sahel was in a continuous state of drought. In 1983 Ethiopia, Somalia, and Sudan confronted their worst dry spell of this century. Within three years more than 10 million people faced starvation and 1.5 million died, 69 percent of them Ethiopians. In 1992 southern Africa encountered that region's most serious absence of precipitation, which impacted nine countries. In all cases the United Nations Children's Fund (UNICEF), the United States, European states, and nongovernmental international aid organizations provided hundreds of millions of dollars in emergency food relief. Once again in 2000, Ethiopia and Eritrea were menaced by drought caused by a three-year absence of rain threatening 9 million people in both countries. The crisis was brought to a halt by the contribution of 1 million tons of food furnished by the European Union and the United States. Between 1986 and 1998, Ethiopia was in a state of drought for six years; Sudan, for five; and Cape Verde, for four. On the other hand, in 2000 and 2001, Mozambique and Malawi were devastated by torrential rains and severe flooding.

The relentless global warming, which many scientists proclaim is already impacting the earth, will only add to the misery of inadequate health care, drought, and famine, as the consequences of climate change will be greatest in developing countries. Since coping with such influences is, according to the Intergovernmental Panel on Climate Change, often a function of technology, education, infrastructure, and access to multiple resources, Africa south of the Sahara can be expected to be hit particularly hard by the warming of the earth's atmosphere.

Often famine has been precipitated not merely by drought but by the ravages caused by civil strife. In both cases cows, goats, and camels also perish; milk and meat vanish; harvests disappear; people flee the smaller villages and towns desperately seeking food; land is left fallow; and the crisis is compounded and intensifies. "Half the world's refugees are African, most of them fleeing drought or civil war or both." One million refugees alone are encamped in Libya, having fled across the Sahara from, among other places, Chad, Niger (where 20 percent of its 10 million people are threatened by famine), Nigeria, Cameroon, Ghana, and the Congo.[11]

Famine can also have profound political repercussions. In Ethiopia, the famine of 1973 was a precipitating factor that led to the military coup d'état which overthrew Emperor Haile Selassie I. Because he was unwilling to "sully" his own and Ethiopia's "responsible" international reputations, he swept the famine under the rug by stifling public commentary. He also refused international relief aid, claiming it was not needed, and barred starving refugees from seeking refuge in the capital city, Addis Ababa. The nation was aghast and initially strongly supported the Marxist military rulers who took over the country. Indeed, I recall being at a dinner at the time, along with 3,000 other guests, celebrating the emperor's birthday. While the country was in the throes of an extraordinary crisis, all the food one could have desired was offered up, including roast pig and various Ethiopian delicacies. I felt it was an abomination, and apparently so did the population and the military. One year later the emperor was deposed.[12]

Survival prospects for Africa's people are grim indeed. Life expectancy in sub-Saharan Africa is 50 years. Infant mortality per 1,000 live births is 92, "food production is 20 percent lower than it was in 1970, when the population was half the size," while together African poverty, abysmal health conditions, and AIDS have generated a frightening 13 million African orphans; in Zambia alone, 25 percent of its children are orphans. In Kenya, 42 percent of the population live below the poverty line; in Malawi, 54 percent. In the world's poorest countries 40,000 deaths occur each day from preventable diseases. The effect of all this misery on Africa's economies is, of course, catastrophic. Thirty sub-Saharan countries have a combined GNP only slightly larger than that of the state of Georgia in the United States; even South Africa, the continent's largest economy, has a GNP smaller than Louisiana's.[13]

Women: A Culture of Privation

One lasting and detrimental effect of colonialism is that women are often excluded from the traditional economy, resulting in their alienation from land they once controlled. "Nutrition undoubtedly suffered as women found it harder and harder to feed their families on the lesser (and often poorer) acreage allotted them, particularly since they still did much of the work on their husband's cash crops."[14] Even as the market women of Ghana, Togo, and the Ivory Coast dominate small-scale trade, a rigid stratification structure currently exists in which the female is often submerged within communal society.[15]

In mud-and-wattle huts throughout the continent, village women feed their families, care for their small children, provide all the needs of the household, and wait on the male adults and male children. Women are the primary caregivers "and take the larger responsibility for the maintenance of family health and care of the sick."[16]

"African women work far longer hours than African men, especially in agriculture, and also in the home collecting water and firewood, and yet due to local customs and legal restrictions, women have less access than men to resources such as land, and other assets like credit, fertilizer, and education." In Uganda women spend 14 percent of their time on farming, while men work the farms only 7.7 percent of the time. Women are three times more active fetching water, while they spend three times as much time collecting firewood then men. "Demand for medical care by women [is] more [negatively] affected by distance and user fees than for men," which plays a role in their maternal mortality rate, which in Uganda is 500 to 2,000 per 100,000 live births, while the infant mortality rate is 97 per 1,000 live births.[17]

Family life is layered along sex lines. The male head of the household is the primary authority figure. In the cities, male authority has been diminished because of western influences, and women play a more powerful role than they do in a rural setting. Still, according to the World Bank, even in the urban arena economic opportunities for women are vastly inferior to those offered men. African culture is ordinarily patriarchic.

In traditional society marriage is most often arranged by the father and other senior male kinsmen. Polygyny and adultery—otherwise known as having inside and outside spouses—are thoroughly accepted values—for men—in much of traditional Africa. In Cape Palmas, Liberia, I knew of an instance where one man, Senator Alan Yancy, had scores of wives, and his children would classify their relationship to one another by bespeaking of their connection as "same father, different mother." *Agatha Moudio's Son,* a novel by the Cameroonian author Frances Bebey, details the complex interaction that occurs in a polygynous household. Chinua Achebe's novel *Things Fall Apart* offers a more sober consideration of the practice among the Ibo of Nigeria at the time of their first rendezvous with colonialism. Currently, the practice of polygyny and adultery has an astounding impact on the diffusion of HIV—in Africa 80 percent of HIV transmissions are accounted for by heterosexual contact—and other sexually conveyed infections.[18]

Forced childhood marriages—a practice deemed a violation of human rights by the United Nations—are common in sub-Saharan Africa. Being married at eight years old is not unusual in Ethiopia and in many parts of West Africa. Largely as a result of giving birth before they are fully biologically developed, in Ethiopia one out of every seven females dies as a result of childbirth or pregnancy. Obviously, for child-mothers who survive, a lifetime of psychological, sexual, and domestic servility is in the offing.

Female Circumcision. A ritual that broadly defines the subordinate role of women in Africa, and speaks to the sexual oppression and social poverty of their gender, is the custom known as female circumcision. Since first recorded in Egypt some 4,000 years ago, more than 100 million women have undergone circumcision, otherwise known as a clitoridectomy, or female cutting. It involves the partial or total removal of the clitoris and/or infibulation, the surgical modification and suturing together of the labia. "Hemorrhaging, infection, and infertility are among the serious complications. The inability to pass urine normally [often it comes out drop by drop], pain during sexual intercourse, and excessively difficult deliveries are common results."[19] The operation, normally completed prior to or during puberty, is usually performed by a female elder in generally unhygienic conditions. As marriage and childbirth near, decircumcisions are performed to open infibulations.

It is a complex moral issue as many African women's groups, some African governments, and most western human rights organizations condemn the practice as barbaric and mutilating. On the other hand, many traditional African women praise the custom and condemn western criticism as an attack on their cultural values by western neocolonial interests. They see it as interference in their culture. Most African leaders, recognizing the power of the ritual in their countries, remain silent. Haji Sasso, who in 1997 was head of the National Council of Muslim Women in Sierra Leone, vociferously defended the rite. "I am only doing this to protect our culture," she said. "I don't want to see this ceremony eradicated because it binds us, we the women, together. We respect each other in this way, and we feel free together because of it."[20]

In Africa, female circumcision is a common practice among Christians, Muslims, and animists, and in many countries and cultures. In Sierra Leone, more than 90 percent of women undergo the procedure, while in Somalia, Sudan, and Chad, it is broadly administered. Many cultures in Nigeria look at it approvingly.

The rite, and often its accompanying celebration, is seen as vital to preserving culture. Men usually perceive it as a mechanism for controlling "unruly" women. Defenders view it as essential to socializing an adolescent into the mores of their tribe and as an instrument for reinforcing respect and authority. Additionally, many adherents claim that in a patriarchal culture when "the women go into the bush for this ceremony [dancing, feasting, and learning about womanhood], it is just about the only time they can drink and dance, let their hair down and enjoy a bit of freedom. It doesn't matter what other people think because we are happy with our customs."[21] Since traditional African males view virginity in their brides as sacrosanct, an intact infibulation demonstrates chastity; an additional motive, of course, is that circumcision also controls female sexuality.

Obviously not all African women appreciate the cultural importance of being mutilated. Numerous Somali women have fled to the United States in the 1990s seeking asylum, claiming that having to undergo circumcision would threaten their lives, and refusal would lead to their being killed. For most, the asylum was granted.

The complexity of the issue, and the tumult surrounding the argument over values, is well represented in *The River Between*, written by Kenya's distinguished novelist Ngũgĩ Wa Thiong'o. Part of the plot line revolves around the bitter conflict created over circumcision as an initiation into womanhood. Muthoni, one of the novel's early protagonists, dies as a result of the operation. Her last words, however, indicate her passion at having succeeded in being "a woman, beautiful in the tribe."[22] To her father, Joshua, a Christian convert, it "was now clear to all that nothing but evil could come out of adherence to tribal customs. . . . Circumcision was wholly evil."[23]

Wherever one stands along this moral divide, it is clear that whether African women appreciate this cultural artifact or not, it is demeaning and oppressive. It negates women's sexual reality, they end up being at the mercy of their husbands, and it oftentimes causes death due to the unsanitary conditions under which this operation is normally conducted. In some circumstances, if they choose to decline the "privilege," women are ostracized from the village community or beaten or even killed by irate fathers or other adult men. A male-dominated village hegemony exists that imposes sexual and social poverty upon women, all in the name of culture. Insofar as female circumcision is concerned, culture is king and individual desires are subordinated to cultural norms. One may support or oppose the ritual, but it is clear that collective or community values override whatever squeamishness exists in the West or among indigenous African critics regarding the procedure. Although it is brutal and debasing, within the context of Africa's ontological nonindividually based norms, kinship and tribe will determine the future of female circumcision.

A CRUMBLING INFRASTRUCTURE

Compounding the overwhelming poverty that afflicts sub-Saharan Africa is a social and economic infrastructure in rapid decay. Abusive warlords and civil, ethnic, and religious strife have permitted the structural foundation of society, which is necessary for providing life-giving services to society, to erode. In many ways social and economic existence is more grinding today than it was before independence, and the rusting away of Africa's substructure is another element to be added to the political equation measuring Africa's self-destruction.

Fully 84 percent of Africa's roads remain unpaved while almost three-quarters of its population has no accessibility to an all-weather road. Even in Kenya, which many outsiders erroneously view as relatively developed, slightly less than 14 percent of primary roads are paved; in Liberia it is 6.2 percent and in Guinea, 16.5 percent. Electricity is generally available only in the larger towns and cities, whereas in most villages kerosene lamps are the standard. Merely 20 percent of Africa's people have recourse to electricity. In Zambia, just 1 percent of the rural population has electricity, while it is available to 36 percent of urban dwellers; in Swaziland, the figures are 5 percent and 14 percent; and in South Africa, 48 percent and 69 percent respectively. Cooking is done over firewood or charcoal. In Africa, clean and safe drinking water is an oxymoronic concept. In villages everywhere water has to be hauled, often from far distances since almost 70 percent of Africans remain without a sufficient reserve of water,[24] or it is collected in rain barrels. Wells are often another source of water.

In terms of sanitation, disposal of sewage and recourse to indoor toilets or adequate outdoor privies, access remains broadly idiosyncratic. While overall less than 50 percent of sub-Sahara's population have appropriate sanitation accommodations, removing Nigeria and South Africa from the list reduces the figure to just over 40 percent. Taking into account the fact that the highest percentage are in urban areas, it is clear that the villages generally suffer. For instance, according to the World Bank data base, only 12 percent of Senegal's villagers have appropriate facilities; in Sudan, 4 percent; Benin, 11 percent; Angola, 4 percent; and Comoros, 16 percent. On the other hand, in Tanzania, the figure is 83 percent; Uganda, 50 percent; Madagascar, 34 percent; Namibia, 37 percent; and Mauritius, 100 percent.[25] Of course, interpreting what "access" means is another question altogether. It should also be noted that in the interior, toilet facilities are often made up of unsuitable outdoor privies since a large proportion of the population lives in stifling hot mud huts with a thatch or zinc roof, or their equivalent. Even in many parts of towns or cities outdoor amenities are the norm.

Because of the extreme humidity affecting the tropical regions, machinery and machine parts must be maintained almost daily to keep them from rusting away. Often such maintenance does not occur. As one travels over laterite roads in the interior of many countries, rusted equipment is often strewn along roadsides that usually front the rain forest. Upkeep, maintenance, and repairs are expensive and are often regarded as an unaffordable luxury.

Education too is part of a nation's heritage and social infrastructure. For most desperately poor sub-Saharan countries, government funding is sometimes less than adequate. In 1995, Niger allocated 3 percent of GNP to education; Ghana, 2.7 percent; Uganda, 1.8 percent; Mozambique, 4 percent; Equatorial Guinea, 1.7 percent; while Botswana allocated a hefty 6.1 percent, and the Seychelles, 7.9 percent. Still, it is important to keep in mind that the bulk of the funding is directed toward urban centers.[26] On the other side of the ledger, less developed countries "also have extremely strong commitments to military expenditure to bolster security and counter threats. Increase in defense expenditure [and] consumption of scarce resources to support the military machine show that . . . taken together [they] were spending about 6.3 percent of their gross output on defense, a staggeringly high amount in absolute terms considering the poverty of most of the countries concerned."[27] The needs of the military always trump education's essentials.

Illiteracy rates are inordinately high: for all of sub-Saharan Africa above 15 years of age, 49 percent of females and 32 percent of males. The corresponding figures for Latin America and the Caribbean are 13 percent and 11 percent.[28] School enrollment is negligible. In Tanzania, an astoundingly tiny 5.5 percent of school-age juveniles are enrolled in secondary school; in Kenya, 24 percent; in Cameroon, 27 percent; and in Mali, 7 percent. Botswana, on the other hand, enrolls 65 percent, and South Africa, an admirable 93 percent.[29] Average schooling for African women increased by only 1.2 years between 1960 and 1990, "the lowest gain for any region."[30]

For all its travails Africa south of the Sahara has perhaps just begun to see how bleak and desperate the future will be. The poverty and misery of life that seems so appalling may be seen in hindsight as a tolerable circumstance, for the continent is at the cusp of a tragedy of pandemic proportions. And although already an extraordinary nightmare, the explosion of AIDS and its cause, the HIV virus, threatens African society in ways almost impossible to imagine. From the Sahara south life is being disrupted and destroyed. Village resilience is crumbling, urban peoples are dying at an accelerated pace, while the basic elements of culture and society are being ripped asunder. The AIDS cyclone has descended on Africa and appears to be developing a ferocious swaggering vortex.

HIV/AIDS

AIDS was initially observed in 1981. In 1983 researchers in Bethesda, Maryland, and Paris, France, isolated the HIV/AIDS virus. The same year the first reported cases were observed in Central Africa, although in December 1982 two AIDS cases were diagnosed in South Africa. By 1989 each African country reported at least one AIDS case. Within a decade 25.2 million sub-Saharan Africans, in a region girding 10 percent of the earth's population, were infected with the HIV virus—70 percent of those contaminated worldwide—and the continent became the epicenter of an AIDS pandemic.[31]

But the virulence of the pestilence for sub-Saharan Africa is even more extraordinary since less than 1 percent of North Africa's population is infected. The virus is more or less concentrated in some 30 countries in Africa south of the Sahara, largely impacting the cup of nations running from Senegal in the west, east through the Central African Republic to Ethiopia, south through the Ivory Coast, Congo, and Kenya, and down to the Republic of South Africa. It has been estimated that over the next decade or so, 25 million more AIDS-affected people will die—over 22 million are reported to have already succumbed—and most of those will be in Africa south of the Sahara. The numbers far surpass the 20 million fatalities resulting from the bubonic plague of the fourteenth century.

The HIV virus, which causes AIDS, spreads exceedingly fast. In 2000, 3.8 million new HIV-infections were reported in sub-Saharan Africa alone—10,500 per day! Thirteen percent were children. The largest number of cases impacts the economically important age group of 15 to 45.[32] The virus is also physically calamitous. During the first stage of HIV—which may last from 1 to 10 years—most people are unaware that they have been infected since they often have no disabling symptoms. As AIDS migrates to its full-blown capacity—a period of one year—pulmonary tuberculosis, prolonged diarrhea, fever, weight loss, bacterial pneumonia, cancers, and fatigue set in. The final phase of a few months brings severe weight loss, recurrent infections, and chronic fever, and by the end the patient is unable to care for her- or himself. Because of the pathetic state of health care, notably in the interior of the continent, traditional healers are often sought out; in Botswana, such country doctors treat 70 percent of AIDS cases.[33] Patients and their families then, for all practical purposes, are usually left to fend for themselves.

In Africa, the transmission of AIDS is largely through heterosexual activity, as the male introduces infection to the wider society. "Unlike the situation in the United States, where the ratio of cases in men to those in women is greater than 10, in most African populations studied the ratio is approximately unity."[34] Polygyny, adultery, prostitution, the migrant labor system (largely in southern Africa), truck drivers plying the transportation grid in East Africa, and refugees, armies, and rebels roaming the countryside are among the primary causal agents in the spread of AIDS.[35] The virus is then diffused to children from the infected mother before birth, during delivery, or while breast feeding. According to the U.S. Centers for Disease Control and Prevention, up to 42 percent of African babies become infected through these channels.

Cultural, traditional, and peculiarly male values constrain the use of condoms. Although protection during intercourse is the key to preventing the spread of the virus, African males ordinarily scoff at the notion since, even beyond a lack of awareness about using prophylactics, it is seen as devaluing their "manhood." In South Africa, "thirteen of 18 male respondents who were asked about condom usage said they would not use condoms. Similarly, in a survey of 429 mineworkers, 66 percent never used condoms."[36] An idiosyncratic response that is not unusual is the concept that westerners dress up for everything they engage in; African males don't "dress up" while involved in sex.

African leaders have been slow to admit publicly that their countries face a human catastrophe. "To admit the existence of the AIDS epidemic became tantamount to admitting the inferiority of African ways of life [because negative images] of the dark continent . . . have long been engraved in the Western view of Africa."[37] Understandable perhaps, but perilous social politics since so much time was lost in coming to grips with the emergency. Public policy was thus dangerously forgone while millions died. In South Africa "the silence on the subject is so great that 'you can hear that proverbial pin drop.'"[38]

As AIDS spreads, the economy goes into a free fall and social norms vanish. In Zimbabwe, maize productions drops 61 percent following the death of a breadwinner. Cotton and vegetable production falls by half. When male adults involved in the modern economy fall ill, families often revert to subsistence farming.[39] As multiple members of a family die, farms are left dormant; surveyed continent-wide the impact is obvious. "The growth rate for developing countries was estimated at 1.5 percent for 1999—which . . . marked the weakest performance for these countries since . . . the early 1980s."[40] According to the World Bank, this was due in no small measure to the impact of AIDS on the overall economy, and the Bank indicated that Africa needed annual growth rates of *more than 7 percent* if it is to *halve* the number of people living in poverty by 2015. On the other hand, should AIDS continue to surge in intensity, sub-Saharan Africa's economic growth rate could be reduced by 25 percent over the next 20 years.

A massive number of orphans are spawned due to parental deaths, forcing other village adults either to care for or to abandon them. In each case the physical and psychological strain on all is unfathomable. Village elders or grandparents who had expected their children to support them in old age must instead feed the grandchildren. Often such families confront starvation. Education too is affected. "Zimbabwean orphans are half as likely to finish school as other children, mainly because their foster parents can't [or won't] afford the minuscule school fees."[41]

In circumstances where AIDS awareness is high, there is often still little that can be done to prevent infection. In Uganda, "the ability of women to avoid being infected is likely to be less than men. For women . . . over one-third said it was because their spouse had multiple partners."[42] Fear of alienating a spouse, or being denied the attention of a sexual partner, constrains women from forcefully insisting that unprotected sex will not be tolerated. In African villages particularly, female adamancy can be dangerous. "Because women are frequently economically dependent upon their partners, they feel that if they become demanding about such a difficult subject, the man may retaliate or leave." In Zimbabwe "we are seeing more women now, usually referred because of HIV-related illness in a child. Often the mother has been tested without the involvement of the husband. Increasingly, the husband declines screening and sometimes rejects the mother and child. These are the realities of AIDS experienced by women in Zimbabwe."[43]

A Sisyphean Nightmare: Nature's Holocaust

In the final analysis, what best maps out the devastation that AIDS has wrought are the specific numbers of people caught up in the disease. The data are electrifying. There is no way to explain away the starkness of their reality. Indeed, the figures jump right off the page and provide a frightening image. They both shock and numb. In fact, World Bank statistics emphasize HIV-seroprevalence in adults. If children below the age of 15 are pulled into the findings, the overall numbers are beyond the capacity of a human being to imagine.

Zimbabwe's adult HIV infection rate is almost 26 percent; Botswana's, 36 percent.[44] For Zimbabwe that amounts to more than 1.5 million people; for Botswana, some 325,000. Of 62,000 babies born yearly in Botswana, 9,000 are infected with the disease. In the Ivory Coast, which has the highest rate of AIDS in West Africa, 11 percent of the adult population are HIV carriers. In 1999, 72,000 Ivoirians died of AIDS; in 1998, 69 percent of all teachers' deaths were AIDS related.[45] In 1993, the HIV virus affected 4 percent of South Africa's adult population; in 2001, the figure was 24.5 percent, or 4.7 million people—the largest number anywhere in the world. Ten percent of skilled and highly skilled finance and insurance executives in South Africa are estimated to have AIDS.[46] In Malawi, 29 government ministers are HIV positive, while 25 percent of the urban workforce is expected to die of AIDS by 2010.[47] In Zambia, the railroad industry has seen its workforce sharply reduced because of the incidence of AIDS. In 1994, in Ghana, where 3.6 percent of its people now have AIDS, 70 percent of the total infected population were female; half the cases were those in the 15 to 45 age bracket, and the remainder children aged 5 to 10.[48]

Between 5 and 10 percent of the adult population have AIDS in Burundi (8.3 percent), Lesotho (8.4 percent), Burkina Faso (7.2 percent), Togo (8.5 percent), Gabon (5 percent), Cameroon (5 percent), Congo-Brazzaville (7.8 percent), Congo (5 percent), and Tanzania (9.4 percent). Ten to 25 percent have AIDS in Djibouti (10.3 percent), Ethiopia (10 percent), Kenya (11.6 percent), the Central African Republic (10.8 percent), Malawi (14.9 percent), Mozambique (14.2 percent), Zambia (19.1 percent), Rwanda (12.8 percent), Namibia (19.9 percent), and Swaziland (25 percent). In Ethiopia alone that amounts to more than 3 million adults; in Congo, 2.5 million; in Zambia, about 1 million; and in Tanzania, 1.5 million. In contrast, less than 0.1 percent of the North African populations of Algeria, Egypt, Libya, Morocco, and Tunisia have AIDS or the HIV virus. In Mauritania, the rate is merely 0.5 percent.[49]

According to Dr. Peter Piot, of the United Nations AIDS research organization UNAIDS, "there is no other single factor in the world today that so systematically undermines the gains of decades of investment in human resources, education, health and the well-being of nations."[50] The question that begs to be answered is: How can African states cope with this crisis?

What Can Be Done? In July 2000, at the thirteenth International AIDS Conference, held in Durban, South Africa, Dr. Piot maintained it would take $3 billion per year to take basic measures to deal with AIDS in Africa and tens of billions in additional yearly funds to provide Africa with the standard drugs used to combat the disease in developed nations. Merely $300 million is now being spent annually on AIDS in Africa. As the conference concluded, the U.S. Export-Import Bank offered 24 sub-Saharan African states $1 billion in annual loans to finance the purchase of drugs and medical services from U.S. pharmaceutical companies. Some states, including Namibia and South Africa, declined the offer, averring they are already overwhelmed by foreign debt. Currently U.S. drug firms only give some developing countries a financial break on the exorbitant cost of drugs used to create an AIDS cocktail for inhibiting the disease, and even then it is an expenditure that is prohibitive for most sub-Saharan African states. Education, establishing free clinics to treat sexually transmitted infections, the distribution of contraceptives along with the cultural education in the use of them so as to break down male attitudes preventing their use, counseling, testing, and the willingness of political and religious leaders to enlighten populations to promote safe sex and reduce the stigma of the disease are vital components against this scourge.

In fact, Senegal, which established a national committee to combat AIDS that emphasizes prevention, has an HIV infection rate of only 1.8 percent. Uganda, under the progressive leadership of President Yoweri Museveni, which in 1988 was the most AIDS-affected country in the world, reduced its infection rate from 14 percent to 8 percent by stressing a response to AIDS that cuts across different preventive venues; through the use of midwives, public health centers, and technology, its rate of maternal mortality, large as it remains, was also halved.[51]

In Malawi, President Bakili Muluzi, who has been in power since 1994, worked with the nation's newspapers to direct the public's attention to how best confront the spread of AIDS. Prior to 1994, former President Hastings Kamuzu Banda disallowed any public discussion of HIV or AIDS. Although AIDS cases remain ruinously high in Malawi, at least the leader is sufficiently concerned with the issue to throw his weight behind a national campaign.

In November 2000, Botswana's president, Festus Mogae, who is leading his nation's crusade against AIDS, spoke forcefully on the subject. He first discussed his government's policy of educating students about HIV/AIDS through school curricula and training teachers how to broach the subject in the classroom. "Parents too," he maintained, should "be more open about the issues of sexuality." He went on to say: "we are faced with the mammoth task of fighting the HIV/AIDS pandemic from all fronts. I am obviously concerned about the low condom usage figure contained in the [Metlhaetsile Women's Information Center] report. The direct result of this is the high rate of teenage pregnancy and the spread of HIV/AIDS. This is a national disaster that is threatening public health, social cohesion, economic development and indeed the very existence of our nation."[52]

Concern does not consistently seem to be the case in South Africa. Thabo Mbeki, the president of South Africa, has emphasized social factors such as poverty rather than HIV as the primary force behind the epidemic, which caused an uproar among HIV/AIDS medical authorities. Given what is known about the disease, and the rapid rise of infection rates in South Africa due to unspent AIDS funds, the lack of adequate treatment, limited government funding for the drug AZT and the distribution of condoms, Mbeki's misplaced emphasis is utterly destructive to South Africa's people. Poverty is an ancillary factor; the HIV virus is *the* cause. His attitude is a major contributing factor to the soaring rate of AIDS in South Africa. Indeed, 40 percent of the nation's clinics do not offer HIV tests.

In 1994, three academic authorities conducting research on AIDS in South Africa concluded that the

> South African political terrain creates added difficulties for health educationists. A government HIV program will meet with extreme suspicion from the black community and be associated with past racist population control initiatives. . . . A program that advocates monogamy and celibacy in the absence of a marriage partner is unlikely to be favorably received by migrant workers. Our interviewees believed that since the mines depend on migrant labor, and as they perceive multiple relationships and prostitution as social consequences of migrant labor, management's concern about HIV must be insincere or have sinister motives.[53]

In 2001, Mbeki's comments will not make it any easier to convince these respondents or, to be sure, many other South Africans, to combat AIDS by wrestling with the HIV virus. And although, due to domestic urgency, he has amended his views somewhat, he still appears to embrace the stance that the HIV virus is merely one of the elements that precipitates AIDS.

Community-based organizations in African countries can do a lot to educate their people about AIDS. They also absolutely require their government's support in conducting their varied activities. Attitudes such as those reflected by Mbeki are hardly helpful. The United States should go out of its way to finance and strengthen those leaders who are willing to take the lead in the battle against AIDS. Expanded financial assistance should be provided to governments, particularly as in the case of Senegal, Malawi, Uganda, and Botswana, when they get out in front of the issue. Indeed in 2000, the Bill and Melinda Gates Foundation (established by Microsoft's cofounder) and Merck and Company donated $50 million each toward helping Botswana's president Mogae battle AIDS in his nation. This is an area where the United States can be helpful and generous; and it should.

Interestingly, in late 2000, the director of the United States Peace Corps program organized a new enterprise to aid African states in dealing with the AIDS epidemic. All 2,400 Peace Corps volunteers serving in Africa, in addition to new recruits, are to be trained as HIV/AIDS educators. Furthermore, in 2001 the Crisis Corps was expanded within the Peace Corps organization to send 200 former volunteers to work on HIV/AIDS-related activities in Kenya, Tanzania, Zambia, Lesotho, Malawi, and Togo. Each Crisis Corps volunteer will be required to sign up for a three- to six-month commitment.

Since there is now no cure for HIV/AIDS, U.S. and European pharmaceutical companies, which hold almost all of the patents, must be urged, even pressured politically by western governments and their populations to lower the cost of all prescription drugs that act as inhibitors. UNAIDS, after intense negotiations, did get five European and U.S. drug firms to substantially reduce the price of HIV drugs to Senegal, Rwanda, and Uganda, while in 2001 the U.S. drug giant Pfizer donated $50 million worth of the drug fluconazole to South Africa to be freely distributed to poor people in public hospitals and clinics for two years. The drug treats an AIDS-related deadly brain inflammation that affects 1 in 10 patients and is effective in dealing with a fungal infection of the esophagus that afflicts up to 40 percent of AIDS sufferers. Normally, one tablet costs $17. Concurrently Merck offered its AIDS drugs crixivan and stocrin to South Africa, and all other states in sub-Saharan Africa, for about $600 per patient; in the United States crixivan alone costs $5,000 per patient per year. For Africa and other regions of the Third World, free drugs or cost reduction are absolute necessities.

All western pharmaceutical companies should, at the least, extend their price reduction initiatives to all sub-Saharan African states—a move that appears to be imminent—otherwise Brazilian, Indian, Thai, and Japanese drug companies, which have offered to provide generic equivalents at rock-bottom prices to African purchasing agents, should be permitted to do so, even though at present doing so would violate World Trade Organization (WTO) patent codes. The regulations should be amended.

In fact, India's Cipla Corporation, which makes a generic form of 4 of the 15 drugs commonly used in the AIDS cocktail therapy—zidovudine, lamivudine, stavudine, and nevirapine—can sell its cocktails for as little as $83 per month as opposed to the $1,000 or more western pharmaceutical companies charge. In 2001, Cipla arranged to provide Doctors Without Borders triple-therapy drug cocktails of stavudine, lamivudine, and nevirapine for $350 a year per patient that the doctor's group will distribute free. Indeed, the same year, the German pharmaceutical firm Boehringer Ingelheim arranged to furnish South Africa and Congo-Brazzaville free supplies of nevirapine—which reduces the risk of AIDS transmission to the fetus—for five years, while Britain's Glaxo Wellcome PLC agreed to provide Ghana, Senegal, and Uganda with another AIDS drug, combivir, at the price of $2 per daily dose. Concurrently Merck, Glaxo Wellcome, the Swiss firm Roche Holdings AG, and Bristol-Myers Squibb Company jointly offered Uganda a reduction in the cost of triple-therapy retroviral AIDS drugs from $1,000 to about $180 per month. Uganda indicated that because it still could not afford to pay for all the therapies its people required, it would provide for them in just five hospitals in the capital, Kampala. Rural areas would not be able to participate in the program. It should also be emphatically noted that even $2 a day is a prohibitive expense for virtually all countries and people in sub-Saharan Africa. They cannot afford it because, quite simply, they don't have the money.

But unless African leaders take the initiative, there is little that can be accomplished over the long run. Too many African rulers remain consumed by the pernicious struggle for power that is ever present in so many countries. Until they move to a political framework that incorporates human rights—the right to life, not death—their budgets will continue to be largely monopolized by their militaries, and there will be precious little revenue left over to deal with socially pressing issues, particularly AIDS. As it is, public health expenditures as a percentage of GDP are merely 2.6 percent for all of sub-Saharan Africa and a minuscule 1.4 percent when South Africa is excluded.[54] For a continent struggling against AIDS, such a lack of commitment of resources is shameful.

Uganda's president Museveni, Malawi's Muluzi, Botswana's Mogae, who is committed to providing free AIDS treatment to his country's population, and both the current president of Senegal, Abdoulaye Wade, and his predecessor, Abdou Diouf, have been successful, to a lesser or greater degree, in changing their country's mind-set about HIV/AIDS. In the case of Senegal and Uganda, AIDS rates have been reduced markedly. These heads of state are role models to be emulated by African leaders when thinking about how to control the AIDS pandemic. They should be helped in their efforts, and others should be prodded to follow suit.

Western nations and the major pharmaceutical companies that continue to oppose Cipla's undertakings in Africa have it in their power to facilitate constraining the HIV/AIDS scourge. In 2001, after Cipla went to court in South Africa so as to gain the right to sell eight generic AIDS drugs at an annual cost of $600 per patient, Bristol-Myers Squibb halted its efforts to stop generic drug producers from selling a variant of its patented drug stavudine throughout Africa. It also reduced the cost of stavudine and didanosine—another AIDS drug—in Africa to a combined price of $1 per day, in sharp contrast to its aggregated U.S. price of $18 a day. Abbot Laboratories followed suit by reducing the cost of each of its AIDS drugs Novir and Kaletra to $1000 a year per patient. Shortly thereafter, 39 major pharmaceutical companies halted their efforts to legally prevent generic drug producers from selling their drugs in South Africa in the face of intense political efforts by various UN agencies and AIDS organizations to get them to drop their lawsuits. In this case public opinion was the crucial element. Even so, the government indicated that providing AIDS drugs to patients, even cheaper generic versions, was not a major priority. Mbeki's benign neglect of the AIDS catastrophe continues to hamper treatment.

But the West and the large drug companies cannot combat AIDS alone even if they were so disposed. Both will need the backing of African leaders who must rule rather than menace or depreciate. But should the battle against AIDS be lost by the all-consuming lust for power and position at whatever cost, which makes even free AIDS drugs inconsequential, then the pandemic will continue to spread, just like a nuclear bomb's mushroom cloud, and Africa will surely not survive the fallout. The Declaration of Commitment to combat AIDS, approved by the General Assembly of the United Nations on June 27, 2001, recognized accountability as vital; without it the destruction of Africa by the equivalent of a nuclear bomb will be ensured.

CHAPTER FIVE

Globalization and Africa

Given the extraordinary malodorous condition of sub-Saharan Africa, it is barely surprising that the industrial world has chosen, in large part, to forgo integrating that geographical sector of the African continent into the new world of globalization. The reigning political disarray, economic disintegration, crumbling infrastructure, and social decay are hardly attractive enticements for absorbing Africa south into the global marketplace. After all, globalization is dominated by giant multinational corporations, largely, although not entirely, based in the United States, whose primary goal is the accretion of huge profits within a political atmosphere of relative stability. Neither is obtainable in most of Africa at the present moment in history.

The sorry condition of the decomposing states that together comprise the worst-performing economies in the world naturally overlays financial restraint when it comes to international commerce within the context of modern technology and long-term consideration of investment capital. Nations, multinational corporations, banks, and international financial lending agencies—such as the World Bank and the International Monetary Fund, whose assets derive largely from the industrial world—have far more attractive regions of the world to address when evaluating where to best invest their resources.

Finance capital seeks to avoid risk, or at least to balance specula-
tion with sufficient reward, but the present equation of risk/reward
holds little enticement for global investors. Institutions, along with
their shareholders—in both bonds and stocks—would be foolhardy
indeed to contemplate overly large commitments of monetary
resources in a region of the world where violence, destruction, chaos,
ethnic strife, civil wars, along with the constant undercurrent of
millions of political refugees are the everyday and never-ending
circumstance.

Even within African urban centers, where indigenous elites may
own and manage globally attractive economic institutions, the com-
bustible nature of internal politics often threatens the cohesion, even
the very survival, of the cities themselves. Monrovia, Freetown,
Kinshasa, Brazzaville, Luanda, Abidjan, Bissau, Bujumbura, Mogadishu, Lagos, and Kigali are among the African capital cities or
commercial centers that have already been either largely destroyed or
corroded, or are cyclic foci of frenzied and violent economic and
political firestorms that cause parts of the towns to be flattened. No
investor, whether large institution or wealthy magnate—a George
Soros, for example—is eager to see his or her economic stake hit by
mortar shells or antiaircraft fire (which is often employed by contending rebel armies in the streets of capital cities), or to have expatriate
employees endlessly seeking refuge from artillery discharged by
opposing military forces. That is never an environment conducive to
stable and securely envisioned profits.

African states relatively free from such tumult, but neighbors to
those that are so embroiled, frequently find that investors are hesitant
to place capital investments even within their boundaries. In South
Africa, for example, "increasingly, the nation's economic managers find
themselves worrying as much about the country's image as its interest
rates, as the nation's AIDS policies and the land-ownership crisis in
Zimbabwe join [its] litany of national worries, among them crime and
poverty . . . despite the country's sounder economic fundamentals."[1]
Indeed, Tito Mboweni, head of the South African Reserve Bank,
indicated frankly and openly that "where I work, people are not
impressed with these little wars. They don't separate Sierra Leone from
Johannesburg. They have no time to find South Africa geographically.

They only have time to find out what return they can make [on their investment capital]."[2] The South African currency, the rand, has tumbled steeply because of negative publicity surrounding events in Zimbabwe. Absolute economic fundamentals are all but scorned by many foreign investors because of the relative fear, rational or not, that Zimbabwe's political climate eventually will seep into South Africa. Globalized investor confidence has undeniably been called into question, even by normally astute investors, because they tend to hear Africa as a whole note rather than as separate quarter notes.

Events in Zimbabwe have also led to investor and foreign citizen unhappiness—which translates into declining foreign investments and sharply reduced tourist revenues—with Botswana, which, along with South Africa, borders President Robert Mugabe's disintegrating nation. Tourist visits have declined precipitously in the animal reserves of Botswana. As a result of the slowdown in the world economy and due to indigenous factors relevant to Botswana, even while productive value is still expected to increase at a startling annual average 6.8 percent until 2003, Botswana's Institute of Development and Policy Analysis contends that the rate of GDP growth is slowing, and points to the crisis in Zimbabwe as one influential causal factor.[3] With an inflation rate of 8.6 percent, however, much of Botswana's economic growth is abraded.[4]

Obviously, in Zimbabwe itself all is financial chaos. The International Bank for Reconstruction and Development (IBRD) and the International Development Association (IDA) placed all Zimbabwean loans and credits on nonaccrual status in late 2000 as a result of their being overdue by six months.[5] Already by 1998 net foreign direct investment in Zimbabwe declined by 22 percent from the previous year, while its present amount of outstanding debt stands at over $4 billion.[6] Tourism in the country is negligible despite its magnificent attractions, such as the animal reserves, elephant camps, and Victoria Falls.

Malawi, which recently received $1.1 billion in development funds from the United States, also suffers from the Zimbabwean malady as its "exports to that country have declined considerably."[7] Zambia, which directly borders Zimbabwe, saw its trade growth decline by 11 percent, while its exports of goods and services has been steadily declining.[8] Mozambique, another neighbor, has, on the other hand, been able to develop "one of the fastest growing economies in Africa" despite its remaining one of the poor countries on the continent. It has the second highest GNP growth rate in sub-Saharan Africa even while its population's life expectancy at birth averages merely 45 years and 70 percent of its people live below the poverty line.[9]

Political upheaval in one state unequivocally upends economic prospects in an entire region. As southern Africa, overall, is mightily impacted by events in Zimbabwe, each separate quadrant of sub-Saharan Africa is financially dislocated by the even more turbulent phenomena occurring in those other regions. East, West, Central, and southern Africa are imprisoned by the catastrophic man-made and natural happenings that have stunned and stunted Africa in the 1990s.

There is little reason to wonder why globalized financial actors have avoided the region and have chosen to direct their investments, arrange their financial transactions, and feature their loans to more politically sensible and economically stable corners of the global marketplace. After all, neither a Charles Taylor nor a Robert Mugabe are the kind of leaders whom foreign investors intent on developing a globalized technological infrastructure can or wish to deal with. Nor are Liberia and Zimbabwe reasonable places to implant expensive infrastructural investments.

A bailiwick where international financial actors *will* invest is in oil exploration. Quite simply, since drilling most frequently takes place offshore, investments and personnel usually can live a protected existence, no mater what turmoil occurs on land. The drilling platforms in the South Atlantic Ocean off Cabinda, in strife-ridden Angola, which are run by the Chevron Corporation, are one stark example. They "produce eight hundred thousand barrels of crude a day. In the last decade the Angolan government has taken in between two billion and three billion dollars a year in oil revenues," despite the never-ending chaos in the country.[10] Nigeria too is a country that, despite decades of turmoil, has been able to attract foreign oil companies to maintain their investments, even though Shell Oil remains at the center of political storms that often swirl about it in the Southeast. Equatorial Guinea is another nation where recently discovered off-shore oil fields promise to bring in billions in receipts.

On the other hand, in landlocked Chad, a $3.5 billion, 663-mile pipeline project was initiated in late 2000 to transport oil from that nation to the Cameroonian port at Kribi. Within four years newly drilled wells are expected to start producing oil in freshly discovered Chadian oil fields. Over the next 25 years the country is expected to receive close to $10 billion in revenues. In the World Bank's initial foray into subsidizing oil production and transmission, the organization is providing 3 percent of the pipeline's funding. The primary financier is the Exxon/Mobil Corporation. "It is the largest single investment project in sub-Saharan Africa and part of a World Bank effort to encourage developing nations to use revenues from their own natural resources to ease poverty."[11] Chadian president Idriss Déby pledged to World Bank officials that 80 percent of the yearly anticipated revenues will be spent on domestic health, education, and agriculture programs. Whether that occurs, of course, remains to be seen.

These kinds of financial transactions are, however, more in the nature of traditional bilateral or multilateral international funding. Globalization is a far more sophisticated and assertive contemporary economic development in which global production facilities are incorporated into a worldwide network where lightning-fast international financial transactions are the sine qua non of commerce. In that arena, with merely a few singular exceptions, sub-Saharan Africa doesn't stand a chance.

WHAT WOULD MICROSOFT DO HERE?

According to the *New York Times* foreign correspondent Thomas Friedman, globalism is the central organizing principle of post–Cold War society, an international order that has replaced the Cold War system so as to develop transparency and improve the efficiencies of economies worldwide.[12] Adamantia Pollis and I have calibrated Friedman's explication and considered it from a more realistic perspective, one not based chiefly on western interests: "Its distinctive feature [is] the contraction of time and space enabling [instantaneous] financial and communications transactions throughout the world. A global economy has come into existence that transcends the state, changing the latter's role and function and/or diminishing state sovereignty in many realms" to the benefit of the industrial powers and their financial and technological corporations.[13]

> Above all, globalization refers to the emergence of a world economy in which international financial transactions: stock, bond and futures market exchanges; and currency mobility are supplemented by a worldwide labor market and global production facilities. The integration of politics, technology, information, and capital has created a global marketplace that is characterized not just by global free trade but more specifically by the free movement of capital.[14]

Turbo-capitalism, or global integration, according to University of Chicago sociologist Saskia Sassen,

> concerns the declining sovereignty of states over their economies. Economic globalization does indeed extend the economy beyond the boundaries of the nation-state. This is particularly evident in the leading economic sectors. Existing systems of governance and accountability for transnational activities and actors leave much ungoverned when it comes to these industries. . . . More generally, the new geography of centrality is transnational and operates in good part in electronic spaces that override all jurisdiction.[15]

The globalized economy is dominated by multinational banks such as Citigroup and the German-based Deutsche Bank; the investment houses Merrill Lynch, Morgan Stanley Dean Witter, and Goldman Sachs; the New York, London, Paris, and Frankfurt stock exchanges and bond markets; the New York based NASDAQ National Market; the Chicago Board of Trade and the Chicago Mercantile Exchange; and the extraordinarily innovative technology companies along the lines of Microsoft, International Business Machines (IBM), Intel, Oracle, Cisco Systems, and Sun Microsystems, all headquartered in the United States.

The computer software, hardware, databases, microprocessors, and Internet routers invented by these corporate technology giants, along with digitization, fiber optics, and satellite communications, developed by corporations such as JDS Uniphase, allow for instantaneous financial activities akin "to a giant circulatory system, sucking capital into the financial markets and institutions at the center [western Europe and the United States] and then pumping it out to the periphery."[16] It is all interrelated: The banks, investment houses, and futures exchanges use the technology, commodity price floors and price ceilings are established on a second-by-second basis, currency values are determined, and multinational blue-chip industries see their value rise or fall on the world's stock exchanges while their profits are configured.

Meanwhile, the nations of the developing world are essentially nonparticipant observers, watching helplessly as their commodity prices rise or fall, bond rates tumble or soar, interest on borrowed capital fluctuates, while currencies flood or evacuate the marketplace. Their domestic businesses can be made or broken in a split second, even as prices received for their agricultural or mineral products and the very amount they can sell abroad are calculated in London, Paris, New York, Chicago, or Milan.

The monopolization and control of the world's economy by the gargantuan conglomerates located in the West is nothing less than astounding. In 1997 the Intel Corporation dominated 60 percent of the world market in microprocessors; by 2001 it was closer to 70 percent. Microsoft's Windows operating system encompasses over 90 percent of the market in software for desktop computers. Four telecommunication companies govern 70 percent of global sales, while just seven medical equipment corporations account for 90 percent of international production. "Analysts foresee a system dominated by a few international investment banks and about 25 major fund managers, along with a consolidated telecommunications industry offering them services spanning the globe."[17]

Because of the elimination of trade barriers resulting from conventions such as NAFTA and the U.S./Vietnamese and U.S./Jordanian free trade agreements, the reduction of other import/export impediments by way of the World Trade Organization, and bilateral contracts agreed to by corporations and nation-states, multinational corporations can readily locate production facilities to such Third World venues as

Mexico, El Salvador, Guatemala, Nicaragua, China, Thailand, Malaysia, South Africa, and the like, avoiding stringent labor agreements, anti-sweatshop regulations, environmental legislation, and the payment of a reasonable and living wage.

Exactly the same kinds of accords are currently being negotiated between the United States and Latin America and bilaterally with both Chile and Singapore, while the European Union is in discussions to eliminate trade barriers with Brazil, after having successfully closed a similar deal with Mexico. Japan too is engaged in its own bilateral free trade talks with South Korea, Singapore, and Mexico.

These global financial, industrial, and technology principals are hardly "accountable to the state for their actions even though they affect hundreds of millions of people. Quite the opposite; states are now accountable to this private economic regime" if they wish to have these conglomerates invest in their nations.[18] It can prudently be argued that globalization is fast becoming "a dictatorship of the world market and appears unstoppable."[19]

Anyone who buys a car, purchases clothing, invests in a computer, acquires electronic equipment or even a telephone, and reads the nonunion label can see for themselves the impact of globalization. Many products obtained in the West appear to be made in Brazil, Mexico, Malaysia, India, Bangladesh, Sri Lanka, China, and other poverty-stricken Third World nations. But almost no tags read "made in X African state."

Asian and Mexican economies have soared or crumpled abetted by the rapid inflow or outflow of capital made possible by the push of a button on a computer's keyboard. But few global and financial Internet "send" messages are directed to Africa, and only an infinitesimal number of free trade agreements are negotiated with African officials. Given the volatile political history of Africa within the past decade, it is no wonder. Even though its people are even poorer than those in Asia, the Middle East, or Spanish America, and would obviously work for as odious a wage rate as they do in those regions of the globe, the violence and tumult that presently defines Africa reasonably prohibits any sane financier, or investing nation, from venturing onto the continent. Obviously, some African states, such as

South Africa, even Nigeria, are exceptions, but as a rule Africa is forbidden investment territory.

Microsoft's Bill Gates clearly indicated why toward the end of 2000. As he put it, with more than 1 billion people living on a dollar per day or less, and with AIDS decimating African populations, what the poor need is food and medical aid, not computers. To that end he appealed to his fellow technology billionaires to stop trying to sell their products to the forlorn of the developing nations and to direct their energies to contributing monies to the poorest of the poor. In other words, what could Microsoft conceivably gain from incorporating Africa into a world globalized network, when its people don't even know if they will survive another 24 hours? The answer, of course, is nothing.[20]

Currently, according to Gates's analysis, it is not European slave traders and colonialists in Africa writing Africans out of history. African leaders, with their tyrannical and pathetic style of abusive rule, in which their people are put through hell (without, it must be said, the least bit of tangible concern by western heads of state), have written their countries—or what is left of them—out of the globalized economy. In effect Gates, today one of the more powerful magnates on the face of the earth, gave his stamp of approval to the exclusion of African states from both the benefits and the liabilities of globalization because of the continent's dire predicament. Thus the new economic ideology has been given the legitimacy to pass Africa by and to let the continent stew in its own pot of bedlam.

Reality from this perspective not only recognizes the present truth of a huge gap between the wealthiest and poorest nations, the north/ south divide, but it creates a stratified hierarchy of the poor and the poorest—a new south/south divide—where the poor nations of Asia, Latin America, and the Middle East will be integrated into a globalized world, while the poorest—read Africa—will be relegated to the margins of the planet's political economy, excluded from globalization's benefits. Handouts and food relief, rather than economic consolidation, will be its lot. And as sub-Saharan Africa's political condition has proceeded to worsen, the likelihood that it will continue to subsist on the periphery of social and pecuniary existence only multiplies.

THE WORLD BANK
AND THE INTERNATIONAL MONETARY FUND

The World Bank and the IMF are the two most important international financial actors of the twenty-first century, as in the era of globalization both the industrial countries and the developing areas seek their input in resolving world financial dilemmas. In this epoch of a new world order, the loan programs instituted by the World Bank, and the economic reform schedules developed, and funding granted, by the IMF, are the sine qua non of development economics. The industrial countries demand that if development aid is to be allocated, bilaterally and multilaterally, both financial giants must grant their imprimatur to individual nations of the Third World. The West thus defers to them a singular amount of power and authority; indeed their influence often far surpasses that wielded by the United Nations, indicating clearly that political economy rather than politics pure and simple is the primary order of the day.

Western dominance of these behemoths is determined by the fact that both rely on the industrial nations for much of their capital, more than 20 percent of all Third World funding is written by the World Bank (i.e., decided by Washington, London, and the like), while the Bank—meaning western nations—remains the fount of virtually all data relating to Africa. The origin of many of the statistics in this book verifies this minor but important fact. It is stark evidence of the extent to which Africa's future is in the hands of the West since statistical measurements often demarcate bilateral aid allocation as well as underwriting support by the World Bank and IMF. And while the United Nations Development Program (UNDP) also produces considerable statistical information, it is by far neither as fulsome nor as influential as that dispensed by the World Bank.

Additionally, voting procedures within the IMF allow the United States and Western Europe to control decision making. The "decisions endorsed as official I.M.F. policies are made by the most powerful market-economy nations. This includes the five permanent members of the Executive Board—the U.S., the U.K., . . . Germany, France, and Japan—as well as Canada, Italy, the Netherlands, Belgium, Sweden [and] Switzerland. This powerful caucus reveals . . . the source of present restraints on Fund activity in regard to the Third World . . ."[21] while fewer restrictions apply to aid directed at the developed nations. The role of the IMF in negotiating and structuring loan programs remains highly controversial. For policies relating to a standby loan—for which a state may draw on funds over a period of three years—*conditionality* must be agreed to. A "government must meet prescribed conditions all along the way: preconditions before drawings are approved, performance criteria which make further drawings contingent, and policy understandings which are broad commitments without specific sanctions."[22]

The World Bank and more specifically the IMF have also adopted a policy procedure known as *structural adjustment*—a practice that emphasizes an export-led growth model which requires "sovereign governments to make economic adjustments, and by doing so at least indirectly dictates social and political objectives."[23] Part of the plan requires that in order for aid to be granted, developing nations must agree to a large-scale reduction of employment in state-run enterprises; an increase in prices and a reduction in wages—so as to control inflation and inflationary expectations; the privatization of major state industries—telecommunications, electricity, railroads, airlines, and the like; and an end to the protection of domestic commerce by agreeing to open up their borders to the international movement of capital and foreign industries. The IMF demands this so-called shock therapy so that, in its view, Third World nations can get their economic house in order—without, it should be added, fouling up their balance of payments or debt rescheduling.

Critics of the policies advocated ("dictated" would be a more accurate appellation) by the World Bank and the IMF "are far less sanguine, alternately referring to the often draconian mix of currency devaluation, price-subsidy elimination and fiscal austerity as 'enslavement by the north of the south' or 'an overdraft for bankrupt economies.'"[24] Since "for low-income countries, the Fund operates as a lender of 'first' or 'only resort,'"[25] western supremacy of the IMF, as well as of the World Bank, does indeed ensure that Third World countries will continue to remain at the economic mercy of western interests. With the demise of the Soviet Union and the undisputed ascendancy of the United States in world politics, the less developed countries depend even more so on the indulgences of the West than they have heretofore.

Clearly, the United States has grown impatient with sub-Saharan Africa's domestic turmoil, as indicated by its relatively isolationist policy toward the continent since 1991. It is unlikely therefore that the World Bank or the IMF will be permitted to liberalize its policies of conditionality or structural adjustment, as both clearly did during the Mexican currency crisis of 1995 and after the fall of President Suharto in Indonesia in 1998. Without such broad-minded generosity, Africa is in for a hard time. In fact, according to an analysis by the World Bank, the demands placed on the Philippines, Indonesia, South Korea, and Thailand by the IMF during the severe Asian economic crisis of 1997 "spread the economic pain far beyond the banks, investment funds and real estate companies that got the countries into trouble to begin with, sending thousands of small businesses into bankruptcy" and more than 100 million people in Indonesia below the poverty line.[26] Will sub-Saharan Africa fare any better? Since its people are already the poorest of the poor, it is hard to see how.

Africa's continuing troubles isolate it from World Bank and IMF development programs. Most countries in sub-Saharan Africa—the Congo, Liberia, Sierra Leone, Somalia, and so on—have largely excluded themselves from any consequential financial relief. As a result, bilateral aid programs are also sharply reduced since World Bank/IMF accreditation is, in most cases, necessary for such projects to go forward. In exceptional circumstances both organizations have been ready to play a role in aiding a few African states to overcome their financial/economic distress. But in large part both institutions are currently part of the globalization apparatus in which

> single-minded policies and legislation, on the part of mostly demo-cratically elected [western] governments, gradually put in place [an] autonomous "money market system" [as] a kind of higher power. Now there is no ideology, no pop culture, no international organiza-tion, no ecological interest even, which binds the nations of the world more closely together than the electronic network of global money machines of the banks, insurance companies and investment

funds. . . . On an average day, currency to the value of 1.5 [trillion] dollars now changes hands. . . .[27]

Very few of those dollars pass through Africa.

GLOBALIZATION IN AFRICA

Private sector investment by U.S. corporations has been negligible. "Development assistance is no longer even accorded much emphasis by US government officials, who in its stead now openly espouse the importance of American corporate *philanthropy* [emphasis mine] in Africa. Democratization and human rights promotion . . . has fallen victim to the sudden continent-wide 'arc of conflict' spreading from Eritrea to Angola."[28] Net foreign direct investment for all of sub-Saharan Africa in 1998 was $3.6 billion, but barely $1.6 billion if the two oil giants Nigeria and Angola are excluded. The latter figure more or less equals the amount of outside direct investment in just Guatemala and Mexico.[29]

Ghana

In Ghana, a country where the World Bank has made great efforts to try to rectify congenital economic problems, structural adjustment has largely misfired. Between 1982 and 1991 Ghana "obtained five IMF programs amounting to approximately US $1.6 billion [while] the government signed more than twenty policy-based program loans with the World Bank. The World Bank also sponsored six consultative group meetings; the first held . . . resulted in pledges of US $190 million. Between 1984 and 1991, almost US $3.5 billion more was raised at five additional meetings."[30]

Yet, already by 1993, even with $5.3 billion in World Bank and IMF assistance, Ghana had "failed to promote food security through appropriate measures to raise productivity. . . . [Its] manufacturing sector, meanwhile, was left to decline, and as Ghana increasingly [became] a 'buying and selling' economy the only real growth [was] in the service sector. Its transportation, wholesale and retail sub-sectors . . . generate[d] little in the way of foreign exchange. After nine years of structural adjustment, Ghana's total external debt has nearly quadrupled. . . ."[31] Currently Ghana's outstanding foreign debt remains an unhealthy $4 billion.

Whatever economic improvements have occurred in Ghana (e.g., between 1988 and 1998, its average annual GNP percentage growth rate per capita has averaged 1.5 percent,[32] modest in absolute terms but a relatively high rate for sub-Saharan Africa) are due largely to black market activity and economic circumstances over which the World Bank, the IMF, and Ghana have no control.[33]

South Africa

Democratic South Africa has tweaked U.S., European, and Japanese interests. As one of the few truly representational and geopolitically important states with diverse economic potential, its access to western markets has broadened since the elimination of apartheid. But to the dismay of the World Bank and the IMF, privatization of large state assets, particularly in the utility and transportation fields, has not occurred, and "few signs of new foreign direct investment have been evident."[34] From 1999 to 2000 the GDP had risen at a yearly rate of merely 1.2 percent while 5 percent is deemed necessary if the 35 percent unemployment rate is to be reduced.

To attract foreign investors, the Ministry of Trade and Industry initiated "an effort," in late 2000, "to make better use of its envoys abroad and turn them into dedicated investment hunters," while the government organized a Marketing Council "aimed at honing the country's image as an investment destination."[35] But in a coordinated European action that had a seriously negative impact on South Africa, Great Britain and a few other European nations sold half their gold reserves in 1999 and 2000, exacerbating the already tumbling price of the mineral on world markets. By January 2001 gold valuations had fallen to about $271 per troy ounce. The country's vast network of gold mines and the employment prospects of its labor force were seriously impaired.

Still, for Europe and the United States, South Africa remains central to their "respective African agendas, a fact underscored by . . .

[their] evocation of South Africa's importance in [their] common foreign and security policy as well as through [their] high-level bilateral trade negotiations" regarding tariff reduction and duty-free concessions.[36] Even financier George Soros has organized an Open Society Foundation, which underwrites science, education, and criminal justice projects.

In 2001, Japanese direct foreign investment in South Africa came to $500 million, while the corporate giants Mitsubishi, Toyota, and Sumitomo play a large role in South Africa's industrial marketplace. Ten percent of Japan's overseas development aid of $10 billion is allocated to Africa, while its trade with South Africa totaled $3 billion in 1999. Whatever occurs in the future, South Africa is surely one of the very few countries in sub-Saharan Africa that will continue to attract the attention of globalization's principal financial and economic contenders.

Kenya

Corruption and President Daniel arap Moi's compulsion in creating a cult of personality has all but gutted World Bank and IMF efforts in Kenya. As early as 1989, Moi constructed

> a new sixty-story office tower to house the headquarters of the . . . country's only legal political party, and a party-run media center. The design called for a large statue of the president as the centerpiece of the building's decoration. Kenya had already moved to borrow $160 million to supplement $40 million in local loans, both steps in violation of agreements with the World Bank and the International Monetary Fund stipulating only limited borrowing—and borrowing only for productive purposes. Moi told . . . the foreign donors that they could take their complaints elsewhere.[37]

Ten years later Moi was still at it. Privatization in Kenya meant selling state-owned enterprises to his political cronies at very low prices, while antipoverty organizations were shut down and their leaders arrested for claiming that corruption permeated the uppermost ranks of the Kenyan state.

By 2000, amid enduring and ever-swirling charges of corruption, most multilateral donors cut Kenya off from any further credit and refused to provide debt relief. Economic growth decelerated, unemployment rose to 25 percent, privatization all but came to a screeching halt, while the mortality rate per 1,000 among children under five years old was a lofty 112; in contrast, Mauritius's child mortality rate was 23.[38] With the economy slowing and foreign aid sharply restricted, it was projected that Kenya's excessively high HIV/AIDS rate would reduce its GDP by close to 15 percent by 2005.

In essence Moi has rejected globalization, except as it suits his own personal interests, while, on the other hand, globalization has been obligated to turn away from Kenya. Future prospects for the country seem dim as Moi continues to alienate formerly sympathetic western donors. Whatever prospects there were of a thriving interconnected globalized Kenyan economy are ever more rapidly vanishing.

Mozambique

Mozambique is an altogether different and more positive story. The World Bank's representative to the country indicated that "up to the year 2000, economic growth has been fueled by growth in agriculture and small and medium industry."[39] U.S. investors have financial interests in the cotton and sugar industries, and insofar as sugar is concerned, 10,000 tons are exported to the United States yearly under a wide-ranging preferential trade agreement that guarantees duty-free access to U.S. markets for most products until 2004, despite "cumbersome regulations imposed by the World Bank and the IMF."[40] Until only recently the world's leading producer of cashew nuts, Mozambique also harvests 1.3 million tons of corn per year along with increasing quantities of beans and manioc, which serve as safety-valve crops to help stave off famine. Net foreign direct investment quadrupled between 1996 and 1998 and currently amounts to 3.3 percent of Mozambique's GDP, while between 1992 and 1998 the country's export growth rate soared 15 percent per annum.[41] Industrial production doubled between 1995 and 1999 while inflation remains a tame 4 percent.

Coal, titanium, natural gas, and hydroelectric power are in abundance. An aluminum smelter joint venture with private firms from Japan, Great Britain, and South Africa recently began production, drawing on aluminum and coke imported from Australia and the United States. Privatization of many banks has taken place while denationalization of the state telecommunications industry and Mozambique Airlines is under way; Mozambique Ports and Railways Corporation, still majority state-owned, partly controls, manages, and operates Malawi's railroad industry. In 2001 access to the Southern African Development Community was realized, giving the country an expanded market of 220 million consumers in 14 countries. According to the executive director of one of Mozambique's larger financial institutions, "international banks are opening credit lines to us which no other bank in the region has."[42]

Currently Mozambique, despite periodic and violent political outbursts in the north of the country, is the darling of the IMF, World Bank, and western investors. The Bank goes so far as to say that "where countries, such as Mozambique . . . have made key economic reforms— liberalizing markets and trade, improving economic management, and promoting private sector activity—growth and personal incomes have risen and poverty has been reduced."[43] As a reward for success, in 1999 the World Bank and the IMF granted Mozambique debt relief of $4.3 billion, which amounted to 72 percent of its outstanding debt; this was among the most significant relief ever granted by either organization in one fell swoop to any sub-Saharan African nation in percentage terms and dollar figures.[44]

Having been felled by extraordinary floods in early 2000, which reduced its growth rate to a still-hardy 6 percent, Mozambique was able, due to the amelioration, to deal relatively swiftly with the floods' calamitous ramifications. It also received abundant help: The United Nations World Food Program helps feed 100,000 people, while donor nations have extended $460 million in assistance. Economic success, while acceding to World Bank/IMF oversight, clearly has its benefits.

GLOBALIZATION'S DIM PROSPECTS

Globalization is hardly likely to embrace sub-Saharan Africa, at least in the early part of the twenty-first century. Despite some success stories, Mozambique being a prime example, and other potential candidates—certainly South Africa, Uganda (with an economy growing at 7 percent per year while, since 1992, the number of Ugandans living in absolute poverty has declined from 56 to 35 percent), Botswana, and Mauritius, perhaps Nigeria—come to mind, much of the continent below the Sahara remains outside the realm of consideration. The infrastructure is not available to support it, and myriad leaders are generally too wrapped up in their own power struggles to create the conditions that would make it attractive. As the World Bank discreetly put it, "Sub-Saharan Africa faces enormous challenges. . . . [M]issed opportunities and conflict [have] marred its prospects during the latter half of the 20th century."[45]

The entire continent of Africa has merely 10 million telephones, half located in South Africa, "with the other 5 million so dispersed that most Africans live two hours away from the nearest telephone."[46] While Europe and Central Asia have 204 telephone main lines per 1,000 people; East Asia and the Pacific, 50; Latin America and the Caribbean, 110; and the Middle East and North Africa, 75; sub-Saharan Africa exclusive of South Africa has just 10; including South Africa, still only 16. Scarcely 2.3 Internet hosts per 10,000 people are available in Africa below the Sahara; Latin America and the Caribbean have 8 times that number.[47]

The meager availability of the basic prerequisites necessary for the Internet to function indicate starkly how singularly unprepared Africa south is for globalization, just in terms of wired infrastructure alone. Even the cost of telecommunications is prohibitive, and most certainly for a continent that remains in the most desperate economic straits. The dollar cost of a three-minute telephone call from sub-Saharan Africa to the United States is $8.11, 26 percent higher than a call placed from the Middle East and North Africa—in a region that encompasses some of the world's poorest countries and where GNP per capita income, at $510, is lower than it was 40 years ago.[48]

On another front, the World Bank reported that as of August 2000, the aggregate principal balance of International Bank for Reconstruction and Development (IBRD) loans in nonaccrual status was $2 billion—1.7 percent of the total outstanding. Overdue interest was

$2.3 billion.[49] The largest share of problematic nations was in sub-Saharan Africa. Earlier, in 1999, President Clinton, in accord with the U.S. Congress, conceded that Africa south would never be able to repay its outstanding loans and that the repayment burden was not only overwhelming but stifling to economic development. As a result, the United States agreed to forgive all the debt owed to Washington by 36 underdeveloped countries as long as the money saved on debt payments was utilized for health, education, water purification, and other urgent human exigencies. Many of the affected countries were in sub-Saharan Africa.

In large part Africa is totally unprepared for globalization, and most of its leaders are unwilling to accept its presence. Some find the demands of the World Bank and the IMF intrusive; others see globalism as eviscerating their power; while additionally there are those who are so engrossed in destroying their people and country that any outside institutional presence is viewed as a mechanism by which their abusive goals will be stifled.

On the other hand, international financial institutions, or western nation-states for that matter, would be foolish even to consider long-term investment in most of sub-Saharan Africa given its decades-long history of waste, corruption, and extraordinary turbulence. The only thing to do is avoid most of the continent as long as the severity of its troubles continue to lay Africa to waste. Individual states, where democracy and suitable economic policies are instituted, can be supported, as is the case with Mozambique, Uganda, and South Africa. Globalization can play a productive role in countries with rational leaders and sensible policies, even though it may offer an economic stringency that is often found to be, in the short term, financially oppressive to its people.

But as long as tyrants continue to rule most of the states in Africa, and as long as they refuse to do *anything* about their political, economic, social, and HIV/AIDS problems, the continent will remain in shambles while its people will have to try to avoid the carnage all about them, on their own and as best they can. There is little any outside force can accomplish as long as the available leadership remains vacuous and, more important, dangerous.

Tribalism or Modernism?

Finally, tribalism itself is an overwhelming impediment to globalization and modern technology. When a former Liberian ambassador to the United Nations can represent the most modern values while engaged in his responsibilities in New York City and then return to the bush in the southeast of his country and subordinate himself to the traditional practitioners of witchcraft whose power lies in the milieu of sorcery, what possible impact can a globalized world have for him?

Or, how can modernization deal with the fact that groups of elite students, the sons and daughters of Liberia's former ruling class, accept the premise that modern medicine is irrelevant, while country doctors, who perform rites with leaves and roots, are viewed as competent? Discussing the normative values of modernism with individuals who hold to that axiom is basically an exercise in frustration. Concession to scientific discourse is hardly a given for people who uphold traditional worth so stringently.

More recently, when a Ph.D. candidate in a first-class university in the United States gives up the effort and returns to his home in the interior of Ghana to become a tribal chief, adopting a system predicated on superstitious awe, isn't globalized interaction pointless?

In many parts of Africa's interior, trial by ordeal rather than a modern judicial process is the norm. In that circumstance, a cutlass is placed in a roaring fire by a group of facially dyed and raffia-bedecked tribal chiefs. After it turns red hot the rapier is placed on the thigh of a suspect. If the leg is scorched—in fact, it just about explodes—he or she is guilty; if the aftermath is benign, the person is innocent.

The ardent conviction in tribalism and the traditional mores passionately held to throughout Africa are formative constraints on modernization and globalization, and as such play a far larger role in inhibiting globalization than the lack of telephones or Internet hosts. The latter can conceivably be dealt with; the former requires long-term socialization so that values which represent centuries of social thought can be modified. After all, when children refuse to wear sandals in Africa's interior, because, despite being told of the hazard entailed in going barefoot, they maintain "we've always done it," changing the mind-set becomes almost superfluous. The health risks involved are serious since various species of infectious organisms enter the body through cracks in the feet. Yet such risks habitually are considered inconsequential.

Although African medicine can sometimes offer a curative, its impact in the twenty-first century is perhaps greater than it has been in the recent past. With a decomposing continent, tribalism and witchcraft may very well be reinforced and more relied upon, since the modern world has been unable to stem Africa's ever present devastation.

The Nigerian novelist Cyprian Ekwensi puts the traditional/ modern dichotomy into perspective. In his book *People of the City,* a western-trained doctor rushes to the West African city home—in a city "which shall be nameless"—of a man who has just had a stroke. He can do little. Shortly thereafter a

> tense crowd hovered in hushed silence along the corridor. Now a man with a black bag—a doctor in the African manner trained by tradition in the ways of the past—this man went down the stairs and began to chalk up the ground and to spatter the blood of a chicken about the house, muttering incantations. He made a great show of ceremony while the gentle wind blew the feathers about the com- pound. . . . The herbalist seemed to be giving the final order to the ghost, to be tilting the balance in a particular direction.[50]

What sinew can globalization have in a society that so adamantly adheres to such traditions—important as they may be to their practi- tioners? More important, can tradition's true believers accept the strictures that motivate modernization and change? Currently it hardly seems likely, and unless the negative vitality of tradition and tribalism is vitiated, the future of globalization in sub-Saharan Africa remains bleak indeed.

CHAPTER SIX

Will Africa Survive?

With the end of the cold war, there remains little motivation for a continuing U.S. interest in the overall political and economic affairs of Africa. Economically, Africa "holds little attraction," and politically "geostrategic global reasons [for] external involvement" have been eliminated.[1] At the same time, the foolish and somewhat romantic notion, upheld by western nations during the era of independence, that they would be able to construct viable nations from territories that often were desperately poor and riddled with tribal and ethnic hatreds, collapsed. After all, these very antagonisms were often developed and helped along by the colonial rulers themselves.[2]

It is obvious that the cold war policies pursued by the United States in sub-Saharan Africa from 1957 to 1991, and the often halting attempts since then to fix broken states, have failed. Liberia, which during the administrations of Presidents William V. S. Tubman (1944-1971) and William R. Tolbert (1971-1980) received extensive U.S. military aid, has all but disintegrated. Ethiopia, which under Emperor Haile Selassie I (1930-1974) received munificent military assistance, segued into a Marxist state in 1974 and remained so until 1991. Now it is a distinctly autocratic nation.

Attempts at peacemaking and nation-building in Somalia by the United States and the United Nations led to catastrophe and influenced the division of the country into three parts. In the Congo and Sierra Leone, wherein western nations and the UN have been immersed, extraordinary strife continues, while in Zimbabwe racial hatred is stirred up to reinforce the rule of an aging tyrant. Concerning Rwanda, where political action could have been taken to stop the slaughter, France and the United States stood by idly and did nothing, even as the French president, François Mitterand, in a monstrous statement (previously stated, but which bears repeating), outrageously claimed, in a comment that can only be taken racially, that "in such countries, genocide is not too important."[3]

The role of western nations in the affairs of Africa has not only been one of disappointment and incompetence but also has often been insulting, condescending, and racist. It has as well been malicious, since it was based almost solely on imperial, colonial, or cold war interests. Indeed, Jacques Foccart, a consummate security aide to former French president Charles de Gaulle, claimed that during the 1960s, France demanded strict obedience from its former African colonies. He maintained that in 1968 he "auditioned" Omar Bongo before allowing him to become president of Gabon, while eight years earlier he had ordered the assassination of Felix Moumié, an opposition leader in Cameroon. "Other African leaders who were made and often broken by France . . . signed blank authorizations of French intervention in case of trouble."[4] In 1958, when Guinea, under the leadership of Sékou Touré, who later became president, opted for independence in a national referendum, France, in a pique because its rule had been rejected and de Gaulle insulted, disengaged from the country for years. Touré insisted that "Guinea preferred poverty in freedom to prosperity in chains"; all other African colonies in the French Union voted to *reject* independence.[5]

In "a perverted moral code that will allow a million innocent civilians of another race to be made destitute because you are not prepared to risk the life of a single professional soldier of your own,"[6] President Clinton refused to act in Rwanda even though he was aware of the ongoing holocaust. Clearly, after 1991, and in particular after the Somalia fiasco, the United States had no coherent foreign policy in Africa other than to have as little to do with the continent as possible.

The IMF's stabilization program of structural adjustment often has strangled the very economies it was meant to help. As Jennifer Seymour Whitaker, of the Council on Foreign Relations, indicated, "people can't eat policy reforms, and the table may look pretty bare before anyone can see the fruits of austerity. Holding onto power while elite privileges are vanishing and the masses grow hungry offers challenges most African politicians would undoubtedly prefer to avoid."[7]

Even in Ghana, where structural adjustment was seen by western financiers as being successful, "the state had become largely irrelevant. . . . [D]evaluation did not have a major effect on consumer prices because almost all imported goods were being sold at black market prices."[8] Indeed, one authority maintains that "Ghana is a state only because the outside world asserts that there is a Ghanaian state."[9] Thus, the claims by the World Bank regarding rising incomes and the expansion of democracy may have less to do with institutional change and more to do with the fact that control over the state by government leaders is tenuous, and the World Bank—given its concentration in Washington, D.C.—may have little direct knowledge of what is occurring in the interior of the country.[10] Ethnic tensions between the Ashanti and the Ewe remain consequential despite some economic reform, and, notwithstanding some improvement, the number of children under five years of age who are malnourished still hovers at 27 percent.

In the Ivory Coast, structural adjustment policies initiated in 1987 were ruinous. "The decision to stabilize commodity prices on behalf of farmers [as the price of cocoa declined steeply] helped precipitate an economic crisis of unprecedented proportion. Likewise, the decision to initiate a restructuring of public enterprises . . . caused layoffs, pay cuts. . . ."[11] Banks collapsed, loans were called, cocoa merchants went bankrupt, jobs were lost, incomes were reduced, while strikes and protests mushroomed. The political, ethnic, and religious discord that confronted the Ivory Coast in the late 1990s and into 2001 can be traced, in part, to the economic policies pursued in the past decade by unpopular and undemocratic leaders.

Whatever the experiences of the past, Africa has now been abandoned by the United States, which, since 1991, has become totally preoccupied with other regions of the world, notably China, the Middle East, and Russia. The members of the European Union, including France, have also limited their exposure, while the World Bank and the IMF have concentrated their efforts and resources toward helping to resolve deep financial crises in Mexico, Asia, and Russia. Even the African AIDS pandemic has drawn only the cursory attention of the West.

The marginalization of Africa, while much of the rest of the world has been incorporated into the global economy, raises profound questions. Given the unchallenged wealth and power of the United States, what role should it have in twenty-first century Africa? Acknowledging its intrusiveness in the continent since 1957, when Ghana received its independence, and recognizing the present dire situation of sub-Saharan Africa, does the United States have a credible role to play?

Then there is the intricate matter of the responsibility of African leaders. In the 1990s far too many tyrants have shot themselves into power, or tried to, and then quite often have proceeded to engage in some of the most horrific violence against their own populations.[12] Given the West's essential disengagement, are these the type of pacesetters the future will offer up, or are the few democrats Africa has experienced the upcoming role models? Do Charles Taylor, Sani Abacha, or Foday Sankoh epitomize what the future will bring, or will it be represented by the likes of Nelson Mandela and Amos Sawyer? Killers or democrats? Annihilators or builders? Will leaders attempt to resolve distress, or will they create it? Will civil wars and ethnic strife be what passes for normal political behavior?

In some fashion the political conduct of African leaders may well determine how the West responds to the continent's economic, social, and political anguish. Yet it may also be that, in the near term at least, it will not matter very much to the West whether democrats or dictators rule. For if no viable or coherent foreign policy framework is developed for Africa, no sensible engagement can be expected. And, at least to this observer, that would lead to additional multiple country-specific cataclysms throughout sub-Saharan Africa.

THE UNITED STATES AND AFRICA
IN THE POST-COLD WAR ERA

"The United States has been retreating from Job's continent since the implosion of the Soviet Union set America free to pursue its own interests in Africa—and it found it did not have any."[13] According to Marguerite Michaels, of the Council on Foreign Relations, U.S. investment in sub-Saharan Africa, which was a minuscule 0.46 percent of the total U.S. abroad in 1990 has been further reduced, while the rate of return on foreign investments declined from 30.7 percent in the 1960s to 2.5 percent by 1990. She goes on to state that "In 1983 . . . Africa received 2.2 percent of total U.S. exports, and it sent 4.1 percent of total U.S. imports. Only five years later, however, American exports to Africa were a mere 1.2 percent, and U.S. imports were halved. The continent's already meager seven percent share of the world's non-oil primary products fell to a paltry four percent [by 1985]."[14]

It is important to note that by 2000, 84 percent of Africa's exports to the United States came from just three countries—Angola, Nigeria, and Gabon—whose vast oil resources made up the bulk of the trade. In truth, that figure may indicate better than anything just how unimportant most of the other 45 sub-Saharan Africa states are within the orbit of the United States. And while trade figures may fluctuate up or down from one year to the next, those changes are often due largely to the oscillating oil needs of petroleum suppliers in the United States.

While Africa spent the last part of the 1990s in an economic free fall—for instance, between 1985 and1995, Malawi's growth rate of real GDP fell from 7.8 percent to -9.8 percent, and Gambia's fell from 4.1 percent to 1.4 percent—in 2001 the IMF and the World Bank participated in a $39.7 billion package of loans and credits to Argentina, the Bank and the Inter-American Development Bank committed $20 billion toward a Free Trade Area of the Americas (FTAA), while in 2000 the IMF provided Turkey with $7.5 billion in new loans. In 1998 the United States pledged $5 billion toward an IMF rescue package for Brazil and provided the IMF an $18 billion assessment to help resolve the financial crises that struck Russia and Asia. In 1995 it participated in a $49.5 billion bailout of Mexico.

Yet in 1993 the United States distributed merely $800 million in loans or grants to the states that make up sub-Saharan Africa, while by 1994 the U.S. State Department saw its African Affairs bureau cut by 9 percent. By 1998 bilateral assistance to Africa was cut to $650 million, while the United States Agency for International Development (USAID) was active in just 26 African states. In 2000 sub-Saharan Africa's external debt had ballooned to close to $200 billion. Full repayment is virtually inconceivable since Africa is so thoroughly indebted that most of its countries are paying more in interest and loan payments to western nations and international financial organizations than they receive in aid or in the initial stages of debt relief from those same sources. Indeed, by 2001 outside investment in Africa amounted to merely 0.5 percent of the total investments made abroad, virtually ensuring that financial growth will be unable to keep up with increasing levels of debt, even taking into account debt relief.

Former President Bill Clinton spoke a lot about Africa but did little. His successor, President George W. Bush, claimed during his 2000 campaign that the United States has no strategic interests in Africa, and vowed to limit the nation's involvement in peacekeeping activities. He also argued that American troops were overstretched during the Clinton years. His secretary of state, Colin L. Powell, secretary of defense, Donald H. Rumsfeld, and his national security advisor, Condoleezza Rice, are well-known advocates of using the U.S. armed forces solely when U.S. national security is threatened, and then only when winning is certain, there are clear goals, and an exit strategy is available. All have vociferously contested using U.S. peacekeepers for humanitarian interests unless such action is firmly grounded in the national interest, which they agree is infrequent. Clearly, their African policy may be even less consequential than it was under Clinton, particularly in light of the fact that in 2001 the United States exacted a budget reduction for UN peacekeeping activities from 30 to 27 percent and an overall abatement of UN dues from 25 to 22 percent. The most likely scenario is that increased financial support will be given for Nigeria to continue its role as an African peacekeeper, while further economic sustenance will be granted Nigeria and South Africa to bolster the two sizable and vital democratic African anchors. Extra funding to combat AIDS will be appropriated, in addition to the $200 million allocated in May 2001.

Those who ran for the U.S. Congress in 2000 headlined their intention to use budget surpluses largely for domestic purposes. And the composition of the Senate and House of Representatives—virtually equally divided between Republicans and Democrats—ensures that divided government will continue and thus expenditures allocated to African affairs certainly will not increase by any substantial amount. Even if aid does not decline, inflation will erode its value. Also, given the political animus that developed between the two political parties as a result of the post-election fiasco in the state of Florida, it is hardly likely that agreement will be reached by the Executive Office and the Congress on an African policy that will measurably raise its status and visibility, other than in South Africa and Nigeria. Even some officials at the World Bank insist that "African aid is a game for losers." [15]

James Schlesinger, formerly secretary of defense and director of the Central Intelligence Agency (CIA), maintains that in the monopolar world where no counterveiling rival exists to contest its power, the United States "should avoid the heady feeling, induced by its triumph in the Cold War, that all things are now possible. It must learn, in this altered context . . . to husband its strength and to choose with care those policy objectives that reflect interests sufficiently weighty that they can garner the public support to sustain them in the long run. . . . Thus, for wise policy it remains imperative that the political capital of public support not be expended on secondary matters but should be reserved to deal with those substantial matters that may pose a direct threat to our interests." [16]

It is evident that the era of the cold war was an aberration vis-à-vis U.S. foreign policy. The epoch that began in 1947 with the Truman Doctrine,[17] in which President Harry Truman admonished and convinced the American people that U.S. national security demanded a policy of worldwide military and economic intervention during peacetime, came to an abrupt end in 1991. Thereafter, overseas engagement was called into question by the American public, even as the citizenry initially felt an imperative for action. The interpositions in Somalia and Iraq are, of course, the prime examples, as President George Bush lost his bid for reelection in 1992 because the public felt he was more concerned with foreign affairs and paid too little attention to domestic matters.

Bill Clinton would not make that mistake. His foreign policy was directed primarily at nudging the world toward the benefits of globalization and free trade. But that effort—symbolized by the creation of NAFTA in 1993, among Mexico, Canada, and the United States; the establishment of the WTO in 1994; the IMF's rescue of Thailand, Indonesia, and South Korea during Asia's financial crisis; the endorsement of China's entrance into the WTO; the Jordanian/U.S. free trade pact signed in 2000; and the discussion of globalization at the UN's 2000 Millennium Summit—has essentially left Africa out in the cold. Globalization has hopscotched around Africa, largely avoiding it and leaving it mired in its own parochial desolation. On one hand the cause is America's concentration on areas of the world conducive to capitalist expansion, and on the other hand it results from Africa's inconsequential economic condition, its political morass, and its wretched infrastructure.

In sub-Saharan Africa electric power per capita (in kilowatt-hours) is a lowly 146. In contrast, for Latin America and the Caribbean the figure is 1,347; for the Middle East and North Africa the indicator is 1,166; and for Europe and Central Asia, 2,788.[18] Nigeria, a regional powerhouse, has just 0.3 telephone lines per 100 inhabitants and only 38 television receivers per 1,000 residents. For Ghana the figures are 0.3 and 16, and for the Ivory Coast, 0.8 and 60. By comparison, Mexico's indicators are 9.3 and 150, while in Lebanon the corresponding statistics are 9.3 and 346. Sub-Saharan Africa has 7 personal computers per 1,000 people. In contrast, the estimate for Latin America and the Caribbean is 34.[19]

With globalization and free trade dependent on brisk financial transactions available only via computers and the Internet, Africa's lack of infrastructure required for integration into a global network indicates that, even given the unlikely scenario that the United States would advance a national interest framework for Africa, it would be impossible to develop a globalized relationship. While the world of the Internet, the necessary ingredient of globalization, requires financial and corporate institutions that populate urban areas, Africa is largely rural, with even village-to-village communication often impossible, either by road or by telephone. In many states there is no interconnecting transportation grid—if routes exit at all, they are usually laterite roads that are basically unusable during the rainy season—and all too often when placing phone calls from one African country to another the link must be routed through Europe. A middle class hardly exists. The lack of a unitary language is also a major hindrance to Africa's participation in a world economy. Linguists view language as a basal characteristic of culture and group identity. In Africa more than 2,000 languages are spoken by as many ethnic cultures. "Of these languages, about half are spoken by communities of 10,000 speakers or fewer, half of these, in turn, are spoken by communities of 1,000 or fewer speakers."[20] In Nigeria alone some 250 languages are voiced, even as a handful are prevalent, while in diminutive Liberia 17 distinct vernaculars exist. Ethiopia has more than 70 languages, 8 of which abound. And although the colonial language is largely used by the bureaucracy in urban areas, or in some few cases an African tongue, such as Swahili in Tanzania, in the interior tribal languages predominate. Tanzania is, in fact, the *only* country in Africa with an African language that is a national language.

As ethnic hierarchies have been developed in more and more African states, multiple cultural groups are often locked out of the prevailing national political economy. In some countries teachers in rural schools are prohibited from using local languages, and instruction may be conducted only in the colonial or predominant ethnic tongue. Thus, the drop out rate among school attendees is enormous. In Ethiopia, almost 75 percent of students drop out between the first and twelfth grades, while merely 17 percent of school-age children are enrolled in primary or secondary schools. In Senegal 37 percent are registered.[21]

"A nightmare scenario may be building: a two-tiered Africa where existing political and economic elites reintegrate with the global economy . . . while increasingly isolated rural populations [or more than 75% of Africa's people] are integrated internationally as perpetual recipients of humanitarian aid."[22] But with western populations suffering from "aid fatigue," it is unlikely that in the future such aid will match its even already paltry levels. United States foreign assistance, which amounted to 1 percent of GNP in 1960, has declined to a lamentable level of 0.3 percent.

James Schlesinger's thesis regarding the importance of establishing foreign policy priorities was certainly implemented during the Clinton administration. Since all things are not possible in the post-

Soviet world, the United States prioritized a strategy of helping to create market economies in Russia and the newly freed states of Eastern Europe. Poland, the Czech Republic, and Hungary were incorporated into the North Atlantic Treaty Organization (NATO) in 1999 so as to advance their political and economic security.

The Balkan region was, for a long time, high on Clinton's agenda. In 1995, after four years of fighting among Croatia, Bosnia and Herzegovina, Yugoslavia, and Serbia, and among Serbs, Croats, and Muslims, Clinton organized the Dayton Accords, which eventually brought an end to the warfare. Twenty thousand U.S. peacekeeping troops were dispatched to the region. In 1999, for 78 days, the United States and its NATO allies organized a ferocious air attack against Yugoslavia to bring to a halt President Slobodan Milosevic's vicious ethnic cleansing campaign in Kosovo, which pitted Serbs against Muslim Kosovo Albanians. European security was also said to be at stake, so with the withdrawal of Yugoslavia from Kosovo Milosevic was prevented from threatening Macedonia and Albania and causing a massive refugee crisis in Europe. To induce the American people to support the action, the domino theory of the cold war was brought out of hibernation. In some part Yugoslavia's defeat led to the eventual overthrow of Milosevic in 2000.

Along with helping to economically stabilize the many states in Asia struck by financial calamity in the late 1990s, improving relations with North Korea and Vietnam was placed on the front burner. Of course, the establishment of normal trade relations with China in 2000 was the culmination of eight years of intense bargaining by Clinton with the U.S. Congress and with the authorities in Beijing.

Immense time and energy certainly went into prodding Israel and the Palestinian Authority to reach a final resolution drawing on the 1993 Oslo Accords as the working framework. Throughout his years in the presidency Middle East leaders endlessly trooped in and out of the White House, while Clinton made countless trips to the region in his failed pursuit of a final arrangement. He also played a marginal role in fostering the signing of the 1994 Jordanian/Israeli peace treaty. Bettering relations with the moderates in Iran and containing Iraqi expansion were notable elements of Washington's Middle East policy.

For Clinton, U.S. involvement in these arenas related to James Schlesinger's "substantial matters" that directly impacted America's national security. Other than in Haiti, the Balkans, and Iraq, Clinton's policy was financial, political, and economic in nature and did not require excessive military involvement. Africa was in the category of "secondary matters" for which no political capital should be expended. The number of people murdered in the Rwanda holocaust of 1994 far exceeded the deaths of Kosovar Albanians (13,000 were killed by Serbian paramilitaries—a horrible statistic but one that pales in comparison to Rwanda's numbers), yet, because Africa was inconsequential, the world stormed to the defense of the Kosovars while allowing Tutsi Rwandans to be butchered.

For political elites in Washington, Africa's economic, political, and ethnic problems are seen as quicksand. Since so much ignorance regarding Africa's multitudinous cultures exists, and so many intractable problems do endure, once involved, as in Somalia, failure is seen as imminent, and an exit strategy is improbable. Thus, after 18 U.S. military deaths, Clinton abruptly went on national television and declared an end to the peacemaking exercise in Somalia. In Burundi, Clinton flew to Tanzania for one day to prod those negotiating for peace, failed in his effort, and promptly flew out. In Rwanda he ignored what was transpiring and, to keep the U.S. public at bay, refused to term it what it was—genocide.

Even Nigeria, the fifth largest supplier of U.S. oil and America's major trading partner in Africa, has been unable to maintain a broad and vital-interest connection to the United States because of its brutal and bloody past. Military support is given to train Nigerian peacekeeping troops for other venues in Africa, and efforts are made at least to preserve a dialogue, but, other than granting a *relatively* large economic aid package while praising the restoration of democracy, the United States has been hesitant to deepen its economic relationship with this potential behemoth. With no crucial interests in sub-Saharan Africa that can fundamentally affect U.S. national security, there can be no foreign policy crusade. That time has passed.

What Is to Be Done?

In an article written for *Foreign Affairs* in 1993, James C. Clad, of the Carnegie Endowment for International Peace, and Roger D. Stone, of the World Wildlife Fund, argued that "After 45 years America's foreign bilateral assistance program lies dead in the water." They then went on to produce an analysis that suggested a development program which would "focus less on governments and more on community-based efforts to alleviate poverty and achieve environmentally sound forms of development. The near-desperate conditions of scores of Third World states will force at least a reluctant acquiescence by their governments in decentralized aid administration."[23] Eight years later one could reasonably suggest that their proposal lies dead in the impenetrable rain forests of Africa. Frustration and apathy toward Africa has only increased since their article was published, and liberal proposals, or what I would term feel-good concepts, have little relevance in the deadly world of African politics.

The conservative approach to Africa's dire straits was taken in a book edited by Jennifer A. Widner and published in 1994. The thrust of the book is that the political and economic failures of African states can more than likely be rectified by a hefty dose of western values exemplified by the fiscal straitjacket demanded by the World Bank and the IMF. Capitalism, democracy, and western perceptions of economic and political thought are seen as a salvation to the orgy of tyranny and dictatorship that Africa has often been. Overall, the ideology and scholarship in the book, with some notable exceptions, represented an attempt to press politically conservative western solutions upon the continent.[24]

In effect, the theses of Widner, and of Clad and Stone were discounted long before their studies were published. In 1985, Irene L. Gendzier, a political sociologist, wrote a compelling book in which she indicated that western theorists of political development were committed to interpreting Third World change in a manner consistent with the expansion of capitalism. Their proposals, she insisted, were bound to fail on both practical and ideological grounds, and she condemned the effort. Perhaps more important, the ideological formulation has, at least in the short term, been laid to rest by the continuing inability of capitalist states to achieve anything close to success in their African endeavors.[25]

Jennifer Seymour Whitaker, in a 1988 book on the emergency in Africa, painted an austere but more realistic picture. Additionally, her thesis was not weighed down by ideological presuppositions. "Africans," she maintained, "rely on the countries of the West only at their own peril. Like that of the Wizard of Oz, Western magic can take its devotees very little further than they are ready to go themselves."[26] Additionally, she argued:

> Structural Adjustment is highly unlikely to have a widely beneficial effect unless African nations get more aid over the next decade than seems likely to be forthcoming. After the Western countries began encouraging and recognizing African "pragmatism" in economic reform, U.S. aid to Africa fell by nearly 50 percent. . . . [D]irect and swift infusions of debt relief are needed to sustain reform now. [And reform] depends greatly on the imponderable of leadership.[27]

Neither African nor western leadership seem to have met Whitaker's expectations, while the external push and internal pull factors that could influence the movement toward reform have been absent. But that was, as she called it, her "optimistic scenario. All our predictions . . . may be overshadowed, at least temporarily, by apocalyptic outbreaks of famine and plague analogous to those that afflicted Europe in the fourteenth century."[28] And that, of course, is precisely what has transpired since her book was published. Still, Whitaker refused to fall into the trap of reaching for sterile solutions and perceptively suggested that major transformation would have to occur within Africa. Without it, any pro-offered western solution is merely chimerical.

In a grandiose attempt to do something, *anything*, in the face of such overwhelming distress, and arguably to soothe their institutional consciences over the fact that in the triage world of international politics Africa remains last in treatment, the World Bank and the IMF agreed in September 2000 to reduce the outstanding foreign debt of a number of African states. The soaring economies and financial markets of western nations provided a huge increase in wealth as a result of rising employment, an explosion in capital gains, and the resulting jump in tax coffers. Because of their economic health, and the pressure placed on governments by antiglobalization forces in Seattle, Washington, D.C., Los Angeles, and Philadelphia, government leaders and finance ministers shifted their priorities to indicate that they care about the future of the poorest nations in Africa.

Thus, during a conference of international lending agencies held in Prague, the Czech Republic, where they were again confronted by furious protesters, the World Bank, the IMF, and western finance ministers agreed on a substantial financial package of relief. The pledge doubled the number of African countries originally offered debt relief by the world's financial institutions in 1999, during a global summit meeting held in Cologne, Germany, in an effort to reduce the financial burden borne by some of the world's poorest nations.

In 1999, to be eligible for relief, however, the lending agencies insisted, because of pressure placed on them by Lawrence H. Summers, the U.S. secretary of the treasury, that debt relief candidates develop a strategy for rural development, school construction, and expansion of health programs. The role of the private sector, charity groups, as well as the government in developing such blueprints had to be codified if relief was to be granted, so as to prevent diversion of monies to corrupt purposes. Compliance was seen as a years-long process, which led to anger and frustration by potential recipients.

In Prague, the lending agencies compromised their magisterial absolutism by allowing the beneficiaries to develop a less rigorous interim strategy, whereby partial relief would be granted, with full relief bestowed when the more comprehensive plan is produced. As a result 16 African states (later expanded to 21) had at least the possibility to begin to use more than $30 billion that they would otherwise have had to set aside for debt payments.

Naturally, the question arises as to where the money for those development schemes is to come from in the first place, since instability within Africa has limited foreign investment and accelerated flight capital. "These ever-broader gyrations of Africa's already wobbly political structures have destroyed what little remains of a viable business climate on the continent."[29] Still, the pledge by rich nations to initially absorb some 15 percent of Africa's debt is at least a first step in developing an alternate strategy for dealing with the continent's ills.

The statistics vis-à-vis debt relief provide a window through which to observe the remarkable amount of debt owed by those polities eligible for assistance.

TABLE 6.1

DEBT RELIEF

	1999			2000	
STATE	DEBT RELIEF (U.S. $ MILLIONS)	OUTSTAND-ING DEBT (%)	STATE	DEBT RELIEF (U.S. $ MILLIONS)	OUTSTAND-ING DEBT (%)
Benin	460	31	Cameroon	2,700	30
Burkina Faso	700	54	Chad	250	27
Mali	870	37	Ethiopia	1,300	23
Mauritania	1,100	50	Guinea	1,150	34
Mozambique	4,300	72	Guinea-Bissau	600	73
Senegal	850	19	Malawi	1,100	43
Tanzania	3,000	54	Rwanda	800	71
Uganda	1,950	57	Zambia	4,500	62

As vociferously as Third World nations have been demanding debt relief, its recognition by the financial powerhouses of the Western world is hardly a short- or long-term solution. Debt relief amounts to the use of a Band-Aid for a profuse hemorrhage. Indeed, shortly after the concession was announced, the World Bank placed all IBRD loans and IDA credits guaranteed by Zimbabwe on nonaccrual status. The IBRD loan of $452 million was overdue by $45 million, and the IDA credit outstanding of $437 million was in arrears by $2 million.[30] And although Zimbabwe was not on the list of those states eligible for debt forgiveness, its plight indicates how difficult it will be for those on the roster to come up with the money to use for development purposes.

Chad, which did qualify, was approved for a further $67 million credit by the World Bank merely one month after Prague. The credit was authorized to assist in the implementation of a national transportation program for financing and upgrading key roads to provide year-round access to markets. Only 0.8 percent of Chadian primary roads are paved. "By the mid-1980s, the only paved roads linking the capital to the interior . . . had disappeared because of insufficient mainte- nance. Of the estimated 31,000 kilometers of dirt roads and tracks, only 1,260 kilometers were all-weather roads. The remainder became impassable during the rainy season."[31]

Toward the end of December, as African states continued their economic free fall, the World Bank announced that Burundi, although laid waste by civil strife and ethnic horrors, would be approved for $440 million in debt relief, reconstruction, and devel- opment aid. In 2001, in accord with the IMF, the United States, Japan, and European states the World Bank expanded the number of countries offered debt relief to include Gambia, Madagascar, Niger, and São Tomé and Príncipe. Western financial officials also agreed to increase spending in a concerted effort to combat AIDS, malaria, and tuberculosis in Africa.

Even as the world's major powers approved the move toward ameliorating Africa's debt crisis, they have opposed the WTO's initia- tives in providing a program to Africa for technical assistance in trade matters. The United States, which in 2000 provided 16 percent—$74 million—of the WTO's budget, along with Japan and Germany implied that Mike Moore, its director general, paid too much attention to developing countries, neglecting broader trade issues, electronic com- merce, the reform of banking regulations, and agriculture.[32] Clearly, western concern with Africa is complicated and contradictory.

Debt relief, increased aid, structural adjustment, loans, and devel- opment grants are not the central solutions to what ails Africa. The data since the 1960s bespeaks otherwise. As Whitaker indicated, transformation must first occur within Africa itself. As long as tyrants rule and civil and ethnic strife convulses African states, no amount of goodwill or financial infusion will have any but parochial effect. A new well, an improved road here or there, the construction of a school, the distribution of seedlings, or the development of fishery, forestry, or agricultural projects on a small scale might help improve the fate of a village but can have no long-lasting impact if populations are turned into refugees and farms and land are abandoned. These limited projects may be helpful but they will not unravel Africa's Gordian knot in a bold or decisive fashion.

Before anything worthwhile can be accomplished, the West's attitude toward Africa also must change. The prevailing demeanor is patronizing. The we-know-best method is a remnant of the earliest stages of imperialism and colonialism, and history is full of examples of how utterly destructive that era was to Africa. "It was the subjugation of the universe, or a vast part of it. . . ."[33]

To move from the racist path that began with the slave trade and the legalization of slavery to an enlightened and egalitarian perspective will not be simple, but it must be done if Africa is to have the opportunity to be considered on the same plane as other continents. Western society has often viewed Africa and its people, in Frantz Fanon's language, as the wretched of the earth, and in so doing could not avoid the accompanying supercilious sentiment; Albert Memmi, whose approach to the subject was less contemptuous, maintained that "only the complete liquidation of colonialism permits the colonized to be freed."[34] Unfortunately, the liquidation has not been complete, even within the United States, as witness the ongoing debate over affirmative action, or the conversation surrounding the issue of reparations for the African American community appertaining to the event of slavery.[35]

To believe that Africa's problem can be solved by throwing money at it or withholding it, which will then act as leverage to force African leaders to confront their predicaments and to do so with a semblance of democracy, symbolizes western fatuousness. At the moment an overall solution for the economic, political, and social quandaries evidenced in one country after another does not exist. Because western values and philosophy are largely based on scientific logic, and individual motivation is seen as the preeminent capitalist virtue, traditional societies and their attendant ontological norms that encompass the clan, tribe, or village community are, more or less, devalued.

Should the West aspire to have influence in helping to untangle Africa's enigmas, it must, first of all, conceptualize a new notion of Africa. It will have to be prepared to negotiate with African leaders whose views and even ideologies may be very different from its own. When responding to issues surrounding human rights, AIDS, ethnic havoc, and civil war become the paramount goal of indigenous leadership, *only then* should the West, particularly the United States, be prepared to offer what it can, irrespective of ideological or political approach. And it should do so within the context of what is important for Africa, not in how it will improve the West. After all, these are issues of dignity, humanity, and civilization.

Western commitment can be accomplished on a country-by-country basis but can come into play only when African political elites renege on their quest for authority for power's sake alone. Until that time approaches, should a singular horrific event, such as famine or genocide, occur, the West can and should use its resources and muscle to intercede. But to continue to push overriding western-based solutions to resolve problems that are intractable because competent and fair leaders are not ascendant, or the obstacles are so utterly pervasive that even African democrats don't know where to begin, is alien and intrusive, and predictably will fail.

Furthermore, stressing western solutions to benevolent African leadership whose sources of authority are based on traditional and nonwestern values will also fail. Good leaders must be listened to, and incompetent potentates must not be supported no matter how supportive of the West they say they are. South Africa is a good example of what can be accomplished. After a nonracial democracy was developed in 1994 under President Nelson Mandela and then reinvigorated by the election of his successor Thabo Mbeki in 1999, the nation began to receive what eventually became the largest share of sub-Saharan aid from the United States. Much of it is apportioned to nongovernmental organizations for needs related to social services, and all of it is conditioned on necessities as diagnosed by South African decision makers. Other countries, even though smaller and far poorer, should be treated similarly.

As far as the United Nations is concerned its position in Africa is highly complicated and deeply flawed. Obviously, many of its organs such as the Food and Agriculture Organization (FAO), the World Health Organization (WHO), and the Economic and Social Council play a vital role in dealing with pertinent matters. But, insofar as the Security Council's peacemaking and peacekeeping operations are concerned, its role is very troubling.

The Security Council is more often than not merely an instrument of the major powers, and has been exceptionally so since 1991. The United Nations, as a result, has been particularly impotent in Sierra Leone, Guinea, Liberia, the Congo, Eritrea, and Ethiopia, among other places. Its pose—truly, that is all it was—during the Rwanda massacres was singularly embarrassing and disturbing. The mien of general feebleness is not going to change as the very creation of the Security Council was developed with the mind-set of maintaining superpower hegemony. At the same time there is no reason to expect that the international organization, with its limited authority, can be any more effective in its efforts than the states that oversee it in the Security Council want it to be—for the Security Council is the only organ that has the jurisdiction to make decisions for the UN regarding peace-keeping operations. The General Assembly can merely recommend.

Those who assert that the UN should do more than it now does do not fully comprehend how lacking in autonomy the organization actually is. It can do only what its Security Council members permit—no more, no less. Many who have served as secretary-general of the United Nations have been frustrated by the stymieing of forceful UN peacekeeping operations by the major powers. Indeed, at the end of his term in 1996, Secretary-General Boutros Boutros-Ghali bitterly attacked the Western powers for what he termed their anti-African bias and general passiveness to events on the continent.

Clearly, the West will have to develop new parameters in its relations with Africa. It is not that in the 1990s it has done too much or too little. What it has done has been imperious and patronizing. Generating rhetoric and giving lip service often have been substituted for policy. Currently there is no coherent design, but one cannot be developed in an abyss. To create a lucid framework, there must be a context that is inherently African. The United States and other western nations must try to use their leverage to nudge democrats into power and then work with them to generate a new approach developed by the African leaders.

Until then, the comments of Ugandan president Yoweri Museveni should be absorbed: "A little neglect would not be so bad. The more orphaned we are, the better for Africa. We will have to rely on ourselves." He then added that "the Euro-American architects of the old postcolonial order were welcome to work with Africa . . . but on Africa's terms. . . . "[36]

TYRANTS OR DEMOCRATS?

In the early years of independence, when Ghana was led by Kwame Nkrumah, the Ivory Coast by Félix Houphouët-Boigny, Kenya by Jomo Kenyatta, Tanganyika (now a part of Tanzania) by Julius Nyerere, Nigeria by Nnamdi Azikiwe and Abubakar Tafawa Belewa, Mali by Modibo Keita, and Senegal by poet-author Léopold Senghor, Africa was bursting with pride and great expectations. These "big men," as the early founding fathers of Africa were called, whether conservative, liberal, or socialist, seemed to hold the future of the continent in their hands. Some were charismatic, others colorless, but most were manifestly impressive and were seen as the living repositories of the grand potential of a future Africa.

Hope was overflowing. Foreign businesspeople poured into the various capital cities so as to participate in the very beginning of what was seen as an assured economic destiny, while in 1961 the first U.S. Peace Corps Volunteers shipped out to Ghana and Tanganyika. United States aid agencies and UN development programs opened offices while their personnel drew up blueprints for projects that would expand the existing infrastructure. Africanists—those academics studying and teaching about Africa in universities throughout the world—often seemed to be messengers of confidence. Debates raged among intellectuals and even among African presidents and prime ministers as to whether the future would be defined by the leftist Pan-African ideas of Nkrumah or the pro-western philosophy represented so well by Houphouët-Boigny and Senghor. Even the leaders were caught up in the thrall of the times, as exemplified by Nkrumah's and Houphouët-Boigny's open courting of Ethiopia's imperial monarch Haile Selassie I. It was a thrilling and heady time to be alive and to be in Africa.

Certainly, civil war had broken out in the Congo, but many outsiders viewed that as a singular event caused in large part by the paternal ideology Belgium pursued in its former colony. As Arthur M. Schlesinger Jr., an advisor to President Kennedy at the time, wrote, "Independence had descended like a hurricane on the unprepared country in July 1960. In a few days the [Congo] was in chaos."[37] Still, as one territory after another heralded the dawn of independence, happenings in the Congo were trumped by the cries of freedom in Central, East, and West Africa. Even Nkrumah got caught up in the excitement of it all. At the very moment when Ghana received independence in 1957 he trumpeted the confidence of the era:

> Today, from now on, there is a new African in the world. . . . We are going to demonstrate to the world, to the other nations, young as we are, that we are prepared to lay our own foundation. . . . Independence is, however, only a milestone on our march to progress. Independence by itself would be useless if it did not lead to great material and cultural advances by our people. . . . If we in Ghana can work out solutions to the problems which beset the tropics, we shall be making a contribution to Africa and to the world as a whole. . . . I believe that this . . . country will be worthy of the responsibility history has entrusted to us and that we will not disappoint those millions of people in other parts of the world to whom our success or failure will mean so much.[38]

Others were not so sure, particularly African literary figures whose writings were cries of protest, and they turned out to be right. In his novel *The Beautyful Ones Are Not Yet Born*, Ghanaian author Ayi Kwei Armah reflects on the Nkrumah years and on the military junta that overthrew him: "In the life of the nation itself, maybe nothing really new would happen. New men would take into their hands the power to steal the nation's riches and to use it for their own satisfaction. That, of course, was to be expected. . . . But for the nation itself there would only be a change of embezzlers and a change of the hunters and the hunted."[39]

In his tale of Africa, *This Earth, My Brother . . .* , Kofi Awoonor is more despairing when speaking of Africa in allegorical form. "They led her away howling, pouring her woes into a bout of tears that streamed down her once beautiful face. Here was the sorrow that was born in the memory of a past which could have been better, the sorrow for a future, now, that would have been different." Being Ghanaian, he also makes reference to a symbolic Nkrumah: "With the cry of Long live the Party, the Party is supreme, he cast us into degradation."[40]

The same theme reverberates in Sembène Ousmane's classic novel, *Xala,* about the Senegalese elite just after independence. His protagonist, who has just been excluded by his Senegalese compatriots, lashes out at them: "Yet what change is there really in general or in particular? The colonialist is stronger, more powerful than ever before, hidden inside us, here in this very place. He promises us the left-overs of the feast if we behave ourselves. . . . What are we? Clodhoppers! Agents! Petty Traders!"[41]

Enthusiasm pivoted to despair. Tyrants such as Jean-Bedel Bokassa in the Central African Republic, Mengistu Haile-Mariam in Ethiopia, Idi Amin in Uganda, Mobutu Sese Seko in the Congo, and Samuel K. Doe in Liberia forcefully took power and then used barbaric methods to retain it. A tumultuous civil war erupted in Nigeria in 1967 and engulfed the nation in ethnic fratricide until 1970. As rebellions took hold in countless countries, new military or civilian warlords appeared who were as brutal, sometimes more so, as their predecessors. By the 1990s Abacha, Taylor, Sankoh, Gueï, Laurent Kabila, and Mugabe had turned Nigeria, Liberia, Sierra Leone, the Ivory Coast, Congo, and Zimbabwe into political and economic infernos, while the Hutu leadership in Rwanda, like the Nazis in Germany, tried to exterminate an entire part of their population. Burundi too was refracted into a charnel house.

Africa appeared to have gone mad and to have transited into an orbit where "Rare is the head of state who acts on behalf of the entire nation. The people are not so much governed as ruled. It is as if they live in a criminally mismanaged corporation where the bosses are armed and have barricaded themselves inside the company safe."[42] Save perhaps for some diplomats and academics, Africa appeared to observers to be in full-blown anarchy while its leadership siphoned billions of dollars into Swiss banks. By 2001 pandemonium had leapt from one nation to another, Africa was on page one of the world's most important newspapers, and most of humanity threw up their hands in despair and consternation.

It could have been different, and Liberia was the place where it might have begun. Amos Sawyer, from the time when I knew him when he was a student at Cape Palmas High School, was an intellectual, a democrat, and a patriot. In 1963 he was the only Liberian pupil to be selected by an American news organization to visit and travel through parts of the United States, along with students from other African nations, and then to meet President Kennedy. Sawyer wanted only what was best for his country and its citizenry, and during his short time as president he endeavored strenuously to create order from chaos. At one time dean of the Social Sciences and Humanities school at the University of Liberia, he also held a Ph.D. from Northwestern University. In 1981 he was selected to help craft a new constitution for Liberia. But academic tools and a fervent intellect were no match for the murderous politics that were Charles Taylor's foremost skill.

Amos Sawyer or Charles Taylor? The dissimilarities in political approach are self-evident. In 1992 Sawyer published a book in which he argued that "given the current state of our understanding of the Liberian social order, one cannot overemphasize the importance of scholarly analyses that penetrate the inner workings of the array of indigenous societies whose existence and interaction tell more about the richness of the Liberian experience and help us understand its complexities."[43] Sawyer's bent was academic and intellectual.

Taylor dealt otherwise with the world of politics. The same year in which Sawyer's book came out, Taylor's bodyguards—adolescent killers—had captured a Nigerian student who was wrongly assumed to be part of an opposition military force. He was tortured near Taylor's encampment. "His face and head were a mess of bloody knots and oozing lacerations, and some of his teeth had been knocked out and both lips split through. His legs were bound. . . . His left leg was swollen monstrously. . . . All of him was swollen."[44]

Unfortunately, the man whose astuteness about Liberian society was profound could not compete in the sordid and tumultuous world of politics that was Taylor's genius. Shortly before Sawyer returned to Liberia to take up his presidency, I had a brief telephone conversation with him. What I recollect most vividly was my warning that he be careful, that he could be killed since he was walking into a maelstrom. He burst into a spirited laugh and said everything would be okay. Of course, it wasn't. The inquisitive high school student who went on to become president of his country was soon forced out of power. But his response was illustrative of his perpetual enthusiasm and confidence. By late 2000 that self-possession must have been sorely tested as Sawyer was severely beaten by Taylor's followers merely for speaking in favor of democracy.

Taylor won. Sawyer lost, but so did Liberia and so did Africa. Amos Sawyer might very well have been an exemplar of a moderate but more rational politics, one in which constituent concern held sway over attaining and maintaining power at whatever cost. The United States lost too. Its response to Sawyer's presidency was cool and it maintained its distance, while Taylor, with his control of Liberia's resources, conducted trade with the West, thus enabling him to obtain the funds necessary to continue his struggle for power. Sawyer vacated the presidency in 1994, although he remained in Liberia as an active proponent of democracy, living, as he put it to me, in "fear and darkness" until March, 2001, at which time he became a resident scholar at the Workshop in Political Theory and Policy Analysis at Indiana University. His optimism and democratic credentials intact, he is currently writing and lecturing on developmental theory, human rights, and Liberian politics. There are, he insists, "too few" African democrats in power. Taylor became president in 1997.

The United States bungled a rare opportunity to reorient its policy toward Liberia. Here was an African head of state who was more than willing to install democratic institutions, but neither President George Bush nor President Bill Clinton seized the moment. Perhaps they didn't recognize what was at stake; more likely, given America's reticence to becoming involved in Africa's wars, they were unwilling to expend the effort to nourish a struggling democrat. So much for the hypothesis that the United States is merely awaiting the emergence of democratic African leaders through whom it can organize a new and creative foreign policy.

In South Africa things were different. In 1994, after spending 27 years in prison as a result of his militant opposition to apartheid, Nelson Mandela led the African National Congress (ANC) to an electoral victory and became the country's first black president. Four years earlier, on February 11, 1990, as millions throughout the world watched in rapt attention via television, this extraordinarily charismatic man of dignity and stature walked out of confinement and, shortly thereafter, before a heartened and enthusiastic crowd at the Cape Town City Hall, spoke of the future: "I have fought against white domination, and I have fought against black domination. I have cherished the idea of a democratic and free society in which all persons live together in harmony and with equal opportunities. It is an ideal which I hope to live for and achieve. But if needs be, it is an ideal for which I am prepared to die."[45] The next day, in Soweto, Mandela's democratic intentions were put sharply into focus. "No man or woman," he said, "who has abandoned apartheid will be excluded from our movement toward a nonracial, united and democratic South Africa based on one-person one-vote on a common voters' role."[46]

A Truth and Reconciliation Commission (TRC) headed by Archbishop Desmond Tutu was formed in 1995 to document the horrors of apartheid in order to cleanse the country by addressing the needs of its victims. To break the cycle of impunity for past human rights abuses, the TRC could offer amnesty and freedom in "exchange . . . for truth." Reconciliation would evolve through confession and forgiveness from which a more open and rights-based society would arise.[47] One year later a new constitution was adopted that strongly emphasized respect for human rights and what was termed a culture of human rights.

Mandela was taking South Africa along a democratic byway that most other African leaders seemed unable and unwilling to wend. His lifelong "struggle for freedom and democracy in South Africa [which] lies inside South Africa itself"[48] was now in full bloom, and President Clinton responded positively.

An American-South African Binational Commission was created in 1994 to deepen the relationship between the two nations "to both 'privilege' the new government in Pretoria and concurrently exercise influence over Africa's potential hegemon."[49] According to Chris Alden, of the London School of Economics, "given South Africa's position as the only African state to be listed as one of the US Commerce Department's ten emerging markets and its status as the continent's most developed economy, it is not surprising that Washington accorded it a special status. . . . [To that end] half of the Southern African Enterprise Development Fund's US $100 million was specifically allocated for South African use."[50] Clinton also nourished a personal relationship with Mandela, often meeting with him in Washington, and even going so far as to travel to Africa to aid in his efforts to bring peace to different parts of the continent.

But as U.S. inertia toward Liberia's Amos Sawyer demonstrated, South Africa is a special case. It is a regional powerhouse whose 1998 GDP of $133 billion was three and a half times that of Nigeria's, its exports of agricultural crops exceed that of every other sub-Saharan African state, while its overseas marketing of manufactured goods is 60 percent of Africa's total merchandise exports, excluding North Africa.[51] Many of its munificent mineral resources are supplied to the United States and used in its space and military programs. Sophisticated technology products comprise 9 percent of its exports.[52]

Unlike most other countries in Africa, South Africa is a country that cannot be ignored, and because of its almost singular condition it calibrates into the larger national security interests of the United States. But since it is in an exceptional position, and knows it, its leadership and population fervently desire to keep the chaos impacting South Africa's neighbors "north of South."[53]

CONCLUSION: A SHAKESPEAREAN TRAGEDY

The diabolical natures of Shakespeare's characters Iago and King Richard III, whose treachery knew no bounds, have been transported to twenty-first century Africa.[54] Murder, corruption, manipulation, deceit, extortion, intimidation, cunning, imprisonment of perceived opponents, and a lust for power were the norms and values subscribed to by both. Kenya's Daniel arap Moi, Zimbabwe's Robert Mugabe, and Liberia's Charles Taylor, among a multitude of other African presidents, prime ministers, and generals, seem to have absorbed the traits and instruments of coercion Shakespeare described so singularly through both Richard and Iago. Currently Africa is populated by contemporary, though perhaps less literarily captivating, versions of Shakespeare's two demonic performers.

According to Robert I. Rotberg of Harvard University's John F. Kennedy School of Government, these "kleptocratic, patrimonial leaders . . . give Africa a bad name, plunge its people into poverty and despair, and incite civil wars and bitter ethnic conflict. They are the ones largely responsible for declining GDP levels, food scarcities, rising infant-mortality rates, soaring budget deficits, human rights abuses, breaches of the rule of law, and prolonged serfdom for millions—even in Africa's nominal democracies."[55] They have, in short, brutally complicated the very severe political, economic, ethnic, health, and environmental issues that challenge Africa.

A continent confronted by the worst plague to strike the earth since the fourteenth century can ill afford such pernicious pacesetters. Yet here they are, and unless something truly fundamental is done to promote democracy, the previous 10 years will have been merely a harbinger of the decade just begun, a destiny that may well encompass a continuing series of coups, countercoups, wars, ethnic explosions, and an elephantine number of AIDS fatalities. States will most probably continue to crumple "until the political leaderships of African countries come to value the long-term betterment of their populations over their own personal and political interests. . . ."[56]

With terribly weak indigenous governmental institutions exacerbating Africa's trauma, the United States, whose timorous approach to the continent has been documented, cannot be expected to take a strong hand in helping to resolve problems. Even as regards peacemaking and conflict prevention, only regions that have high priority— "Europe, the Middle East, countries near U.S. borders, and the Pacific Rim, especially Korea and Taiwan"—are likely to see U.S. activity.[57] Africa, where peacemaking has largely failed due to the U.S. political retreat, hardly registers on America's foreign policy radar screen, despite Susan Rice's fulminations to the contrary.

When she served as assistant secretary of state for African affairs, Rice claimed the Clinton administration had provided a "new paradigm for Africa" that encompassed globalization and national security vis-à-vis preventing terrorism and disease.[58] Yet globalization's impact on Africa remains negligible; terrorism—witness the bombings of the U.S. embassies in Kenya and Tanzania in 1998, which resulted in the deaths of 269 people, mostly Kenyans and Tanzanians—does not afford Africa much aid beyond dollars to provide construction of and security for American installations; and the United States has done very little regarding disease, particularly AIDS, although in 2000 U.S. bilateral aid to "promote child survival . . . through inoculations, micronutrient supplements, and oral rehydration therapy" reached $715 million *worldwide*.[59] Tariff-free imports of African textiles, exported to the United States under the African Growth and Opportunities Act of 2000, have helped Madagascar and Nigeria, among others, but have had only limited economic impact on desperate African economies.

Rhetoric, lip service, and periodic trips to Africa where a president speaks of democracy and "feels your pain" do not make a viable and coherent foreign policy. To make bread requires flour, yeast, water (or perhaps milk), sugar, and butter; sugar and yeast alone won't cut it. So too with foreign policy; words by themselves are meaningless.

Within Africa, certainly, elections have taken place from 1991 to 2001. They were held in, among other countries, Ghana, Senegal, Botswana, Mozambique, Ethiopia, Namibia, Cape Verde, São Tomé and Príncipe, Benin, Nigeria, Tanzania, Malawi, Kenya, Uganda, the Ivory Coast, Madagascar, the Central African Republic, and Mauritius. But elections are merely one indicator of the democratic process, and they are not worth very much if one leader, party, or group totally dominates the system and if opponents are harassed, intimidated, often shot at, even arrested, and obligated to campaign fearing for their very lives. Sometimes they are even killed. After all, Togo has elections but it is a totalitarian state dominated by President Gnassingbé Eyadéma, who has been in power for some three decades, while in Liberia Charles Taylor was elected president in 1997 through a process of controlled mayhem.

As for economies, while the Ivory Coast and Zimbabwe had once experienced impressive economic growth rates, by 2000 they had both collapsed into political anarchy that decimated the prudence both countries once partook in. Sierra Leone, the Congo, Somalia, Angola, Sudan, among many others, have no functioning productive power. In Botswana the GDP growth rate is a strong and sustainable 3.5 percent and in Mauritius it is an impressive 5.6 percent, while in Lesotho it is a remarkably desperate -3.6 percent.[60]

The lack of political democracy overall, the generally weak although often sporadic bursts of economic growth, the AIDS pestilence, and a sweeping neglect of the continent by the United States does not bode well for Africa's near-term future. An exceptionally fair and democratic leader, such as South Africa's Nelson Mandela, Liberia's Amos Sawyer, and Ghana's recently elected president John A. Kufuor, is unique. As Rotberg indicates, Africa's positive role models "need to be offered to emerging African leaders. . . ."[61] Unfortunately, far too many African potentates spurn the Mandela appellation but choose to emulate the behavior of Shakespeare's Richard III and Iago.

It hardly seems to matter to them that their attitude corresponds precisely to the voice of an actual monarch, France's King Louis XV, as, in words attributed to him, he assured his people *"après moi le déluge."*

Notes

INTRODUCTION

1. The optimism of that era is indicated in a few lines from different segments of a speech that I gave on behalf of the first group of Peace Corps Volunteers shortly before leaving Liberia. On June 27, 1964, in a countrywide broadcast from the capital, Monrovia, on radio station ELBC, I stated: "Idealism and altruism may not always be the easiest way, yet, as in Robert Frost's poem, the easiest way may not be the best. Even up against the test of realism, idealism does not necessarily die. . . . Many of us came here with the spirit of wanting to do something to aid in the growth and maturity of the world. . . . Within one's lifetime one hopes for a great number of things that can be done, but having the chance to further understanding does not come to everyone and for this opportunity one can be grateful." It was also an age in which a cold warrior like President John F. Kennedy could be described as "old enough to dream dreams, and still young enough to see visions." See Ted C. Sorensen, *Kennedy* (New York: Harper & Row, 1965), p. 752.

2. *Public Papers of the Presidents of the United States, John F. Kennedy, 1961* (Washington, D.C.: United States Government Printing Office, 1962).

3. *New York Times*, September 6, 2000, p. A16.

4. Chinua Achebe, *A Man of the People* (Garden City, NY: Anchor Books, 1967), p. 141.

5. Vicente Blasco Ibañez, *The Four Horsemen of the Apocalypse* (New York: E. P. Dutton, 1918), p. 177.

6. *New York Times*, August 27, 2000, p. 5.

7. *New York Times*, May 1, 1997, pp. C1, C10. See also Wole Soyinka, *Idanre and Other Poems* (New York: Hill and Wang, 1967), and *The Interpreters* (New York: Collier Books, 1970).

8. World Bank, News Release No. 2000/363/AFR, Washington, D.C., June 2, 2000.

CHAPTER ONE

1. Gerald Moor and Ulli Beier, eds., *Modern Poetry from Africa* (Middlesex: Penguin Books, 1966), p. 18.

2. Melville J. Herskovitz, cited in preface to Jacob Drachler, ed., *African Heritage: Intimate Views of the Black Africans from Life, Lore, and Literature* (New York: Collier Books, 1964), p. 106.

3. Moore and Beier, *Modern Poetry*, p. 51.

4. Drachler, *African Heritage*, p. 106.

5. Exact numbers of those who reached the New World and those who died are unknown. The problem of reaching accurate figures is discussed in Basil Davidson, *The African Slave Trade: Precolonial History 1450-1850* (Boston: Little, Brown, 1961), p. 79, and in Philip D. Curtin, *The Atlantic Slave Trade: A Census* (Madison: University of Wisconsin Press, 1970), pp. 3-13. According to Davidson, some authorities estimate the total of those "landed alive" at over 50 million. Curtin's analysis is more conservative. See also Paul E. Lovejoy, *Transformations in Slavery: A History of Slavery in Africa*, 2nd ed. (Cambridge: Cambridge University Press, 2000).

6. Barry Unsworth, *Sacred Hunger* (New York: W. W. Norton, 1993).

7. Davidson, *African SlaveTrade*, pp. xv-xvi.

8. Lawrence W. Henderson, *Angola: Five Centuries of Conflict* (Ithaca, NY: Cornell University Press, 1979), pp. 94, 96; Geoff Simons, *Cuba: From Conquistador to Castro* (New York: St. Martin's Press, 1996), p. 101.

9. Helen Chapin Metz, *Nigeria: A Country Study* (Washington, D.C.: Department of the Army, 1992), p. 17.

10. LaVerle Berry, ed., *Ghana: A Country Study* (Washington, D.C.: Department of the Army, 1995), p. 11.

11. Davidson, *African SlaveTrade*, p. 59.

12. Curtin, *Atlantic Slave Trade*, pp. 35, 237.

13. Davidson, *African SlaveTrade*, p. 90.

14. Henderson, *Angola*, p. 95.

15. Davidson, *African SlaveTrade*, p. 278.

16. André Schwarz-Bart, *A Woman Named Solitude* (New York: Atheneum, 1973), p. 20.

17. D. Elwood Dunn and S. Byron Tarr, *Liberia: A National Polity in Transition* (London: Scarecrow Press, 1988), p. 16.

18. Chinua Achebe, *Things Fall Apart* (Greenwich, CT: Fawcett, 1959).

19. J. Gus Liebenow, *Liberia: The Quest for Democracy* (Bloomington: Indiana University Press, 1987), p. 11.

20. Basil Davidson, *The Lost Cities of Africa* (Boston: Little, Brown, 1959), p. 91.

21. S. E. Crowe, *The Berlin West African Conference: 1884-1885* (Westport, CT: Negro Universities Press, 1970), pp. 174-175.

22. Albert Memmi, *The Colonizer and the Colonized* (Boston: Beacon Press, 1967), pp. xii, 70, 74.

23. Ibid., pp. 83, 85, 91, 92.

24. Ferdinand Oyono, *Boy!* (New York: Collier Books, 1970), p. 5.

25. Nuruddin Farah, *Sweet and Sour Milk* (St. Paul, MN: Graywolf Press, 1992), p. 124.

26. Frantz Fanon, *The Wretched of the Earth* (New York: Grove Press, 1968), p. 43.

27. Berry, *Ghana*, p. 19.

28. Metz, *Nigeria*, p. 32.

29. Chinua Achebe, *Arrow of God* (Garden City, NY: Anchor Books, 1969), pp. 36, 39.

30. Robert E. Handloff, ed., *Côte d'Ivoire: A Country Study* (Washington, D.C.: Department of the Army, 1991), pp. 12, 16.

31. Ibid., p. 14; Samuel Decalo, *Coups and Army Rule in Africa: Studies in Military Style* (New Haven, CT: Yale University Press, 1976), p. 133.

32. Sembène Ousmane, *God's Bits of Wood* (Garden City, NY: Anchor Books, 1970), p. 306, 322.

33. Memmi, *Colonizer and Colonized*, pp. 71, 73.

34. See the section on the Congo in chapter 2 of this book, and on Burundi and Rwanda in chapter 3.

35. Tsitsi Dangarembga, *Nervous Conditions* (Seattle: Seal Press, 1989), pp. 200-201.

36. Ibid., p. 202.

37. Frantz Fanon, *A Dying Colonialism* (New York: Grove Press, 1967), p. 179.

38. For the Truman Doctrine, see H. L. Trefousse, *The Cold War: A Book of Documents* (New York: Capricorn Books, 1966), pp. 97-102. The message President Harry Truman enunciated was that the United States must "support free peoples" everywhere through a vigilant application of the containment and domino theories. Contain the Soviet Union and its communist ideology, or countries will fall under its control like dominos, one after the other.

39. Arthur M. Schlesinger Jr., *A Life in the Twentieth Century: Innocent Beginnings, 1917-1950* (Boston: Houghton Mifflin, 2000), p. 406.

40. Peter Schwab, "Cold War on the Horn of Africa." *African Affairs* 77, 306 (1978): 12; see also *A History of Kagnew Station and American Forces in Eritrea* (1973).

41. *U.S. Security Agreements and Commitments Abroad, Ethiopia* (Washington, D.C.: Committee on Foreign Relations, U.S. Senate, part 8, June 1, 1970), pp. 1902, 1904-1905, 1940.

42. Schwab, "Cold War on the Horn of Africa," p. 12.

43. Peter Schwab, *Ethiopia: Politics, Economics and Society* (Boulder, CO: Lynne Rienner Publishers, 1985), p. 99.

44. For more on Ethiopia, Eritrea, and Somalia, see chapters 2 and 3 in this volume.

45. Fanon, *Wretched of the Earth*, p. 101.

46. Ibid., pp. 102-103. Italics in original.

47. Ibid., p. 67. On neocolonialism, see David Birmingham, *The Decolonization of Africa* (Athens: Ohio University Press, 1995).

48. For a book dealing with the economic pressures placed on Nkrumah, which helped to create the conditions for his overthrow by Ghana's pro-West military, see Bob Fitch and Mary Oppenheimer, *Ghana: End of an Illusion* (New York: Monthly Review Press, 1968).

49. Thomas Hodgkin, *Nationalism in Colonial Africa* (New York: New York University Press, 1957), p. 15.

50. Chinua Achebe, *No Longer at Ease* (London: Heinemann, 1966), p. 92.

51. A phrase borrowed from the title of Ama Ata Aidoo, *No Sweetness Here* (Garden City, NY: Anchor Books, 1972).

CHAPTER TWO

1. Carol Lancaster, "Redesigning Foreign Aid." *Foreign Affairs* (September/October 2000): 74-88.

2. Philip Gourevitch, "Forsaken: How a Seven-Nation War Engulfed Congo." *New Yorker,* September 25, 2000, pp. 3-67.

3. Chinua Achebe, *No Longer at Ease* (London: Heinemann, 1966), pp. 43-44.

4. Chinua Achebe, *A Man of the People* (Garden City, NY: Anchor Books, 1967), p. 34. For analyses of the political, social, and cultural criticism evident in Achebe's novels, see: John Povey, "Political Protest in the African Novel in English." In *Protest and Power in Black Africa,* pp. 823-853, edited by Robert I. Rotberg and Ali A. Mazrui (New York: Oxford University Press, 1970); Kofi Awoonor, *The Breast of the Earth: A Survey of the History, Culture and Literature of Africa South of the Sahara* (Garden City, NY: Anchor Books, 1976); Annie Gagiano, *Achebe, Head, Marechera: On Power and Change in Africa* (Boulder, CO: Lynne Rienner Publishers, 2000); and Chinwe Christina Okechukwu, *Achebe the Orator: The Art of Persuasion in Chinua Achebe's Novels* (Westport, CT: Greenwood Press, 2001).

5. Buchi Emecheta, *Destination Biafra* (Oxford: Heinemann, 1988), p. 186.

6. Bonnie Campbell, "The Ivory Coast." In *West African States: Failure and Promise,* pp. 66-116, edited by John Dunn (Cambridge: Cambridge University Press, 1978), p. 93. For what has become a classic study of the Ivory Coast, see Aristide R. Zolberg, *One-Party Government in the Ivory Coast* (Princeton, NJ: Princeton University Press, 1964).

7. As quoted in Campbell, "Ivory Coast," p. 91; *United Nations World Statistics Pocketbook* (New York: United Nations, 1997), p. 45.

8. *New York Times,* October 25, 2000, p. A5.

9. *African Development Indicators 2000* (Washington, D.C.: World Bank, 2000), p. 34.

10. James Traub, "Sierra Leone: The Worst Place on Earth." *New York Review of Books,* June 29, 2000, pp. 106. See Web site at nybooks.com.

11. *African Development Indicators 2000,* pp. 95, 96, 99, 239; Christopher Allen, "Sierra Leone." In *West African States: Future and Promise,* pp. 189-210, edited by John Dunn (Cambridge: Cambridge University Press, 1978), p. 203.

12. See *NewsHour with Jim Lehrer* (television program), May 16, 2000.

13. For a theoretical discussion of military intervention, but of the more traditional kind, see Henry Bienen, ed., *The Military Intervenes: Case Studies in Political Development* (New York: Russell Sage Foundation, 1968), p. 189. Also see John L. Hirsch, *Sierra Leone: Diamonds and the Struggle for Democracy* (Boulder, CO: Lynne Rienner Publishers, 2001).

14. *African Development Indicators 2000,* pp. 10, 95, 96, 99; *World Bank Little Data Book 2000* (Washington, D.C.: World Bank, 2000), p. 189; Traub, "Sierra Leone," p. 1.

15. Marguerite Michaels, "Retreat from Africa." *Foreign Affairs* 71, 1 (1993): 94, 95.

16. Jeffrey Clark, "Debacle in Somalia." *Foreign Affairs* 72, 1: 121.

17. Christopher Clapham, "Liberia." In Dunn, ed., *West African States,* p. 119. See also D. Elwood Dunn and S. Byron Tarr, *Liberia: A National Polity in Transition* (London: Scarecrow Press, 1988), pp. 9-26. For a fascinating study of the family structure of the Kru ethnic group and its interface with Monrovia's Americo-Liberian "civilized" society, see Merran Fraenkel, *Tribe and Class in Monrovia* (New York: Oxford University Press, 1964).

18. J. Gus Liebenow, *Liberia: The Quest for Democracy* (Bloomington: Indiana University Press, 1987), p. 263.

19. See ibid., pp. 247-315, for an absorbing discussion of this period in Liberian history. See also Amos Sawyer, *The Emergence of Autocracy in Liberia* (San Francisco: Institute for Contemporary Studies, 1992), pp. 293-299.

20. Sawyer, *Emergence of Autocracy in Liberia,* p. 294. As Doe stated in Sawyer's presence, "My advisors may have MA, but I have M-16."

21. Dunn and Tarr, *Liberia,* pp. 98, 112-115. Chester A. Crocker, Reagan's assistant secretary of state for African affairs, upheld the views of Perkins.

22. See Denis Johnson, "The Small Boys Unit: Searching for Charles Taylor in a Liberian Civil War." *Harper's* (October 2000): 41-60.

23. D. Elwood Dunn and S. Byron Tarr, *Liberia: A National Polity in Transition* (London: Scarecrow Press, 1988), pp. 90, 93.

24. See Stephen Ellis, *The Mask of Anarchy: The Destruction of Liberia and the Religious Dimension of an African Civil War* (New York: New York University Press, 1999), for a remarkable description of Liberia's apocalypse. Also note Ryszard Kapuściński, *The Shadow of the Sun* (New York: Alfred A. Knopf, 2001), pp. 233-260.

25. Karl Maier, *Into the House of the Ancestors: Inside the New Africa* (New York: John Wiley & Sons, 1997), p. xx.

26. *African Development Indicators 2000*, p. 6.

27. See Richard Sherman, *Eritrea: the Unfinished Revolution* (New York: Praeger, 1980).

28. In 1985 I wrote a book analyzing Ethiopia under Mengistu. Originally I viewed that government as a necessary analeptic to the harsh and forbidding rule of Emperor Haile Selassie I. I judged that after the purging of the structures and officials of the ancien régime, and of the intolerant radical opposition, it would moderate its views. I was wrong. See Peter Schwab, *Ethiopia: Politics, Economics and Society* (Boulder, CO: Lynne Rienner Publishers, 1985). Note also Fred Halliday and Maxine Molyneux, *The Ethiopian Revolution* (London: Verso Editions, 1981). For an analysis of politics, government, and the feudal land policies of Haile Selassie's government, see Peter Schwab, *Decision-Making in Ethiopia: A Study of the Political Process* (London: C. Hurst, 1972).

29. See Robert D. Kaplan, *Surrender or Starve: The Wars Behind the Famine* (Boulder, CO: Westview Press, 1988), and Dawit Wolde Giorgis, *Red Tears: War, Famine and Revolution in Ethiopia* (Trenton, NJ: Red Sea Press, 1989). Note also Nega Mezlekia, *Notes from the Hyena's Belly: An Ethiopian Boyhood* (New York: Picador, 2001).

30. *New York Times*, April 23, 2000, p. 4.

31. *New York Times*, April 5, 2000, p. A5.

32. *New York Times*, September 17, 2000, p. 12.

33. See chapter 1 in this book; note also Peter Schwab, "Cold War on the Horn of Africa." *African Affairs* 77, 306 (1978): 6-20.

34. David Martin and Phyllis Johnson, *The Struggle for Zimbabwe: The Chimurenga War* (London: Faber and Faber, 1981), pp. 330, 331.

35. Robert I. Rotberg, "Africa's Mess, Mugabe's Mayhem." *Foreign Affairs* (September/October 2000): 47.

36. *New York Times*, December 15, 2000, p. A8.

37. *New York Times*, November 1, 2000, p. A10.

38. *New York Times*, November 11, 2000, p. C2; *Mmegi/The Reporter*, November 3-9, 2000, B2.

39. *World Bank Little Data Book 2000*, p. 231; Rotberg, "Africa's Mess," p. 52.

40. *World Bank Little Data Book 2000*, p. 231.

41. *New York Times*, December 15, 2000, p. A8.

42. Ama Ata Aidoo, *No Sweetness Here* (Garden City, NY: Anchor Books, 1972), pp. 12, 13, 14.

43. Kenneth L. Adelman, "Zaïre's Year of Crisis." *African Affairs* 77, 306 (January 1978): 37; *United Nations World Statistics Pocketbook* (New York: United Nations, 1997), p. 42; *World Bank Little Data Book 2000*, p. 69.

44. Gourevitch, "Forsaken," p. 55.

45. *African Development Indicators 2000*, pp. 82, 318, 322, 324.

46. Adelman, "Zaïre's Year of Crisis," p. 37; *United Nations World Statistics Pocketbook*, p. 42; *World Bank Little Data Book 2000*, p. 69.

47. M. Crawford Young, "Rebellion and the Congo." In *Protest and Power in Black Africa*, pp. 969-1011, edited by Robert I. Rotberg and Ali A. Mazrui (New York: Oxford University Press, 1970), p. 969.

48. See ibid. and Catherine Hoskyns, ed., *Case Studies in African Diplomacy: The Organization of African Unity and the Congo Crisis, 1964-65* (Dar Es Salaaam: Oxford University Press, 1969), for analyses and documents from this period.

49. Gourevitch, "Forsaken," p. 54.

50. See chapter 3 in this book.

51. Gourevitch, "Forsaken," p. 55.

52. *NewsHour with Jim Lehrer*, May 16, 2000.

53. Young, "Rebellion and the Congo," p. 1011. For additional readings on chaotic Africa, see Maier, *Into the House of the Ancestors;* George B. N. Ayittey, *Africa Betrayed* (New York: St. Martin's Press, 1993); and Ayittey, *Africa in Chaos* (New York: St. Martin's Press, 1998).

54. Inis L. Claude Jr., *Swords into Plowshares: The Problems and Progress of International Organization* (New York: Random House, 1964), pp. 227-228.

55. J. L. Brierly, *The Law of Nations* (New York: Oxford University Press, 1963).

CHAPTER THREE

1. *United Nations Economic and Social Council, Commission on Human Rights* (New York: United Nations, February 3-March 14, 1986), E/CN.4/1986/20, p. 3.

2. Adamantia Pollis and Peter Schwab, eds., *Human Rights: Cultural and Ideological Perspectives* (New York: Praeger Publishers, 1979).

3. Ibid., p. xiii.

4. See *Universal Declaration of Human Rights* (New York: United Nations, December 10, 1948).

5. Adamantia Pollis and Peter Schwab, "Human Rights: A Western Construct with Limited Applicability." In *Human Rights: Cultural and Ideological Perspectives*, ed. Pollis and Schwab, pp. 1-18.

6. *New York Times*, November 18, 2000, p. 7.

7. Pollis and Schwab, "Human Rights," p. 13.

8. As quoted in ibid., p. 3.

9. Adamantia Pollis and Peter Schwab, eds., *Human Rights: New Perspectives, New Realities* (Boulder, CO: Lynne Rienner Publishers, 2000), p. 2. See also Peter Schwab and Adamantia Pollis, eds., *Toward a Human Rights Framework* (New York: Praeger Publishers, 1982).

10. Pollis and Schwab, *Human Rights: New Perspectives*, p. 3.

11. Julius K. Nyerere, *Freedom and Development/Uhuru na Maendeleo* (Dar Es Salaam: Oxford University Press, 1973), p. 2.

12. Samuel Decalo, *Psychoses of Power: African Personal Dictatorships* (Boulder, CO: Westview Press, 1989), p. 149.

13. Ibid., pp. 102, 13. For a book describing the Amin regime in all its beastliness, see Henry Kyemba, *A State of Blood: The Inside Story of Idi Amin* (New York: Ace Books, 1977).

14. *Mail & Guardian*, November 10-16, 2000, p. 11

15. Jennifer A. Widner, *The Rise of a Party-State in Kenya: From "Harambee!" to "Nyayo!"* (Berkeley: University of California Press, 1993), p. 170. Widner's study is a brilliant analysis of Moi's growing intolerance and his use of the one-party state to solidify his control. For an articulate and prescient analysis of Kenya's first leaders and its incipient party politics, see John J. Okumu, "Charisma and Politics in Kenya: Notes and Comments on the Problems of Kenya's Party Leadership." *East Africa Journal* 5, 2 (1968): 9-16. A fascinating discussion of Tom Mboya, Kenya's most significant nationalist and independence figure next to Kenyatta, who was assassinated in 1969, is found in "Tom Mboya: A Commemorative Issue." *East Africa Journal* 6, 9 (1969): 6-37. See also Jomo Kenyatta, *Facing Mount Kenya: The Traditional Life of the Gikuyu* (London: Heinemann, 1979).

16. Peter Woodward, *Sudan, 1898-1989: The Unstable State* (Boulder, CO: Lynne Rienner Publishers, 1990), p. 93. Regarding the Islamization of the Sudan, see Scott H. Jacobs, "The Sudan's Islamization." *Current History* (May 1985): 205-208, 230-232.

17. Woodward, *Sudan,* p. 219.

18. Jeffrey Clark, "Debacle in Somalia." *Foreign Affairs* 72, 1 (1993): 117. For a discussion of Somalia's exigency even prior to the 1991 emergency, see: David D. Laitin and Said S. Samatar, *Somalia: Nation in Search of a State* (Boulder, CO: Westview Press, 1987); and *Somalia, a Government at War with Its Own People: Testimonies about the Killings and the Conflict in the North* (Washington, D.C.: Africa Watch/Human Rights Watch, 1990).

19. Clark, "Debacle in Somalia," p. 112.

20. A phrase borrowed from *Somalia, a Government at War.*

21. Decalo, *Psychoses of Power,* p. 1. For a respectable historical and social overview of Congo-Brassaville, albeit one that is politically dated, see Gordon C. McDonald et al., *Area Handbook for People's Republic of the Congo (Congo Brassaville)* (Washington, D.C.: Foreign Area Studies of the American University, 1971).

22. René Lemarchand, "Social Change and Political Modernisation in Burundi." *Journal of Modern African Studies* 4, 4 (1966): 401.

23. Ibid., p. 407.

24. See Lucy S. Dawidowicz, *The War Against the Jews: 1933-1945* (New York: Bantam Books, 1979); François Ponchaud, *Cambodia: Year Zero*

(New York: Holt, Rinehart and Winston, 1978); and David Chandler, *Voices from S-21: Terror and History in Pol Pot's Secret Prison* (Berkeley: University of California Press, 1999).

25. Philip Gourevitch, *We Wish to Inform You That Tomorrow We Will Be Killed with Our Families: Stories from Rwanda* (New York: Farrar, Straus and Giroux, 1999), p. 57.

26. Ibid., p. 125. Gourevitch's book is the most extraordinary and thorough analysis of the Rwanda genocide. It is unlikely that any other study will be as penetrating, absorbing, or descriptive. It is *the* definitive work on the subject.

27. Ibid., pp. 150, 149.

28. Ibid., p. 325.

29. Leland M. Goodrich, *The United Nations* (New York: Thomas Y. Crowell, 1964), pp. 255-256.

30. For a scholarly analysis of the history of civil conflict in Angola, see Lawrence W. Henderson, *Angola: Five Centuries of Conflict* (Ithaca, NY: Cornell University Press, 1979), pp. 162-258.

31. On the missing $900 million, see *New York Times,* April 9, 2000, p. 3; Jon Lee Anderson, "Letter from Angola: Oil and Blood." *New Yorker,* August 14, 2000, p. 49.

32. *African Development Indicators 2000* (Washington, D.C.: World Bank, 2000), pp. 322, 324; *New York Times,* December 24, 2000, p. A8.

33. Quoted in Peter Schwab, ed., *Biafra* (New York: Facts On File, 1971), p. 9.

34. Karl Maier, *This House Has Fallen: Midnight in Nigeria* (New York: Public Affairs, 2000), p. 3.

35. For analyses of Saro-Wiwa's life and work, see Craig W. McLuckie and Aubrey McPhail, eds., *Ken Saro-Wiwa: Writer and Political Activist* (Boulder, CO: Lynne Rienner Publishers, 2000).

36. As quoted in Maier, *This House Has Fallen,* p. 106.

37. *New York Times,* August 27, 2000, p. 1.

38. *African Development Indicators, 2000,* p. 322.

39. Ibid., pp. 276, 329, 334, 335, 397; *World Bank Little Data Book 2000* (Washington, D.C.: World Bank, 2000), p. 166.

40. *Nelson Mandela Speaks: Forging a Democratic, Nonracial South Africa* (New York: Pathfinder Press, 1993), p. 255.

41. See Willie Henderson, "Review Article: Metaphors, Narrative and 'Truth': South Africa's TRC." *African Affairs* 99, 396 (July 2000): 459.

42. *New York Times,* November 10, 2000, p. A9.

43. *Mail & Guardian,* November 10-16, 2000, p. 4.

44. Ibid., p. 8.

45. Daryl Glaser, "The Media Inquiry Reports of the South African Human Rights Commission: A Critique." *African Affairs* 99, 396 (July 2000): 385-386. For a dazzling novel that captures the complex social and

racial jostling enveloping the new South Africa see J. M. Coetzee, *Disgrace* (New York: Penguin Books, 2000).

46. Chris Alden, "From Neglect to 'Virtual Engagement': The United States and Its New Paradigm for Africa." *African Affairs* 99, 396 (July 2000): 359.

47. Adamantia Pollis, "A New Universalism." In *Human Rights: New Perspectives, New Realities*, pp. 9-30, ed. Pollis and Schwab, p. 26.

48. Ibid.

49. *Charter of the United Nations* (New York: United Nations, 1945), article 2, paragraph 7.

50. Goodrich, *United Nations*, p. 76.

CHAPTER FOUR

1. Arthur N. Strahler, *Physical Geography* (New York: John Wiley & Sons, 1969), p. 644, plate 1. By comparison, Chile receives 14 inches of rainfall per year, Mali gets 30 inches, and San Francisco receives 22 inches.

2. Elizabeth Eiselen, "Africa South of the Saraha." In *World Geography*, pp. 492-543, edited by John W. Morris and Otis W. Freeman (New York: McGraw-Hill, 1965), p. 503.

3. Paul Hutchinson, *Health Care in Uganda: Selected Issues* (Washington, D.C.: World Bank, 1999), pp. 73, 159, 161.

4. LaVerle Berry, ed., *Ghana: A Country Study* (Washington, D.C.: Department of the Army, 1995), pp. 111-112.

5. Jennifer Seymour Whitaker, *How Can Africa Survive?* (New York: Council on Foreign Relations Press, 1988), p. 116.

6. *Washington Post*, June 2, 2000, p. A26; *African Development Indicators 2000* (Washington, D.C.: World Bank, 2000), pp. 318, 324.

7. *African Development Indicators 2000*, p. 326.

8. Ibid., p. 328. For contrast, in Cuba, a nation under siege as a result of the U.S. embargo, there is 1 medical practitioner for every 180 people. Ninety-six percent of the population is attended by physician-and-nurse teams living in the neighborhood they serve. For information on Cuban healthcare, see Peter Schwab, *Cuba: Confronting the U.S. Embargo* (New York: St. Martin's Press, 2000), pp. 53-78; see pp. 60-61 for the data cited.

9. *Family Planning Methods and Practice: Africa* (Atlanta: U.S. Department of Health and Human Services, Centers for Disease Control and Prevention, 2000), p. 213.

10. Ifi Amadiume, *Male Daughters, Female Husbands: Gender and Sex in an African Society* (London: Zed Books, 1987), pp. 69, 75.

11. Marguerite Michaels, "Retreat from Africa." *Foreign Affairs* 72, 1 (1993): 96; *New York Times*, January 4, 2001, pp. A1, A16.

12. Peter Schwab, *Ethiopia: Politics, Economics and Society* (Boulder, CO: Lynne Rienner Publishers, 1985), pp. 14-21.

13. *World Bank Little Data Book 2000* (Washington, D.C.: World Bank, 2000), p. 14; Michaels, "Retreat from Africa," pp. 95-96; Brian O'Reilly, "Death of a Continent." *Fortune*, November 13, 2000, pp. 264, 272; *World Development Report 2000/2001: Attacking Poverty* (New York: Oxford University Press, for the World Bank, 2001), p.280. Corresponding data for Cuba stands in stark contrast to sub-Saharan Africa. Life expectancy in Cuba is 76 years, while the infant mortality rate per 1,000 live births is 7. See World Bank, News Release no. 2000/363/AFR, June 2, 2000. 74.

14. Whitaker, *How Can Africa Survive?* p. 132.

15. Garcia Clark, *Onions Are My Husband* (Chicago: University of Chicago Press, 1994); Adamantia Pollis, "A New Universalism." In *Human Rights: New Perspectives, New Realities,* pp. 9-30, edited by Adamantia Pollis and Peter Schwab (Boulder, CO: Lynne Rienner Publishers, 2000), p. 19; Berry, *Ghana,* p. 28.

16. Mary T. Bassett and Marvellous Mhloyi, "Women and AIDS in Zimbabwe: The Making of an Epidemic." In *AIDS: The Politics of Survival,* pp. 125-139, edited by Nancy Krieger and Glen Margo (Amityville, NY: Baywood Publishing, 1994), p. 129.

17. World Bank, News Release no. 2000/363/AFR, June 2, 2000, Washington, D.C.

18. *Family Planning Methods and Practice: Africa,* p. 75.

19. Asha Samad, "Afterword." *Natural History* (August 1996): 52. See also Bettina Shell-Duncan and Ylva Hernlund, eds., *Female "Circumcision" in Africa: Culture, Controversy, and Change* (Boulder, CO: Lynne Rienner Publishers, 2001).

20. *New York Times,* January 31, 1997, p. A4.

21. Ibid.

22. Ngũgĩ Wa Thiong'o, *The River Between* (Oxford: Heinemann, 1965), p. 53.

23. Ibid., pp. 58-59.

24. World Bank, News Release no. 2000/363/AFR, pp. 1-4; *African Development Indicators 2000,* pp. 257, 400, 401, 404.

25. *African Development Indicators 2000,* p. 325.

26. *United Nations World Statistics Pocketbook* (New York: United Nations, 1997), pp. 26, 58, 71, 127, 137, 191; *Human Development Report 2000.* (New York: Oxford University Press, for the United Nations Development Program, 2000), 215.

27. Saadet Deger, "Human Resources, Government Education Expenditure, and the Military Burden in Less Developed Countries." *Journal of Developing Areas* 20, 1 (October 1985): 37. Although written some years ago, the ratio between military and educational expenditures retains its resonance.

28. World Bank, News Release no. 2000/363/AFR, pp. 11, 14.

29. *African Development Indicators 2000,* p. 335.

30. World Bank, News Release no. 2000/363/AFR, p. 3.

31. See *New York Times,* August 14, 2000, p. A6, and *New York Times,* November 25, 2000, p. A5. By 2000, 36.1 million people worldwide were infected with the HIV virus or had contracted AIDS: 920,000 in the United States and Canada; 540,000 in Western Europe; 700,000 in Eastern Europe and central Asia; 6.4 million in Asia and the Pacific region; 400,000 in North Africa and the Middle East; 1.8 million in Latin America and the Caribbean; 15,000 in Australia and New Zealand; and 25.2 million in sub-Saharan Africa. Of the 3 million people who died of AIDS in 2000, 2.4 million (80 percent) perished in sub-Saharan Africa and 52 percent were women.

32. *Family Planning Methods and Practice: Africa,* p. 75; Bassett and Mhloyi, "Women and AIDS in Zimbabwe," p. 125; *New York Times,* November 25, 2000, p. A5.

33. *Family Planning Methods and Practice: Africa,* p. 80; O'Reilly, "Death of a Continent," p. 263. For an extraordinary description and analysis of the progression of HIV/AIDS, see Peter Piot et al., *AIDS in Africa: A Manual for Physicians* (Geneva: World Health Organization, 1992).

34. *Confronting AIDS: Directions for Public Health, Health Care, and Research* (Washington, D.C.: National Academy Press, 1986), p. 75. For a study of homosexuality in East Africa, see Deborah P. Amory, "Mashoga, Mabasha, Magei: 'Homosexuality' in the East African Coast." In *Boy Wives and Female Husbands: Studies in African Homosexualities,* pp. 67-87, edited by Stephen O. Murray and Will Roscoe (New York: St. Martin's Press, 1998).

35. Karen Jochelson, Monyaola Mothibeli, and Jean-Patrick Leger, "Human Immunodeficiency Virus and Migrant Labor in South Africa." In *AIDS: The Politics of Survival,* ed. Krieger and Margo, pp. 143-152. Note the trans-African transportation routes in Gary W. Shannon, Gerald F. Pyle, and Rashid L. Bashshur, *The Geography of AIDS: Origins and Course of an Epidemic* (New York: Guilford Press, 1991), p. 81.

36. Jochelson, Mothibeli, and Leger, "Human Immunodeficiency Virus," p. 153.

37. Bassett and Mhloyi, "Women and AIDS," p. 127.

38. O'Reilly, "Death of a Continent," p. 260.

39. Ibid., p. 263.

40. *Global Economic Prospects and the Developing Countries 2000* (Washington, D.C.: International Bank for Reconstruction and Development/ World Bank, 2000), p. 1.

41. O'Reilly, "Death of a Continent," p. 264.

42. Hutchinson, *Health Care in Uganda,* p. 12.

43. *Family Planning Methods and Practice: Africa,* p. 97; Bassett and Mhloyi, "Women and AIDS in Zimbabwe," p. 135.

44. World Bank, News Release no. 2000/363/AFR, p. 2; O'Reilly, "Death of a Continent," p. 268; *African Development Indicators 2000*, p. 322; *New York Times*, May 8, 2001, pp. A1, A14.
45. *New York Times*, August 14, 2000, p. A6.
46. *New York Times*, July 10, 2000, p. A6; *New York Times*, March 21, 2001, p. A. 8; O'Reilly, "Death of a Continent," p. 268. If children below the age of 15 are also considered, the total number of South Africans afflicted with AIDS would exceed 5 million.
47. *New York Times*, November 7, 2000, p. A12.
48. *African Development Indicators 2000*, p. 322; Berry, *Ghana*, p. 115.
49. *African Development Indicators 2000*; O'Reilly, "Death of a Continent," p. 268.
50. *New York Times*, August 14, 2000, p. A6.
51. World Bank, News Release no. 2000/363/AFR, p. 3; *New York Times*, July 16, 2000, p. 6. See *AIDS: Guidelines for Counseling about HIV Infection and Disease*, series 1-11 (Geneva: World Health Organization, 1989-1992).
52. *Mmegi/The Reporter*, November 3-9, 2000, p. 10.
53. Jochelson, Mothibeli, and Leger, "Human Immunodeficiency Virus," p. 155.
54. *African Development Indicators 2000*, p. 327. Also see Tina Rosenberg, "How to Solve the World's AIDS Crisis," *New York Times Magazine*, January 28, 2001, pp. 26-31, 52, 58, 62-63.

CHAPTER FIVE

1. *New York Times*, November 11, 2000, p. C1.
2. Ibid.
3. *Mmegi/The Reporter*, November 3-9, 2000, p. B2.
4. Ibid., p. B4.
5. World Bank, Press Release, October 3, 2000, Washington, D.C.
6. *African Development Indicators 2000* (Washington, D.C.: World Bank, 2000), p. 82; *World Bank Little Data Book 2000* (Washington, D.C.: World Bank, 2000), p. 231.
7. *Mmegi/The Reporter*, November 3-9, 2000, p. B20.
8. *African Development Indicators 2000*, p. 89; *World Bank Little Data Book 2000*, p. 230.
9. World Bank, News Release no. 2000/363/AFR, June 2, 2000, Washington, D.C.; *African Development Indicators 2000*, p. 6; *New York Times*, December 4, 2000, p. A6.
10. Jon Lee Anderson, "Letter from Angola: Oil and Blood." *New Yorker*, August 14, 2000, p. 46.
11. *New York Times*, October 19, 2000, p. A15.
12. See Thomas L. Friedman, *The Lexus and the Olive Tree* (New York: Farrar Straus and Giroux, 1999).

13. Peter Schwab and Adamantia Pollis, "Globalization's Impact on Human Rights." In *Human Rights: New Perspectives, New Realities,* pp. 209-223, edited by A. Pollis and P. Schwab (Boulder, CO: Lynne Rienner Publishers, 2000), p. 210.

14. Ibid.; George Soros, "Capitalism's Last Chance." *Foreign Policy* (Winter 1998/1999): 56.

15. Saskia Sassen, *Globalization and Its Discontents* (New York: New Press, 1998), p. xxvii.

16. Soros, "Capitalism's Last Chance," pp. 56-57.

17. Eric Toussaint, *Your Money or Your Life!: The Tyranny of Global Finance* (Dar Es Salaam: Mkuki na Nyota Publishers, 1999), p. 33; Saskia Sassen, "Global Financial Centers." *Foreign Affairs* 78, 1 (1999): 80-81.

18. Schwab and Pollis, "Globalization's Impact on Human Rights," p. 212.

19. Ibid., p. 213.

20. Sam Howe Verhovek, "Bill Gates Turns Skeptical on Digital Solution's Scope," *New York Times,* November 3, 2000, p. A18.

21. Andrew I. Schoenholtz, "The I.M.F. in Africa: Unnecessary and Undesirable Western Restraints on Development." *Journal of Modern African Studies* 25, 3 (1987): 405-406.

22. Ibid., p. 415.

23. Ibid., p. 431.

24. Marguerite Michaels, "Retreat from Africa." *Foreign Affairs* 72, 1 (1993): 98.

25. Schoenholtz, "I.M.F. in Africa," p. 433.

26. World Bank, *Annual Report* (Geneva: World Bank, 1998).

27. Hans-Peter Martin and Harald Schumann, *The Global Trap: Globalization and the Assault on Prosperity and Democracy* (London: Zed Books, 1998), p. 48.

28. Chris Alden, "From Neglect to 'Virtual Engagement': The United States and Its New Paradigm for Africa." *African Affairs* 99, 396 (July 2000): 367-368.

29. *African Development Indicators 2000,* p. 82; *World Bank Little Data Book 2000,* pp. 102, 150.

30. LaVerle Berry, ed., *Ghana: A Country Study* (Washington, D.C.: Department of the Army, 1995), p. 187.

31. Michaels, "Retreat from Africa," p. 100.

32. *African Development Indicators 2000,* p. 6.

33. Jeffrey Herbst, "The Dilemmas of Explaining Political Upheaval: Ghana in Comparative Perspective." In *Economic Change and Political Liberalization in Sub-Saharan Africa,* pp. 182-198, edited by Jennifer A. Widner (Baltimore: Johns Hopkins University Press, 1994), p. 193.

34. *New York Times,* November 11, 2000, P. C2.

35. Ibid.

36. Alden, "From Neglect to 'Virtual Engagement,'" pp. 369, 361.

37. Jennifer A. Widner, *The Rise of a Party-State in Kenya: From "Harambee!" to "Nyayo!"* (Berkeley: University of California Press, 1993), p. 1.
38. *African Development Indicators 2000*, pp. 265, 322.
39. *New York Times*, December 4, 2000, p. A6.
40. Ibid.
41. *African Development Indicators 2000*, pp. 21, 38, 82.
42. *New York Times*, December 4, 2000, p. A7.
43. World Bank, News Release no. 2000/363/AFR, p. 1.
44. *New York Times*, September 17, 2000, pp. 1, 12.
45. World Bank, News Release no. 2000/363/AFR, p. 1.
46. Ibid., p. 3.
47. Ibid., p. 4; *World Bank Little Data Book 2000*, pp. 11, 14.
48. World Bank, News Release no. 2000/363/AFR, p. 4; *World Bank Little Data Book 2000*, p. 14.
49. World Bank Press Release, Washington, D.C., October 3, 2000.
50. Cyprian Ekwensi, *People of the City* (Greenwich, CT: Fawcett Publications, 1969), pp. 7, 110. On African religion overall, see Laurenti Magesa, *African Religion: The Moral Traditions of Abundant Life* (Maryknoll, NY: Orbis Books, 1997), and John S. Mbiti, *Introduction to African Religion* (Westport, CT: Heinemann, 1991). Note Margaret Trowell, "Form and Content of African Art." In *African and Oceanic Art*, pp. 6-201, by M. Trowell and Hans Nevermann (New York: Harry N. Abrams Publishers, 1968), for an incisive discussion on the relationship among African religion, art, dance, and country medicine.

CHAPTER SIX

1. M. Crawford Young, "Democratization in Africa: The Contradictions of Political Imperative." In *Economic Change and Political Liberalization in Sub-Saharan Africa*, pp. 230-250, edited by Jennifer A. Widner (Baltimore: Johns Hopkins University Press, p. 247).
2. See Patricia M. E. Lorcin, *Imperial Identities* (London: I. B. Tauris, 1995), for a superb study of the imposition of French colonialism in Algeria within the context of divide and rule.
3. As quoted by Philip Gourevitch, *We Wish to Inform You That Tomorrow We Will Be Killed with Our Families: Stories from Rwanda* (New York: Farrar, Straus and Giroux, 1999), p. 325, from an article in *Le Figaro*.
4. See *New York Times*, February 28, 1994, p. 8. R. W. Johnson speaks of Foccart's aborted attempts to have Guinean president Sékou Touré liquidated: R. W. Johnson, "Guinea." In *West African States: Failure and Promise*, pp. 35-65, edited by John Dunn (Cambridge: Cambridge University Press, 1978), p. 45.
5. See Johnson, "Guinea." L. Gray Cowan maintains that in its anger, France went about "destroying vital files [while] destruction of telephone instruments and plumbing facilities were not uncommon":

"Guinea." In *African One-Party States,* pp. 149-236, edited by Gwendolen M. Carter (Ithaca, NY: Cornell University Press, 1964), p. 171. For a brilliant novel depicting how France maintained control of Senegal after independence, see Sembène Ousmane, *Xala* (Westport, CT: Lawrence Hill & Co., 1976).

6. As quoted by Roger Cohen, "Eyewitness Account." *New York Times Book Review,* October 29, 2000, p. 5, from Timothy Garton Ash, *Essays, Sketches, and Dispatches from Europe in the 1990s* (New York: Random House, 2000).

7. Jennifer Seymour Whitaker, *How Can Africa Survive?* (New York: Council on Foreign Relations Press, 1988), p.208.

8. Jeffrey Herbst, "The Dilemmas of Explaining Political Upheaval: Ghana in Comparative Perspective." In *Economic Change and Political Liberalization in Sub-Saharan Africa,* pp. 182-198, edited by Widner, p.193.

9. Richard Hodder-Williams, *An Introduction to the Politics of Tropical Africa* (London: Allen and Unwin, 1984), p. 233.

10. Herbst, "Dilemmas of Explaining Political Upheaval," pp. 188-189. Michaels insists the World Bank is arrogant and ignorant: Marguerite Michaels, "Retreat from Africa." *Foreign Affairs* 71, 1 (1993): 101.

11. Jennifer A. Widner, "Political Reform in Anglophone and Francophone African Countries." In *Economic Change and Political Liberalization in Sub-Saharan Africa,* pp. 49-79, edited by Widner, p. 71. In the late 1980s, "the IMF insisted that 585 of the 650 foreign experts on government payrolls be let go": see Robert E. Handloff, ed., *Côte d'Ivoire: A Country Study* (Washington, D.C.: Department of the Army, 1991), p. 106.

12. In earlier decades, the condition was similar. Between 1960 and 1969, "no less than twenty-six unconstitutional changes of government took place in independent Africa": Victor T. Le Vine, "The Coups in Upper Volta, Dahomey, and the Central African Republic." In *Protest and Power in Black Africa,* pp. 1035-1071, edited by Robert I. Rotberg and Ali A. Mazrui (New York: Oxford University Press, 1970), p. 1038. See also Samuel Decalo, *Coups and Army Rule in Africa: Studies in Military Style* (New Haven, CT: Yale University Press, 1976); Samuel Decalo, *Psychoses of Power: African Personal Dictatorships* (Boulder, CO: Westview Press, 1989); Ruth First, *The Barrel of a Gun: Power in Africa and the Coup d'État* (London: Allen Lane, Penguin Press, 1970); and Henry Kyemba, *A State of Blood: The Inside Story of Idi Amin* (New York: Ace Books, 1977).

13. Michaels, "Retreat from Africa," p. 94.

14. Ibid., p. 95.

15. Virtually all candidates in the 2000 U.S. national elections argued vociferously that the budget surplus should be used to shore up the Social Security system and both Medicare and Medicaid. Foreign policy had a minute presence in the presidential and congressional candidate

debates. With the end of the cold war, domestic issues trump foreign policy. See also Michaels, "Retreat from Africa," p. 99; *United Nations World Statistics Pocketbook* (New York: United Nations, 1997), pp. 68, 113; Chris Alden, "From Neglect to 'Virtual Engagement': The United States and Its New Paradigm for Africa." *African Affairs* 99, 396 (July 2000): 362.

16. James Schlesinger, "Quest for a Post-Cold War Foreign Policy." *Foreign Affairs* 72, 1 (1993): 17, 19.

17. See H. L. Trefousse, *The Cold War: A Book of Documents* (New York: Capricorn Books, 1966), pp. 97-102, for the Truman Doctrine.

18. World Bank, News Release No. 2000/363/AFR, June 2, 2000, Washington, D.C., p. 4.

19. *United Nations World Statistics Pocketbook* (New York: United Nations, 1997), pp. 45, 71, 104, 122, 138. *World Bank Little Data Book 2000* (Washington, D.C.: World Bank, 2000), pp. 11, 14.

20. Barbara Rose Johnston, "Human Environmental Rights." In *Human Rights: New Perspectives, New Realities,* pp. 95-113, edited by Adamantia Pollis and Peter Schwab (Boulder, CO: Lynne Rienner Publishers), p. 111 n.

21. *United Nations World Statistics Pocketbook,* pp. 61, 165. *African Development Indicators 2000* (Washington, D.C.: World Bank, 2000), p. 387.

22. Michaels, "Retreat from Africa," p. 93.

23. James C. Clad and Roger D. Stone, "New Mission for Foreign Aid." *Foreign Affairs* 72, 1 (1993): 196, 199.

24. Widner, "Political Reform."

25. Irene L. Gendzier, *Managing Political Change: Social Scientists and the Third World* (Boulder, CO: Westview Press, 1985).

26. Whitaker, *How Can Africa Survive?* p. 223.

27. Ibid., p. 231.

28. Ibid., p. 223.

29. Michaels, "Retreat from Africa," pp. 98-99. From 1997 to 1998, foreign direct investment in sub-Saharan Africa declined by 43 percent; *World Bank Little Data Book 2000,* p. 14. See also *World Investment Report 1999: Foreign Direct Investment and the Challenge of Development* (New York: United Nations, 1999).

30. World Bank, Press Release, Washington, D.C., October 3, 2000.

31. World Bank, Press Release, Washington, D.C., October 26, 2000; *African Development Indicators 2000,* p. 257; Thomas Collelo, ed., *Chad: A Country Study* (Washington, D.C.: Department of the Army, 1990), p. 91.

32. *New York Times,* October 31, 2000, p. W1.

33. As quoted by Edward W. Said, *The Question of Palestine* (New York: Vintage Books, 1980), p. 78.

34. Frantz Fanon, *The Wretched of the Earth* (New York: Grove Press, 1968); Albert Memmi, *The Colonizer and the Colonized* (Boston: Beacon Press, 1967), p. 151.

35. William E. Gary, et al., "Making the Case for Racial Reparations." *Harper's* (November 2000): 37-53 for a discussion surrounding racial reparations and the Reparations Assessment Group Project.

36. Gourevitch, *We Wish to Inform You*, pp. 326, 332. The first quote is Museveni's; the second is a paraphrase by Gourevitch.

37. Arthur M. Schlesinger Jr., *A Thousand Days: John F. Kennedy in the White House* (Boston: Houghton Mifflin, 1965), p. 574.

38. Kwame Nkrumah, *I Speak of Freedom* (New York: Frederick A. Praeger, 1962), pp. 107, 109, 110.

39. Ayi Kwei Armah, *The Beautyful Ones Are Not Yet Born* (New York: Collier Books, 1973), p. 160.

40. Kofi Awoonor, *This Earth, My Brother* . . . (Garden City, NY: Anchor Books, 1972), pp. 134, 29.

41. Sembène Ousmane, *Xala* (Westport, CT: Lawrence Hill & Co., 1976), p. 93.

42. Karl Maier, *This House Has Fallen: Midnight in Nigeria* (New York: Public Affairs, 2000), p. xxiii.

43. Amos Sawyer, *The Emergence of Autocracy in Liberia* (San Francisco: Institute for Contemporary Studies, 1992), p. 3.

44. Denis Johnson, "The Small Boys Unit: Searching for Charles Taylor in a Liberian Civil War." *Harper's* (October 2000): 3.

45. *Nelson Mandela Speaks: Forging a Democratic, Nonracial South Africa* (New York: Pathfinder Press, 1993), p. 28. See also Mary Benson, *Nelson Mandela: The Man and the Movement* (New York: W. W. Norton, 1986).

46. Nelson Mandela, *Long Walk to Freedom* (New York: Little, Brown, 1994), p. 497.

47. See Desmond Tutu, *No Future Without Forgiveness* (London: Rider Books, 1999). See Willie Henderson, "Review Article: Metaphors, Narrative and 'Truth': South Africa's TRC." *African Affairs* 99, 396 (July 2000): 457-465.

48. Mandela as quoted by Benson, *Nelson Mandela*, p. 112.

49. Chris Alden, "From Neglect to 'Virtual Engagement': The United States and Its New Paradigm for Africa." *African Affairs* 99, 396 (July 2000): 359.

50. Ibid.

51. *World Bank Little Data Book 2000*, pp. 166, 195; *African Development Indicators 2000*, pp. 37, 105, 245.

52. *World Bank Little Data Book 2000*, p. 195.

53. I appropriated the concept "north of south" from Shiva Naipaul, *North of South: An African Journey* (New York: Penguin Books, 1980), although it has become a conventional motif among many South Africans.

54. William Shakespeare's play *Othello, the Moor of Venice* was first printed in 1622 in a quarto edition, while *The Tragedy of King Richard III* was published in 1597, also in quarto form.
55. Robert I. Rotberg, "Africa's Mess, Mugabe's Mayhem." *Foreign Affairs* (September/October 2000): 47.
56. Carol Lancaster, "Redesigning Foreign Aid." *Foreign Affairs* (September/October 2000): 80.
57. Ibid., pp. 75-76.
58. Africa News Service, October 22, 1997.
59. See Lancaster, "Redesigning Foreign Aid," p. 81.
60. *World Bank Little Data Book 2000*, pp. 51, 72, 132, 148, 231.
61. Rotberg, "Africa's Mess," p. 61. The modesty of leaders such as Sawyer and Mandela is indicated by a story Amos Sawyer related to me in June 2001. While president, Sawyer met Mandela at an OAU meeting in Cairo. He said to Mandela: "When I was first thrown in prison for political reasons I felt sorry for myself; then I thought of your lengthy prison term, and I felt ashamed of myself." Mandela threw his arms around Sawyer and replied: "Anyone who spends even one minute in prison for political activity has nothing to be ashamed of."

Bibliography

A History of Kagnew Station and American Forces in Eritrea. 1973. Arlington, VA: Information Division IACS-I, Headquarters, U.S. Army Security Agency.

Achebe, Chinua. 1959. *Things Fall Apart.* Greenwich, CT: Fawcett Publications.

———. 1966. *No Longer at Ease.* London: Heinemann.

———. 1967. *A Man of the People.* Garden City, NY: Anchor Books.

———. 1969. *Arrow of God.* Garden City, NY: Anchor Books.

Adelman, Kenneth L. 1978. "Zaïre's Year of Crisis." *African Affairs* 77, 306 (January): 36-44.

Africa News Service. 1997. (October 22).

African Development Indicators 2000. 2000. Washington, D.C.: World Bank.

Aidoo, Ama Ata. 1972. *No Sweetness Here.* Garden City, NY: Anchor Books.

AIDS: Guidelines for Counseling about HIV Infection and Disease. Series 1-11. 1989-1992. Geneva: World Health Organization.

Alden, Chris. 2000. "From Neglect to 'Virtual Engagement': The United States and Its New Paradigm for Africa." *African Affairs* 99, 396 (July): 355-371.

Allen, Christopher. 1978. "Sierra Leone." In *West African States: Future and Promise,* pp. 189-210. Edited by John Dunn. Cambridge: Cambridge University Press.

Amadiume, Ifi. 1987. *Male Daughters, Female Husbands: Gender and Sex in an African Society.* London: Zed Books.

Amory, Deborah P. 1998. "Mashoga, Mabasha, Magei: 'Homosexuality' in the East African Coast." In *Boy Wives and Female Husbands: Studies in African Homosexualities,* pp. 67-87. Edited by Stephen O. Murray and Will Roscoe. New York: St. Martin's Press.

Anderson, Jon Lee. 2000. "Letter from Angola: Oil and Blood." *New Yorker* (August 14): 46-59.

Armah, Ayi Kwei. 1973. *The Beautyful Ones Are Not Yet Born.* New York: Collier Books.

Awoonor, Kofi. 1972. *This Earth, My Brother. . . .* Garden City, NY: Anchor Books.

———. 1976. *The Breast of the Earth: A Survey of the History, Culture and Literature of Africa South of the Sahara.* Garden City, NY: Anchor Books.

Ayittey, George B. N. 1993. *Africa Betrayed.* New York: St. Martin's Press.

————. 1998. *Africa in Chaos.* New York: St. Martin's Press.

Bassett, Mary T., and Marvellous Mhloyi. 1994. "Women and AIDS in Zimbabwe: The Making of an Epidemic." In *AIDS: The Politics of Survival,* pp. 125-139. Edited by Nancy Krieger and Glen Margo. Amityville, NY: Baywood Publishing.

Bebey, Francis. 1973. *Agatha Moudio's Son.* New York: Lawrence Hill.

Benson, Mary. 1986. *Nelson Mandela: The Man and the Movement.* New York: W. W. Norton.

Berry, LaVerle, ed. 1995. *Ghana: A Country Study.* Washington, D.C.: Department of the Army.

Bienen, Henry, ed. 1968. *The Military Intervenes: Case Studies in Political Development.* New York: Russell Sage Foundation.

Birmingham, David. 1995. *The Decolonization of Africa.* Athens: Ohio University Press.

Brierly, J. L. 1963. *The Law of Nations.* New York: Oxford University Press.

Campbell, Bonnie. 1978. "The Ivory Coast." In *West African States: Failure and Promise,* pp. 66-116. Edited by John Dunn. Cambridge: Cambridge University Press.

Chandler, David. 1999. *Voices from S-21: Terror and History in Pol Pot's Secret Prison.* Berkeley: University of California Press.

Charter of the United Nations. 1945. New York: United Nations.

Clad, James C., and Roger D. Stone. 1993. "New Mission for Foreign Aid." *Foreign Affairs* 72, 1: 196-205.

Clapham, Christopher. 1978. "Liberia." In *West African States: Failure and Promise,* pp. 117-131. Edited by John Dunn. Cambridge: Cambridge University Press.

Clark, Gracia. 1994. *Onions Are My Husband.* Chicago: University of Chicago Press.

Clark, Jeffrey. 1993. "Debacle in Somalia." *Foreign Affairs* 72, 1: 109-123.

Claude, Inis L., Jr. 1964. *Swords into Plowshares: The Problems and Progress of International Organization.* New York: Random House.

Coetzee, J. M. 2000. *Disgrace.* New York: Penguin Books.

Cohen, Roger. 2000. "Eyewitness Account." *New York Times Book Review* (October 29): 5.

Collelo, Thomas, ed. 1990. *Chad: A Country Study.* Washington, D.C.: Department of the Army.

Confronting AIDS: Directions for Public Health, Health Care, and Research. 1986. Washington, D.C.: National Academy Press.

Cowan, L. Gray. 1964. "Guinea." In *African One-Party States,* pp. 149-236. Edited by Gwendolen M. Carter. Ithaca, NY: Cornell University Press.

Crowe, S. E. 1970. *The Berlin West African Conference: 1884-1885.* Westport, CT: Negro Universities Press.

Curtin, Philip D. 1970. *The Atlantic Slave Trade: A Census.* Madison: University of Wisconsin Press.

Dangarembga, Tsitsi. 1989. *Nervous Conditions.* Seattle: Seal Press.

Davidson, Basil. 1959. *The Lost Cities of Africa.* Boston: Little, Brown.

———. 1961. *The African Slave Trade: Precolonial History 1450-1850.* Boston: Little, Brown.

Dawidowicz, Lucy S. 1979. *The War Against the Jews: 1933-1945.* New York: Bantam Books.

Decalo, Samuel. 1976. *Coups and Army Rule in Africa: Studies in Military Style.* New Haven, CT: Yale University Press.

———. 1989. *Psychoses of Power: African Personal Dictatorships.* Boulder, CO: Westview Press.

Deger, Saadet. 1985. "Human Resources, Government Education Expenditure, and the Military Burden in Less Developed Countries." *Journal of Developing Areas* 20, 1 (October): 37-48.

Drachler, Jacob, ed. 1964. *African Heritage: Intimate Views of the Black Africans from Life, Lore, and Literature.* New York: Collier Books.

Dunn, D. Elwood, and S. Byron Tarr. 1988. *Liberia: A National Polity in Transition.* London: Scarecrow Press.

Eiselen, Elizabeth. 1965. "Africa South of the Sahara." In *World Geography*, pp. 492-543. Edited by John W. Morris and Otis W. Freeman. New York: McGraw-Hill.

Ekwensi, Cyprian. 1969. *People of the City.* Greenwich, CT: Fawcett Publications.

Ellis, Stephen. 1999. *The Mask of Anarchy: The Destruction of Liberia and the Religious Dimension of an African Civil War.* New York: New York University Press.

Emecheta, Buchi. 1988. *Destination Biafra.* Oxford: Heinemann.

Family Planning Methods and Practice: Africa. 2000. Atlanta, GA: U.S. Department of Health and Human Services, Centers for Disease Control and Prevention.

Fanon, Frantz. 1967. *A Dying Colonialism.* New York: Grove Press.

———. 1968. *The Wretched of the Earth.* New York: Grove Press.

Farah, Nuruddin. 1992. *Sweet and Sour Milk.* Saint Paul, MN: Graywolf Press.

First, Ruth. 1970. *The Barrel of a Gun: Power in Africa and the Coup d'État.* London: Allen Lane, the Penguin Press.

Fitch, Bob, and Mary Oppenheimer. 1968. *Ghana: End of an Illusion.* New York: Monthly Review Press.

Fraenkel, Merran. 1964. *Tribe and Class in Monrovia.* New York: Oxford University Press.

Friedman, Thomas L. 1999. *The Lexus and the Olive Tree.* New York: Farrar, Straus and Giroux.

Gagiano, Annie. 2000. *Achebe, Head, Marechera: On Power and Change in Africa.* Boulder, CO: Lynne Rienner Publishers.

Garton Ash, Timothy. 2000. *Essays, Sketches, and Dispatches from Europe in the 1990s.* New York: Random House.

Gary, William E., et al. 2000. "Making the Case for Racial Reparations." *Harper's* (November): 37-53.

Gendzier, Irene L. 1985. *Managing Political Change: Social Scientists and the Third World.* Boulder, CO: Westview Press.

Glaser, Daryl. 2000. "The Media Inquiry Reports of the South African Human Rights Commission: A Critique." *African Affairs* 99, 396 (July): 373-393.

Global Economic Prospects and the Developing Countries 2000. 2000. Washington, D.C.: International Bank for Reconstruction and Development/ The World Bank.

Goodrich, Leland M. 1964. *The United Nations.* New York: Thomas Y. Crowell.

Gourevitch, Philip. 1999. *We Wish to Inform You That Tomorrow We Will Be Killed with Our Families: Stories From Rwanda.* New York: Farrar, Straus and Giroux.

———. 2000. "Forsaken: How a Seven-Nation War Engulfed Congo" *New Yorker* (September 25): 53-67.

Halliday, Fred, and Maxine Molyneux.1981. *The Ethiopian Revolution.* London: Verso Editions.

Handloff, Robert E., ed. 1991. *Côte d'Ivoire: A Country Study.* Washington, D.C.: Department of the Army.

Henderson, Lawrence W. 1979. *Angola: Five Centuries of Conflict.* Ithaca, NY: Cornell University Press.

Henderson, Willie. 2000. "Review Article: Metaphors, Narrative and 'Truth': South Africa's TRC." *African Affairs* 99, 396 (July): 457-465.

Herbst, Jeffrey. 1994. "The Dilemmas of Explaining Political Upheaval: Ghana in Comparative Perspective." In *Economic Change and Political Liberalization in Sub-Saharan Africa,* pp. 182-198. Edited by Jennifer A. Widner. Baltimore, MD: Johns Hopkins University Press.

Hirsch, John L. 2001. *Sierra Leone: Diamonds and the Struggle for Democracy.* Boulder, CO: Lynne Rienner Publishers.

Hodder-Williams, Richard. 1984. *An Introduction to the Politics of Tropical Africa.* London: Allen and Unwin.

Hodgkin, Thomas. 1957. *Nationalism in Colonial Africa.* New York: New York University Press.

Hoskyns, Catherine, ed. 1969. *Case Studies in African Diplomacy: The Organization of African Unity and the Congo Crisis, 1964-65.* Dar Es Salaam: Oxford University Press.

Human Development Report 2000. 2000. New York: Oxford University Press, for the United Nations Development Program.

Hutchinson, Paul. 1999. *Health Care in Uganda: Selected Issues.* Washington, D.C.: World Bank.

Ibañez, Vicente Blasco. 1918. *The Four Horsemen of the Apocalypse.* New York: E. P. Dutton.

International Covenant on Economic, Social and Cultural Rights. 1976. (January 3). New York: United Nations.

Jacobs, Scott H. 1985. "The Sudan's Islamization." *Current History* (May): 205-208, 230-232.

Jochelson, Karen, Monyaola Mothibeli, and Jean-Patrick Leger. 1994. "Human Immunodeficiency Virus and Migrant Labor in South Africa." In *AIDS: The Politics of Survival,* pp. 141-158. Edited by Nancy Krieger and Glen Margo. Amityville, NY: Baywood Publishing.

Johnson, Denis. 2000. "The Small Boys Unit: Searching for Charles Taylor in a Liberian Civil War." *Harper's* (October): 41-60.

Johnson, R. W. 1978. "Guinea." In *West African States: Failure and Promise,* pp. 36-65. Edited by John Dunn. Cambridge: Cambridge University Press.

Johnston, Barbara Rose. 2000. "Human Environmental Rights." In *Human Rights: New Perspectives, New Realities,* pp. 95-113. Edited by Adamantia Pollis and Peter Schwab. Boulder, CO: Lynne Rienner Publishers.

Kaplan, Robert D. 1988. *Surrender or Starve: The Wars Behind the Famine.* Boulder, CO: Westview Press.

Kapuściński, Ryszard. 2001. *The Shadow of the Sun.* New York: Alfred A. Knopf.

Kenyatta, Jomo. 1979. *Facing Mount Kenya: The Traditional Life of the Gikuyu.* London: Heinemann.

Kyemba, Henry. 1977. *A State of Blood: The Inside Story of Idi Amin.* New York: Ace Books.

Laitin, David D., and Said S. Samatar. 1987. *Somalia: Nation in Search of a State.* Boulder, CO: Westview Press.

Lancaster, Carol. 2000. "Redesigning Foreign Aid." *Foreign Affairs* (September/October): 74-88.

Lemarchand, René. 1966. "Social Change and Political Modernisation in Burundi." *Journal of Modern African Studies* 4, 4: 401-433.

Le Vine, Victor T. 1970. "The Coups in Upper Volta, Dahomey, and the Central African Republic." In *Protest and Power in Black Africa,* pp. 1035-1071. Edited by Robert I. Rotberg and Ali A. Mazrui. New York: Oxford University Press.

Liebenow, J. Gus. 1987. *Liberia: The Quest for Democracy.* Bloomington: Indiana University Press.

Lorcin, Patricia M. E. 1995. *Imperial Identities.* London: I. B. Tauris.

Lovejoy, Paul E. 2000. *Transformations in Slavery: A History of Slavery in Africa,* 2nd ed. Cambridge: Cambridge University Press.

Lystad, Robert A. 1977. *The Ashanti: A Proud People.* Westport, CT: Greenwood Press.

Magesa, Laurenti. 1997. *African Religion: The Moral Traditions of Abundant Life.* Maryknoll, NY: Orbis Books.

Maier, Karl. 1997. *Into the House of the Ancestors: Inside the New Africa.* New York: John Wiley & Sons.

————. 2000. *This House Has Fallen: Midnight in Nigeria.* New York: Public Affairs.

Mail & Guardian (South Africa newspaper). November 10-16, 2000.

Mandela, Nelson. 1994. *Long Walk to Freedom.* New York: Little, Brown.

Martin, David, and Phyllis Johnson. 1981. *The Struggle for Zimbabwe: The Chimurenga War.* London: Faber and Faber.

Martin, Hans-Peter, and Harald Schumann. 1998. *The Global Trap: Globalization and the Assault on Prosperity and Democracy.* London: Zed Books.

Mbiti, John S. 1991. *Introduction to African Religion.* Westport, CT: Heinemann.

McDonald, Gordon C., et al. 1971. *Area Handbook for People's Republic of the Congo (Congo Brazzaville).* Washington, D.C.: Foreign Area Studies of The American University.

McLuckie, Craig W., and Aubrey McPhail, eds. 2000. *Ken Saro-Wiwa: Writer and Political Activist.* Boulder, CO: Lynne Rienner Publishers.

Memmi, Albert. 1967. *The Colonizer and the Colonized.* Boston: Beacon Press.

Metz, Helen Chapin. 1992. *Nigeria: A Country Study.* Washington, D.C.: Department of the Army.

Mezlekia, Nega. 2001. *Notes from the Hyena's Belly: An Ethiopian Boyhood.* New York: Picador.

Michaels, Marguerite. 1993. "Retreat from Africa." *Foreign Affairs* 72, 1: 93-108.

Mmegi/The Reporter (Botswana newspaper). November 3-9, 2000.

Moore, Gerald, and Ulli Beier, eds. 1966. *Modern Poetry from Africa.* Middlesex: Penguin Books.

Naipaul, Shiva. 1980. *North of South: An African Journey.* New York: Penguin Books.

Nelson Mandela Speaks: Forging a Democratic, Nonracial South Africa. 1993. New York: Pathfinder Press.

NewsHour with Jim Lehrer (television program). 2000. May 16.

New York Times. Editions from 1994 to 2001.

Ngũgĩ Wa Thiong'o. 1965. *The River Between.* Oxford: Heinemann.

Nkrumah, Kwame. 1962. *I Speak of Freedom.* New York: Frederick A. Praeger.

Nyerere, Julius K. 1973. *Freedom and Development/Uhuru na Maendeleo.* Dar Es Salaam: Oxford University Press.

Okechukwu, Chinwe Christina. 2001. *Achebe the Orator: The Art of Persuasion in Chinua Achebe's Novels.* Westport, CT: Greenwood Press.

Okumu, John J. 1968. "Charisma and Politics in Kenya: Notes and Comments on the Problems of Kenya's Party Leadership." *East Africa Journal* 5, 2: 9-16.

O'Reilly, Brian. 2000. "Death of a Continent." *Fortune* (November 13): 259-274.

Ousmane, Sembène. 1970. *God's Bits of Wood.* Garden City, NY: Anchor Books.

———. 1976. *Xala.* Westport, CT: Lawrence Hill & Co.

Oyono, Ferdinand. 1970. *Boy!* New York: Collier Books.

Piot, Peter, et al. 1992. *AIDS in Africa: A Manual for Physicians.* Geneva: World Health Organization.

Pollis, Adamantia. 2000. "A New Universalism." In *Human Rights: New Perspectives, New Realities,* pp. 9-30. Edited by Adamantia Pollis and Peter Schwab. Boulder, CO: Lynne Rienner Publishers.

Pollis, Adamantia, and Peter Schwab. 1979. "Human Rights: A Western Construct with Limited Applicability." In *Human Rights: Cultural and Ideological Perspectives,* pp. 1-18. Edited by Adamantia Pollis and Peter Schwab. New York: Praeger Publishers.

Pollis, Adamantia, and Peter Schwab, eds. 1979. *Human Rights: Cultural and Ideological Perspectives.* New York: Praeger Publishers.

———. 2000. *Human Rights: New Perspectives, New Realities.* Boulder, CO: Lynne Rienner Publishers.

Ponchaud, François. 1978. *Cambodia: Year Zero.* New York: Holt, Rinehart and Winston.

Povey, John. 1970. "Political Protest in the African Novel in English." In *Protest and Power in Black Africa,* pp. 823-853. Edited by Robert I. Rotberg and Ali A. Mazrui. New York: Oxford University Press.

Public Papers of the Presidents of the United States, John F. Kennedy, 1961. 1962. Washington, D.C.: United States Government Printing Office.

Rosenberg, Tina. 2001. "How to Solve the World's AIDS Crisis." *New York Times Magazine* (January 28): 26-31, 52, 58, 62-63.

Rotberg, Robert I. 2000. "Africa's Mess, Mugabe's Mayhem." *Foreign Affairs* (September/October): 47-61.

Rotberg, Robert I., and Ali A. Mazrui, eds. 1970. *Protest and Power in Black Africa.* New York: Oxford University Press.

Said, Edward W. 1980. *The Question of Palestine.* New York: Vintage Books.

Samad, Asha. 1996. "Afterword." *Natural History* (August): 52.

Sassen, Saskia. 1998. *Globalization and Its Discontents.* New York: New Press.

———. 1999. "Global Financial Centers." *Foreign Affairs* 78, 1: 75-87.

Sawyer, Amos. 1992. *The Emergence of Autocracy in Liberia.* San Francisco, CA: Institute for Contemporary Studies.

Schlesinger, James. 1993. "Quest for a Post-Cold War Foreign Policy." *Foreign Affairs* 72, 1: 17-28.

Schlesinger, Arthur M., Jr. 1965. *A Thousand Days: John F. Kennedy in the White House.* Boston: Houghton Mifflin.

———. 2000. *A Life in the Twentieth Century: Innocent Beginnings, 1917-1950.* Boston: Houghton Mifflin.

Schoenholtz, Andrew I. 1987. "The I.M.F. in Africa: Unnecessary and Undesirable Western Restraints on Development." *Journal of Modern African Studies* 25, 3: 403-433.

Schwab, Peter. 1972. *Decision-Making in Ethiopia: A Study of the Political Process.* London: C. Hurst.

————. 1978. "Cold War on the Horn of Africa." *African Affairs* 77, 306: 6-20.

————. 1985. *Ethiopia: Politics, Economics and Society.* Boulder, CO: Lynne Rienner Publishers.

————. 2000. *Cuba: Confronting the U.S. Embargo.* New York: St. Martin's Press.

Schwab, Peter, ed. 1971. *Biafra.* New York: Facts On File Publishers.

Schwab, Peter, and Adamantia Pollis, eds. 1982. *Toward a Human Rights Framework.* New York: Praeger Publishers.

Schwab, Peter, and Adamantia Pollis. 2000. "Globalization's Impact on Human Rights." In *Human Rights: New Perspectives, New Realities,* pp. 209-223. Edited by Adamantia Pollis and Peter Schwab. Boulder, CO: Lynne Rienner Publishers.

Schwarz-Bart, André. 1973. *A Woman Named Solitude.* New York: Atheneum.

Shakespeare, William. 1961. *The Tragedy of King Richard III.* In *The Complete Works of Shakespeare,* pp. 302-339. Edited by Hardin Craig. Chicago, IL: Scott, Foresman.

————. 1961. *Othello, the Moor of Venice.* In *The Complete Works of Shakespeare,* pp. 947-979. Edited by Hardin Craig. Chicago, IL: Scott, Foresman.

Shannon, Gary W., Gerald F. Pyle, and Rashid L. Bashshur. 1991. *The Geography of AIDS: Origins and Course of an Epidemic.* New York: Guilford Press.

Shell-Duncan, Bettina, and Ylva Hernlund, eds. 2001. *Female "Circumcision" in Africa: Culture, Controversy, and Change.* Boulder, CO: Lynne Rienner Publishers.

Sherman, Richard. 1980. *Eritrea: The Unfinished Revolution.* New York: Praeger.

Simons, Geoff. 1996. *Cuba: From Conquistador to Castro.* New York: St. Martin's Press.

Somalia, A Government at War with Its Own People: Testimonies About the Killings and the Conflict in the North. 1990. Washington, D.C.: Africa Watch/Human Rights Watch.

Sorensen, Theodore C. 1965. *Kennedy.* New York: Harper & Row.

Soros, George. 1998/1999. "Capitalism's Last Chance." *Foreign Policy* (Winter): 55-65.

Soyinka, Wole. 1967. *Idanre and Other Poems.* New York: Hill and Wang.

————. 1970. *The Interpreters.* New York: Collier Books.

Strahler, Arthur N. 1969. *Physical Geography.* New York: John Wiley & Sons.

"Tom Mboya: A Commemorative Issue." 1969. *East Africa Journal* 6, 9: 6-37.

Toussaint, Eric. 1999. *Your Money or Your Life!: The Tyranny of Global Finance.* Dar Es Salaam: Mkuki na Nyota Publishers.

Traub, James. 2000. "Sierra Leone: The Worst Place on Earth." *New York Review of Books* (June 29): 1-6. See Web site at nybooks.com.

Trefousse, H. L. 1966. *The Cold War: A Book of Documents.* New York: Capricorn Books.

Trowell, Margaret. 1968. "Form and Content of African Art." In *African and Oceanic Art,* pp. 6-201. Texts by Margaret Trowell and Hans Nevermann. New York: Harry N. Abrams Publishers.

Tutu, Desmond. 1999. *No Future Without Forgiveness.* London: Rider Books.

United Nations Economic and Social Council, Commission on Human Rights. 1986. E/CN.4/1986/20 (February 3-March 14): 1-8. New York: United Nations.

United Nations World Statistics Pocketbook. 1997. New York: United Nations.

Universal Declaration of Human Rights. 1948 (December 10). New York: United Nations.

Unsworth, Barry. 1993. *Sacred Hunger.* New York: W. W. Norton.

U.S. *Security Agreements and Commitments Abroad, Ethiopia.* 1970 (Part 8, June 1). Washington, D.C.: Committee on Foreign Relations, United States Senate.

Verhovek, Sam Howe. 2000. "Bill Gates Turns Skeptical on Digital Solution's Scope." *New York Times* (November 3): A18.

Washington Post. June 2, 2000.

Whitaker, Jennifer Seymour. 1988. *How Can Africa Survive?* New York: Council on Foreign Relations Press.

Widner, Jennifer A. 1993. *The Rise of a Party-State in Kenya: From "Harambee!" to "Nyayo!"* Berkeley: University of California Press.

————. 1994. "Political Reform in Anglophone and Francophone African Countries." In *Economic Change and Political Liberalization in Sub-Saharan Africa,* pp. 49-79. Edited by Jennifer A. Widner. Baltimore, MD: Johns Hopkins University Press.

Wolde Giorgis, Dawit. 1989. *Red Tears: War, Famine and Revolution in Ethiopia.* Trenton, NJ: The Red Sea Press.

Woodward, Peter. 1990. *Sudan, 1898-1989: The Unstable State.* Boulder, CO: Lynne Rienner Publishers.

World Bank, 1998. *Annual Report.*

————. 2000. News Release No: 2000/363/AFR. Washington, D.C., June 2.

————. 2000. Press Release. Washington, D.C., October 3.

————. 2000. Press Release. Washington, D.C., October 26.

World Bank Development Committee-Communiqué. 2000 (September 25). Prague: World Bank.

World Bank Little Data Book 2000. 2000. Washington, D.C.: World Bank.

World Development Report 2000/2001: Attacking Poverty. 2001. New York: Oxford University Press, for the World Bank.

World Investment Report 1999: Foreign Direct Investment and the Challenge of Development. 1999. New York: United Nations.

Young, M. Crawford. 1970. " Rebellion and the Congo." In *Protest and Power in Black Africa,* pp. 969-1011. Edited by Robert I. Rotberg and Ali A. Mazrui. New York: Oxford University Press.

————. 1994. "Democratization in Africa: The Contradictions of Political Imperative." In *Economic Change and Political Liberalization in Sub-*

Saharan Africa, pp. 230-250. Edited by Jennifer A. Widner. Baltimore: Johns Hopkins University Press.

Zimmermann, Warren, et al. 1999. *War in the Balkans.* New York: Council on Foreign Relations Press.

Zolberg, Aristide R. 1964. *One-Party Government in the Ivory Coast.* Princeton, NJ: Princeton University Press.

Index